Robert Herrick, Alexander Balloch Grosart

Early English Poets

The Complete Poems of Robert Herrick. Vol. I

Robert Herrick, Alexander Balloch Grosart

Early English Poets
The Complete Poems of Robert Herrick. Vol. I

ISBN/EAN: 9783744687737

Printed in Europe, USA, Canada, Australia, Japan

Cover: Foto ©Thomas Meinert / pixelio.de

More available books at **www.hansebooks.com**

Early English Poets.

ROBERT HERRICK.

PRINTED BY ROBERT ROBERTS,
BOSTON.

Robert Hearick.

Early English Poets.

THE
COMPLETE POEMS
OF
ROBERT HERRICK.

EDITED,

WITH

Memorial-Introduction and Notes,

BY THE

REV. ALEXANDER B. GROSART.

IN THREE VOLUMES.—VOL. I.

London:
CHATTO AND WINDUS, PICCADILLY.
1876.

To
ALGERNON CHARLES SWINBURNE, Esq.

My Dear Sir,

It is a very great pleasure to be allowed to dedicate this first adequate edition of the Poetry of Herrick—to you. I asked this, in order to express my sense of the privilege with which you honour me in your old-fashionedly long and full letters on literary matters ; and also, of the rare combination in your person, of supreme original genius in many directions with the most painstaking and laborious research into our earlier literature, and a swift, almost prodigal recognition of others, whether dead or living.

No more than can any, will you admire everything in the *Hesperides.* But I shall be disappointed if you do not ratify my decision to reproduce the whole rather than excise.

I have worked prolongedly and thoroughly on these three volumes. I place them beneath penetrative but most human eyes in yours.

I am,

My dear Sir,

Ever faithfully,

ALEXANDER B. GROSART.

Preface.

THERE have been EIGHT complete and distinct editions of the Poems of HERRICK, since he himself, in 1647-8, published his "Hesperides, or Works Both Humane and Divine of ROBERT HERRICK, *Esq*," —the 'Divine' moiety being dated 1647 (=1647-8), and separately paged and forming the closing and not the opening portion of the book. It seems clear that a very large impression must have been taken of the first edition; for it sufficed for the demands of the Cavaliers and of The Restoration and until well on in the 19th century. One curious typographical difference in copies of the same-dated volume suggests that the types may have been kept standing for awhile. In the *Hesperides* page 207, while the catchword " 11. Where " is found in some—as in my own—the stanza to which it belongs is dropped out and page 208 commences with

" 12. It is vain to sing or stay."

In most copies that I have examined and had reported on, the stanza appears as in our Vol. II. page 129.

To SYLVANUS URBAN, Esq., (NICHOLS)—*clarum et venerabile nomen* to every one who really loves our olden literature and to whom he is a genuine personality—

belongs the honour of having been the first in later times to recall attention to the (then) long-neglected Poet. This was in the *Gentleman's Magazine* for 1796 and 1797. Following his " Letters " came in 1798 DR. NATHAN DRAKE's still most pleasant *Literary Hours* (Vol. III., 1st edition : Nos. 42, 43, and 44, 3rd edition, 1804) on the *Life, Writings and Genius* of HERRICK, with well-put quotations, and genial if not always accurate criticism. Some years later (1810) Dr. NOTT, of Bristol, published the following :—" Select Poems from the Hesperides or Works both Human and Divine, of Robert Herrick, Esq, with Occasional Remarks by J. N. Accompanied also with the Head, Autographe [*sic*] and Seal of the Poet. Bristol, Printed and published by J. M. Gutch, 15 Small Street. Sold also by Messrs. Longman, Hurst, Rees, and Orme, Paternoster Row, and I. Miller, 72, Chancery Lane, London, n.d. (8vo pp. viii and 253)." On this Selection the well-known friend of Coleridge and Lamb and other contemporary ' mighties '—Mr. BARRON FIELD (not SOUTHEY as frequently stated) wrote a chatty *critique* in the *Quarterly Review* (for August 1810).* Not until

* Peter Cunningham, Esq., in Notes and Queries, 1st s. x. 27, compared with Walford's edition of the Hesperides, p. iii., and 1846 edition. (*infra*) I. xviii.

1823 was a complete edition furnished. This was done
with admirable carefulness and enthusiasm by the late
accomplished THOMAS MAITLAND, Esq.,of Dundrennan,
Advocate, afterwards as a Judge of the Scottish Court
of Session, named LORD DUNDRENNAN. It was in
two volumes, post 8ᵛᵒ, and a few copies in small
4ᵗᵒ : " Edinburgh Reprinted for W. and C. Tait.
MDCCCXXIII." On the title-page is a woodcut of the
bust of Herrick with his autograph. Prefixed is a
Biographical Notice (pp. v.—xxx.) : Vol. I. pp. 288 :
Vol. II., pp. 296, followed by pp. 38 Table of Contents
to both volumes. In 1825 a limited number of " remainder " copies of Lord Dundrennan's edition having
been purchased by the late WILLIAM PICKERING, he
gave them fresh title-pages with his original motto
" Perennis et Fragrans," and a steel portrait by
WORTHINGTON. Otherwise the books are identical.

In August 1822, in *The Retrospective Review* (Vol. V.
p. 156) Lord Dundrennan's edition was examined in a
delightful Paper — the Writer of which one would
gladly know. In 1839 appeared " Selections from the
Hesperides and Works of the Rev. Robert Herrick
(Antient) Vicar of Dean-Prior, Devon. By the late
CHARLES SHORT, Esq., F.R.S. and F.S.A. London :
John Murray, Albemarle Street. MDCCCXXXIX. (pp.

xiv. and 216.)   In 1844 was published in paper covers
2 vols. 16mo. an unpretentious but not at all an un-
worthy little edition intrinsically "edited by HENRY G.
CLARKE" (London : H. G. Clarke & Co.).   In 1846
came William Pickering's typographically beautiful
and attractive edition : 2 vols., cr. 8ᵛᵒ, and a few on
large paper.   The Editor was neither vigilant nor
capable.   The Writer of the Memoir disclaimed the
editing.†   He was the late SAMUEL WELLER SINGER.
He might equally have relinquished any merit for his
Memoir seeing that as Mr. Hazlitt not unjustly remarks,
it is "but a lame paraphrase of that attached to the
edition of 1823," and altogether is perfunctorily done.‡
In 1848 was published "Selections from Herrick for
Translation into Latin Verse with a short Preface by
the Rev. A. J. Macleane, M.A., Trinity College, Cambridge, Principal of Brighton College (London : George
Bell; pp. 79, 16mo.)   Other complete editions appeared
in 1850 and 1852—each in 2 vols.   That of 1852, two
vols. 12mo., was published by Bohn (Vol. I. pp. 213 :
Vol. II., pp. 238).   In 1856, Pickering's of 1846 was
reprinted in the United States : " Boston : Little,
Brown, & Co. : Vol. I., pp. 340 : Vol. II., pp. 298)

† Notes and Queries, 1st s. Vol. I. p. 459.
‡ Vol. I. p. v.

In 1859 we have the following : " The Poetical Works of Robert Herrick, containing his " Hesperides " and " Noble Numbers." With a Biographical Memoir by E. Walford, M.A., Late Scholar of Baliol Coll., Oxford. London : Reeves and Turner, 238 Strand. 1859. (Post 8ᵛᵒ, pp. xi. and 608) ; and finally in 1869, this :—" Hesperides the Poems and other Remains of Robert Herrick now First Collected. Edited by W. Carew Hazlitt. London : John Russell Smith, Soho Square, 1869. (2 vols., cr. 8ᵛᵒ : Vol. I. pp. xxx. and 1—255 : Vol. II., pp. 256— 526 : copies also on large paper). Mr. HAZLITT disavows responsibility for the text, which is virtually that of Pickering's of 1846 ; but in the Biographical Notice he has intercalated some additions and corrections within brackets, and in Appendices added Poems from MSS., etc. Of these and the different editions enumerated more will be found in the Memorial-Introduction (II. Critical).

For all these Eight editions the admirer of Herrick is grateful. None is without its own merits. Therefore none ought to be undervalued.

Now for the present edition. It is distinguished from preceding by these things :—

1. The text is for *the first time* reproduced in integrity

    (a) from the Author's own edition of 1647-8—

Italics, capitals and punctuation being his own, save that his list of errata and a few others overlooked by him have been put right : *(b)* from other books and from MSS. with exact collation of the originals whether printed or MS.

2. For *the first time* an effort has been made to annotate and illustrate wherever there seemed a call for it.   Hitherto except Dr. Nott's occasional Notes to his " Selections," nothing has been done worthwhile even to explain words and allusions, or to inform on names, &c.   The Author's own few Notes bear his initial (H); a few from Dr. Nott bear his initial (N).   For the rest, in Thomas Fuller's phrase " my meannesse is responsible " (Abel Redevivus : Ep. ded. 1651).

3. For *the first time* the facts and circumstances of the Life are fully told.   Hitherto the Memoirs have been meagre and fragmentary.   On almost every point in the Biography new information is now given, previous errors corrected, and old data brought into their places.

4. For *the first time* an attempt at an adequate Estimate of these Poems and of the Man is made.   This forms the second division of the Memorial-Introduction.

5. For *the first time* there is given a thorough Glossarial Index, Index of first lines, and other helpful apparatus.

6. The Portrait (on steel) is for *the first time* true to the original of 1647-8. Of it I speak in relation to others elsewhere.

As I must fully concede, Herrick is one of those Poets of whom more than most of equal kind and quality of genius, a Selection rather than a Collection in entirety, might plausibly be deemed preferable and at this day sufficient. Dr. Nott's and Short's and Macleane's were very acceptable, as far as they went; and still more so I do not doubt will be Mr. FRANCIS TURNER PALGRAVE'S announced "Selections" for the "Golden Treasury" series of Messrs. Macmillan & Co. "Selections" such as the last, will carry Herrick whither we would scarcely choose to have the whole carried; for we would not choose to have our wives or children come on the sorrowful nastinesses of too many of the (so-called) Epigrams and occasional lines of the other Poems. But seeing that the existence of Nott's and Short's and Macleane's and now of Mr. Palgrave's "Selections" makes it unnecessary for such to possess Herrick completely, there remains consideration for others. For my part I am clear that in the interest of students of our Literature and of our national *morals* and progress, it is a thing of truthfulness that any book that is called for ought to be furnished honestly. Only so can genuine verdicts be arrived at ; only so can the History of our national Literature be written in the knowledge of its formative and informing elements ; and above all, only so is it possible to solve questions that are thickening on us, questions that take us to the very roots of our national life and activity. Personally, I frankly acknowledge that I should not elect to publish completely either Herrick or Donne or others ; but since they are imperatively and encreasingly demanded, it is, I must repeat, a thing of truth as against falsehood that the Works shall be made accessible in integrity of text—all save students of our Literature being warned off to " Selections " specially provided. It isn't a matter of casuistry but of indisputable honour if the thing is to be done at all —not to say that your compiler of " Selections " like your fine-nosed searcher after heresy, is too often extremely unpoetic, unsympathetic and narrow in his vision, and grubs up the Passion-flower or moth-wing-like Pansy because forsooth, a slug has trailed across it, sightless to the glory of bloom and tint as to the iridiscence of even the slug's pathway.

I have right cordially to thank several literary friends for willing aid rendered me in these volumes. Foremost, as usual, is my very dear friend DR. BRINSLEY NICHOLSON with his ever-fecund resources and untiring painstaking, and next to him MR. FRANCIS T. PALGRAVE. When I had finished my annotation, the 'copy' was submitted to these two good friends, with the result of enriching my Notes considerably. The Rev. W. E. BUCKLEY, M.A., of Middleton Cheney, Banbury, the Rev. THOMAS ASHE, M.A. (now of Crewe), JOHN SHELLY, Esq., Plymouth, GEORGE H. WHITE, Esq., Glenthorn, Devon, have favoured me with their occasional notes and suggestions. For genealogical and other *data* I owe emphatic thanks to COLONEL CHESTER, of Bermondsey, the Rev. THOMAS PELHAM DALE, M.A., St. Vedast, London, the Rev. W. T. FREER, M.A., Houghton-on-the-Hill, Leicester, and Miss HERRICK MACAULAY, Leicester, the Rev. L. R. CARTER, M.A., Brantham, Suffolk, the late W. PERRY-HERRICK, Esq., Beaumanor, W. A. ABRAM, Esq., Blackburn, and W. H. CHAPPELL, Esq., London. In certain of the patristic references (all loose) I was helped by PROFESSOR LIGHTFOOT, of Cambridge; and FATHER PURBRICK, of Stonyhurst, as always, freely opened to me the noble Library of the College. I must add that, repeatedly, the Printer of these books (MR. ROBERT ROBERTS, of Boston), who is of the nearly defunct type of literary craftsmen, has laid me under pleasant obligation in various ways.

And so I commend ROBERT HERRICK to the present generation and coming generations :—

> " Thou living voice from olden times,
> That like a spirit travellest on
> From lip to lip, from heart to heart
> Linking our own to those long gone :
> 'Tis with a throbbing heart I hear
> Thy well-known voice of harmonies,
> Float—like past boyhood,—on my ear,
> With old ancestral memories !
> Oh ! thou art as an unseen soul
> That communes with us, till we be
> Quite space-and-time free, blended all
> With thy deep essence lovingly :
> Thou art a stirring note, blown on
> Imagination's magic horn,
> But out of date in these dull days,
> When Faith is of her visions shorn."
> (HENRY ELLISON.)

ALEXANDER B. GROSART.

St. George's Vestry,
June 19th, 1876.

POSTSCRIPT.

In my Essay I give reasons for rejecting poems
ascribed to Herrick by Mr. W. C. Hazlitt in his
edition of the Works; here it may be well to repeat
that one of the Poems (I. Description of a Woman)
that he imagined had not before been printed,
appeared in "Wit's Recreations" (1640); and that one
of the alleged new pieces (On Julia's Weeping) forms
one of the couplets in *Hesperides.* More remarkable
still, instead of the " six or eight " poems of the *Hesperides* that Mr. Hazlitt states had originally appeared
in "Wit's Recreations," no fewer than 62 so appeared—
all as noticed in the places.

Contents.

MEMORIAL-INTRODUCTION.

Memorial-Introduction.

I. BIOGRAPHICAL.

ERRICK himself proudly recalls his " deare ancestrie " generally, and specifically works into his Book " of the Just "—of which more in the sequel—celebrations of many members of his family on both sides, as well direct as indirect (by marriages). It seems therefore only fitting that in the outset his Biographer should avail himself of recently-given details of Pedigree, corrective of and supplementary to Nichols, and others.[1]

The earliest known seat in England of the Herricks was Stretton Magna or Great Stretton, (Leicestershire)

[1] Nichols' History and Antiquities of the County of Leicester (Vol. II. part ii. p. 615 and pp. 502-3) has been displaced in so far as the district embraced by the later book is concerned, by the following most laborious local history : " The History of Market Harborough with that portion of the Hundred of Gartree, Leicestershire, containing the parishes of Baggrave, Billesdon [etc., etc., etc.] . . . . . . .with an account of the Lords of the Manors and their Pedigrees ; and a list of the Patrons and Rectors of each Living ; a Description of the Churches, Monuments, &c., by John Harwood Hill, B.A., F.S.A., Leicester : printed for the subscribers (and not

and which is sometimes called Bishop Stretton, from being the birth-place of Robert Eyrick, Bishop of Lichfield, who in 1378 founded a 'Chantry' there. It is told of him that at the time of his consecration he was " obliged to have some one to read the profession of canonical obedience before the Archbishop, as he could not read "[2]—no unusual thing then. Earlier still, viz. in 1334, Isabella, wife of Ivo Herrick—Ivo suggesting the Norse traditionary lineage from Erik—"recovered seisin in relation to the Manor of Stretton, from Matilda, daughter of Ivo Eyrick, of three and a half acres and one messuage."[3] The following is the Pedigree of Eyrick of Great Stretton.

——Eyrick of Stretton, temp Henry III.══—

Alan Eyrick, of Stretton ══— 2. Henry Eyrick, of Stretton ══—

Robert Eyrick, of Stretton.   John Eyrick, of Stretton ══—

Robert Eyrick, of Stretton ══ Joanna

1. Sir William Eyrick, of Stretton, Kent, from whom descend the Eyricks of Houghton.   2. Robert Eyrick, Bp. of Lichfield, ob. 1385.   John Eyrick, of Adelena, Stretton.[4]

published) by Ward and Sons, 1875, folio pp. xvi. and 345. In these genealogical details Mr. Hill is my authority, unless otherwise marked. [2] Hill, as before, p. 110. [3] *Ibid.* [4] *Ibid*, p. 123.

The Stretton Eyricks—as represented by Sir William Eyrick, Knt.—are next found at Houghton, anciently called Houkton, Hohtone, Houltone, and Houghton-on-the-Hill, about six miles from Leicester. The story of this 'Lordship' is a stirring and various-coloured one. Many lustrous names figure in it, especially the Zouches or La Zouches, Ferrers, Erdingtons, and Beaumonts, and later the Freers. The Church—dedicated to St. Catharine—lies in a light of ancient glory. One of the most venerable 'Rectors' was Tobias Heyricke B.D. 1605, who died in 1627. The branches of the Houghton Herricks are manifold. I can only record the more noticeable. As at Stretton the spelling of the name was Ericke, Eyreke or Eyrick. Robert Ericke of Houghton, had two sons, by Agnes his wife : Robert, who died without issue, and Thomas, "of Houghton-on-the-Hill, Gent," who afterwards settled at Leicester. This Thomas is the first of the name that appears in the Corporation-Books of Leicester, where he is mentioned as a member of that body in 1511. He died "about six years afterwards, most probably in early life, as he never executed the office of chief magistrate of Leicester." His Will is dated 1517. Nicholas and John, the two sons of this Thomas Eyrick, became freemen of Leicester in 1535 Nicholas, the eldest,

c

was Mayor of Leicester in 1552, and "had, it is believed, two sons, Thomas and John." John, as appears by the Corporation-Books was made free in 1568; and he had a son (probably named John) for "old John, in his Will dated in 1588, gives a small legacy to his godson, the son of his cousin John Eyrick; and it is well known that in those days uncles called their nephews cousins."[5] John Eyrick, the younger son of Thomas, was twice Mayor of Leicester; and by Mary, his wife, daughter of John Bond, of Ward End, otherwise Little Bromwich, in the county of Warwick, Esquire, had five sons and seven daughters.[6] The following curious epitaph of this John Heyrick and Mary, his wife, is in St. Martin's Church, Leicester, on an upright marble, at the East end of the North aisle, in what is still called Heyrick's Chapel :—

" Here lieth buried the body of JOHN HEYRICKE, late of
    this parish, who departed this life ye 2nd of April, 1589,
    beinge about the age of 76. He did marrie the
    daughter of John Bond, of Wardend, of the county of
    Warwicke, Esquire, who lived with ye saide Marie in

    [5] See this curiously illustrated by " The London Prodigal" who invariably calls his uncle " uncle," while the uncle as invariably calls the nephew " cousin."

    [6] *Ibid*, p. 118. Interesting *data* are here given on all these " sons' and daughters "—not necessary to be furnished by us.

one house, full 52 years; and in all that time never
buried man, woman, nor childe, though they were
sometimes 20 in a household. He had issue by the
said Marie, 5 sonns and 7 daughters, viz : Robert,
Nicholas, Thomas, John, and William ; and daughters,
Ursula, Agnes, Elizabeth, Ellen, Christian and Alice.
The said John was Mayor of this towne in anno 1559;
and again in anno 1572. The said MARIE departed
this life ye 8th of December, 1611, being of the age 97
years. She did see before her departure, of her children, and her children's children, to the number
of 142.''[7]

Robert Heyricke, the first son of John and Mary
thus celebrated, was three times Mayor of Leicester,
and was M.P. for the borough, with John Chyppyndale,
Esq., " the indenture of whose return is dated 11th of
October.—30 Elizabeth."[8] He had large property,
being possessed of the Franciscan or Grey, and the
Augustus Friars, in Leicester, with a considerable
estate adjoining to the latter, besides other estates;
and although he had eleven children, was a great bene-
factor to the town of Leicester.

In 1598, " were granted from the Herald's office,
unto Robert and William Herrick, the sonns of John
Heyrick, the sonne of Thomas Herick, *alias* Erick, of

---

[7] *Ibid*, p. 118.   [8] *Ibid*, pp. 118-19.

Houghton, in the county of Leicester, gent, and their posterity for ever.—A certain creast or badge, ivy, on a wreath of these colours, a bull's head Argent, yssuing forth of a laurell garland, the mussell, ears, and hornes tipped Sable, to be annexed and borne with their auncient coat of armes, which is, Silver, a fess verrey Or, and Gules."[9]

The old Alderman Heyrick died in 1618, and is thus described on an upright stone in St. Martin's.—

" Here lieth the bodie of Robert Herick, Ironmonger and Alderman of Leicester, who had been thrise Maior thereof. Hee was the eldest son to John Herrick and Marie, and had two sonnes and 9 daughters by one wife, with whom he lived 51 years. At his death he gave away 16 pound 10 shillings a yeare to good uses. He lived 78 years : and after dyed very godly the 14th of June, 1618. All flesh is grasse : but younge and ould must die : and so we pass in judgment by and by."[1]

The Portrait of this Robert Herrick is still preserved in the Town Hall of Leicester, thus inscribed :

" His picture whom you here see,
When he is dead and rotten ;
By this shall he remembered be,
When he would be forgotten.

[9] *Ibid*, p. 119.   [1] *Ibid*, p. 116.

The descendants of these Leicester Herricks gave various clergymen to the Church of England and eminent citizens to London and elsewhere.[2] Two things in their descent and intermarriages claim passing notice from their linking on to still greater modern names, viz., 1. That an Abigail Erick, of Leicester, (probably of the family of the first Nicholas) married in 1665, Jonathan Swift, of Leicestershire, father of the Dean of St. Patricks. 2. That Anne, daughter of the Rev. Samuel Heyrick, M.A., Rector of Bramton Ash, co. Northampton, married the Rev. Aulay Macaulay, vicar of Rothley and brother of Zachary Macaulay, father of Lord Macaulay.

Turning back now to Nicholas Heyrick, the second son of John and Mary of the epitaph before given, he was "articled in or before the year 1556, to a goldsmith of eminence in Cheapside, London, in which place and profession he afterwards himself settled."[3] By a lucky accident I have obtained the record of his marriage-license as granted by the Bishop of London. It was issued "8 Dec. 1582" and the parties are described as "Nicholas Herycke, Goldsmith, and Julian Stone, spinster, of the city of London." They were

---

[2] *Ibid*, pp. 119—121.   [3] *Ibid*, p. 121.

"to marry at St. Leonard's, Bromley, co. Middlesex."[4]
This Julian Stone is usually described as a daughter of
William Stone, of Segenhoe, in Bedfordshire, Esquire;
but Segenhoe did not come to the Stones until 1632;
so that such description is by prolepsis.[5] She was
sister to Anne, Lady Soame, wife of Sir Stephen
Soame, Knight, Lord Mayor of London (1598). For-
tunately the Registers of their Parish Church—St.
Vedast, Foster Lane, London—escaped the fire; and
I am enabled by the kindness of the present Rector
(the Rev. Thomas Pelham Dale, M.A.) to furnish
hitherto unknown family details, as follows :—

1. William Herricke sonne to Nicholas Herricke was
baptized the xxiiii. day of November 1585.

2. Martha Herricke the daughter of Nicholas Herricke
was baptized the xxii[th] day of January, 1586.

3. Mercie the daughter of Nicholas Herricke was baptized the xxii[th] day of December, 1586.

4. Thomas Herricke sonne to Nicholas Herricke was
baptized the vii[th] day of May, 1588.

5. Nicholas Herricke sonne to Nicholas Herricke was
baptized the xxij[th] of April 1589.

6. Anne Herricke the daughter of Nicholas Herricke was
baptized the xxvi day of July 1590

7. Robert Herricke sonne to Nicholas Herricke was baptized the xxiiii day of August 1591.

[4] Through Colonel Chester, Bermondsey, London.

[5] *Ibid,*—who has supplied me with the facts.

There was a posthumous son, William (born 1593)
as appears by a poem in the *Hesperides*. The 'Robert'
of this Register was our Poet. So that it is seen his
great-grandfather was Thomas Eyrick of Houghton-on-
the-Hill (ob. 1517)—his grandfather, John Eyrick of
Leicester, son of Thomas (ob. 1589)—his father,
Nicholas Herricke or Heyrick, 2nd son of John of
Leicester. He was named 'Robert' after the famous
Robert of Leicester as is proved by a small legacy to
him as his 'godsonne.'[6] Very soon after the birth of
Robert a dark shadow fell across the hearth and household in Cheapside—for the father died in 1592, and
was buried on "the ix^th day" of the month.[7] Family
papers at Beaumanor inform us that the death was
caused by a fall from an upper window of his own
house. These also reveal that at the time the fall was
suspected to have been not accidental but intentional.
The Will—which it is our privilege to print for the first

[6] In his Will in 1617 he leaves "To Robert Heyricke my
brother Nicholas's son, my godson, five pounds."

[7] Usually he is said to have died on the 9th November, but the
entry in the Register of Vedast, Foster Lane, is:—"Nicholas
Herricke a goldsmith was buried the ixth day of November 1592."
This would seem to indicate that he died on the very day of making
his Will (7th). He could hardly have been buried on the same day
that he died.

time from the original, and which is dated only two days
before the funeral, gives no suspicion of suicide.   It
thus runs—*literatim :*—

" In the name of God Amen The seaventhe Daye of
November A thousand ffive hundreth ninety twoe I Nicholas Hericke goldsmith of perfecte memorye in sowle but
sicke in bodye Doe make and ordayne this my Last will
and testament wherein I Doe commend my Sowle to the
handes of Almighty god And my Bodye to be buryed in the
parrishe Churche of S[t] ffosters My worldly goods I will and
give as the Lorde hathe given me freely in this sorte My
state is worthe three thowsand poundes I giue to my
Loving wyfe Julyan Hericke the thirde parte which is one
thowsand poundes And the twoe partes to be Devided my
funeralls being Discharged amongest my six children my
twoe Brothers Robert and William chefe overseers And my
sonnes Thomas and Nicholas wholle and sole Executors
This I request my brethren to see performed   Nicholas
Hericke   Witnesses William Herricke Helyn Holden[8]
V.H."

This Will is stated by Mr. Hazlitt[9] and others not to
have been forthcoming on the death ; but as it bears

---

[8] Letters of Administration were granted in the Prerogative Court
of Canterbury 13 Feb. 1592-3 to Robert Herricke, brother of testa-
tor, during the minority of Thomas and Nicholas Herricke the sons
and executors named in the will, the relict Julian Herricke having
renounced.   Recorded in Book " Nevell," folio 95.

[9] Biographical Notice, as before, p. xiii.

that Letters of Administration were granted in the Prerogative Court of Canterbury so early as Feb. 13th 1592-3, this must be a mistake. All the more deplorable consequently was it that rumours swiftly taken up by Dr. Fletcher, Bishop of Bristol, as High Almoner, led to a claim by him on the whole "goods and chattels" of the alleged suicide. After weary and wearing litigation, the matter was referred to arbitration, and the Bishop was awarded £220 only, "in satisfaction of all pretensions." It was £220 taken graspingly from the "widow and the fatherless"—one of, alas! many unscrupulous actions of this constantly impecunious Bishop. (Sorrow it is to us thus to speak of the father of John Fletcher and a brother of the noble Dr. Giles Fletcher, father of Phineas and Giles Fletcher.)[1]

The surroundings of Robert as a child, then little more than a year old, as of the entire family, were thus black enough; but their worldly prospects were not altogether inauspicious. If not to be regarded as wealthy, Nicholas Herrick must have been in fairly easy circumstances. By his Will *(supra)* he himself estimated his entire property at £3000 ; but it realized actually £5000, which may be set down as equal to £25,000 to-day. Early in 1593 came a posthumous child, who

[1] Beaumanor MSS.

was named William, the " dying brother " of some
touching lines in the *Hesperides*.[2]   As he was born
at Harry Campion's house at Hampton, [Court] the
widow appears to have retired thither.   From an enigmatical reference to his father's burial-place it looks as
though a shadow of mystery was allowed to hang over
his memory.[3]   He thus writes of him :—

> " *To the reverend shade of his religious Father.*
> That for seven *Lusters* I did never come
> To doe the *Rites* to thy Religious Tombe ;
> That neither haire was cut, or true teares shed
> By me, o'r thee, *(as justments to the dead)*
> Forgive, forgive me ; since I did not know
> Whether thy bones had here their Rest, or no.
> But now 'tis known, Behold ; behold, I bring
> Unto thy Ghost th' Effusèd Offering :
> And look, what Smallage, Night-shade, Cypresse, Yew,
> Unto the shades have been, or now are due,
> Here I devote ; And something more then so ;
> I come to pay a Debt of Birth I owe.
> Thou gav'st me life (but mortal) ; For that one
> Favour, Ile make full satisfaction ;
> For my life mortall, Rise from out my Herse,
> And take a life immortall from my verse."[4]

[2] Vol. I. p. 125.
[3] Probably the body had been secretly buried and the place kept
secret in fear of its being buried as that of a suicide.   The rapidity
of the burial, two days or less after death, is significant certainly.
[4] Vol. I., pp. 45-6.

As annotated in the place 'seven Lusters' is = 35 years, and gives 1626 as the date of the long-delayed filial tribute. This was only three years before the mother's death. It is not easy in our dim light to explain the son's ignorance of his father's burial-place ; but if the litigation extended over years and years, he may intend a sub-allusion in ' Rest' to the undecided question as to suicide or accident—the former involving ecclesiastically an unconsecrate grave and a darkened memory—for the Bishop in his greed made no pitiful allowance for so much as temporary insanity, even supposing his intended self-destruction had been true. As an infant of 14 months only, he could himself have no personal recollections. Be this as it may, by the Will the children were confided to the guardianship of their uncle, William Herrick, (afterward from the boring skilfully of a diamond for the King, created Sir William) —who was also a goldsmith in Cheapside and prosperous in every way.[5] From our Poet's kindly recollections of "beloved Westminster" it may be pretty safely assumed that that venerable School may claim

---

[5] In Appendix A to this Memorial-Introduction will be found genealogical and other details on the Beaumanor Herricks ; and also in Appendix B a fuller notice than hitherto of one eminent member of the family, the Warden of Manchester College.

? much dis·cussed. Unpartable !

him for a pupil. Mr. Walford observes on this : " He certainly speaks of the youthful amusements of rowing and swimming in connection with his " beloved Westminster " in a way which would all but warrant us in asserting that he was educated at Westminster School ; and the assertion would be strongly confirmed by the evident saturation of his mind with the writings of classical authors, to an extent scarcely ever found except in the case of those whose early years have been spent at an English public school," (p. v.). It is to be regretted that the early Registers of this renowned School have all perished ; but I agree with Mr. Walford that his way of celebrating his " beloved Westminster" seems to indicate the School and not his after home-residence. The amusements point to boyhood, not to the later abode in " St. Anne's, Westminster." The fact that his little brother William was born at Hampton gives vividness to his mention of the villages on the Thames, whither he steered, " Richmond, Kingstone and Hampton-Court." If he came and went to School at Westmimster from Hampton it is not difficult to understand his " Tears to Thamasis."

There were four boys in all, and their guardian seems to have seen to their several occupations with characteristic carefulness (in a double sense, as will

appear). The post-natus William died young : Thomas
was placed with Mr. Massam, a merchant in London ;
but in 1610 he retired to the country and settled in a
small farm—as immortalized in one of his brother's most
Horatian and sustained poems (" A Country Life : to
his brother M. Tho: Herrick "),[6] and Nicholas, was similarly settled early in life in London, and traded to the
Levant. Another poem, addressed to him, shows that
he had travelled much by sea and land, including
Jerusalem (" To his Brother, Nicholas Herrick ").[7]
Robert was in like manner destined to follow in his
father's footsteps; for from the original Indentures which
are at Beaumanor, we learn he was " bound apprentice "
on the 25th September, 1607, "for ten years " to his
uncle and guardian. Ten years would bring us forward
to 1617-18 ; but the pact must have been broken,[8]

---

[6] Hill, as before, p. 122. It is supposed that this Thomas was
father of Thomas Heyricke, who in 1668, resided at Market Harborough and issued a trader's token there; and grandfather to a
Thomas Herrick who was curate of Market Harborough, and who
published some Sermons and Poems.

[7] *Ibid*, p. 122. In 1634 his pedigree is entered in the Visitation
of London ; and he had then by his wife Susanna, d. of William
Salter, 3 sons and 3 daughters. He was living in 1648 when
the *Hesperides* was published.

[8] ' Broken.' That is in so far as young Herrick was concerned,

seeing that he is found addressing his uncle from (probably) Cambridge so early as September, 1613, and in all likelihood he had proceeded thither some time previously. In 1613 he was in his 21st year, and youths went to College from their 14th to their 17th year. From the loss of the University and College registers and other documents, it is impossible to trace him exactly; but there can be no question that he proceeded to the University. Mr. Walford casts doubt on his ever having been of St. John's College, and in all Professor Mayor's bulky tomes from the Baker MSS. his name is sought for in vain, albeit innumerable nobodies (or bodies only) have found, perhaps inevitably, devout record and eulogy therein.[9] It is singular that both these scholars should have overlooked the fact that two of his Letters are expressly dated " Cambridg : St. Johns " and that in a third in a receipt, he designates himself a " Fellow Commoner of S^t. Johns Colledg in

who certainly ceased to be an ' apprentice.' It has been suggested to me that his dependence upon his uncle for the quarterly doles of his own patrimony even after his coming of age, is to be accounted for by the apprentice bond being still in force. It is noteworthy in regard to this that the money-letters cease about the date of the expiry of the apprentice term.

[9] Memoir, as before, p. v.: and History of St. John's College, Cambridge, 2 vols., 8vo, 1869.

Cambridg." There is thus absolute certainty as to his having entered and attended at S.t John's College.

His guardian-uncle, though the " Fellow Commoner " was in his 21st-23d years, kept a discreditably tight rein on his nephew's expenditure. In the first of fourteen letters preserved at Beaumanor, the student seeks " fifteen pounds " for his brother Thomas.[1] It has all the stiffness and stateliness of etiquette demanded from young men (and eke young ladies) of the period, in their approaches to their seniors and (technically) superiors—even in the case of sons and daughters to their parents. We must pause to read it :

LETTER I.

[September, 1613.]

" SR.—Syth the qvallitie of the Time, and extreamitie of my Brothers occasions forse me, I first shew my deutie, and next entreat you to furnish my Brother with 15 pounds, which he would needes borrow of me, and because his vrgent occasions stand in so vehement a manner, I am willing to pleasure him, still relying vpon your Worships

---

[1] Nichols in his Leicestershire was the first to print some of these Letters. Mr. Hazlitt printed them *in extenso* as an Appendix, but faultily. I have had the advantage of collating his text with the originals, through their owner, the late W. Perry-Herrick, Esq., of Beaumanor. Eheu! He has recently died, and in him the English Herricks become apparently extinct. There are others in the United States.

fauour, and trusting that I shall not seem offensiue to you nor engender any cause of dislike in my proceeding : I haue writ thus much at the request of my Brother, though indeed I was vnwilling to acquaint you in this busines, yet pray, S*, iustly waigh each thing in equall ballances : I still runn headlong into your Worships debt. I trust you will be pleased, though I vnwillingly acquaint you with this. Thus hauing rudely made known the effect of the matter, I with my endles deutie take my leaue, liuing to be comanded by you and yours for euer :

ROBERT HERICK."

[Endorsement :]
" To the right worl. Sr William Hearick
at Beaumanor or els where."

A second Letter but without time-date, though from echo of words used in the preceding, most probably written very soon after it—has under all its phrases of respect an under-tone of plaint if not complaint of his "constrained necessitie." The explanation of the evident *sore* feeling of the Writer is to be found in this, that every one of the payments in these letters was simply out of his own "little fortune," which amounted to from £470 to £660 (= £2500 now). It was hard to have what was his own doled out meagrely, in this knowledge. This second letter intimates a very bare 'setting up' at the University.   Had the nephew-apprentice irritated the old knight by violating his indenture to him ? We can only conjecture.   Here is

LETTER II.

" Cambridg : St. Johns.

" S^r.—Considering the importunitie of my own affaires, and the last testimonie of your so euident loue, makes me to run headlong between two ineuitable difficulties, but desirous of equall performance : the shortness of this shall not hinder the one, nor I trust detract from the other : S^r, vnderstand that my hart (more feruently then my pen can express) speaks my deuout thanks, and ioyes in no greater thing then this, that it can see some sparkes of your conceald affection : I haue not as hitherto acquainted you with the chardg I liue in, but your self can iudg, by my often (as now at this time) writing for mony, which when I doe, it is for no impertinent expens, but for constraind necessitie : for be your self the iudg, when aboue twentie pounds will not suffice the house, not reckening with it commoditie for my self (I meane apparell nor other complements) nor tuition mony nor other sundrie occasions for chardges, this but considered, there is no reasonable soule, but will kindly and indulgently censure of my lyfe and me. Had I but a competent estate to mayntayne my self, to my title, I could presume of as soone atayning to ye end of the efficient cause—my coming,—as he that hath stronger cause and fortune : S^r, I know you vnderstand me, and did you but know how disfurnished I came to Cambridg, without bedding (which I yet want) and other necessaries, you would (as I now trust you will) better your thoughts towards me, considering of my forc't expence. S^r, I entreat you to furnish me with ten pounds this quarter; for the last mony which I receaud came not till

d

the last quarter had almost spent it self, which now con-
straines me so suddenly to write for more.   Good S^r,
forbeare to censure me as prodigall, for I endeuour rather
to strengthen (then debilitate) my feeble familie fortune.
I should fill much paper, if I should follow my passions ;
but I will break off, only entreating you (yf there be no
waye for me to leade a lyfe here) that then you would
write me your counsell how I maye learn to liue.   In hope
that you will some waye effectuate my desires, with all
respect of deutie and obseruance, I forstop [2] my passage.

   " Euer to be at comand and studious to please,

                      " R. HEARICK."

    [Endorsement :]

      " To his most carefull Vncle Sr Willi :
         Hearick dwelling at London in
         Wood-streete."

There was a little break of sarcasm surely in that
endorsement "To his most *carefull* Vncle" as within
in the phrase, " *concealed* affection."

Still at S^t. John's College, a third letter brings the
student before us in the same attitude of formal and
punctilious obeisance to the grand city-uncle and evidently hampered for books and scholarly necessities,
after a fashion not at all creditable to his guardian.
In the last letter he had said " I should fill much paper
if I should follow my passions ; but I will break off,
only entreating you (yf there be no waye for me to leade

    [2] I stop my going on earlier than I otherwise would.

a lyfe Here) that then you would write me your counsell how I maye leame to liue." Surely this was most
reasonable? With his youth passing away and his
future indefinite, he now still more passionately longs
to be and to do something, e.g. "because that *Time
hath devoured some yeeres,* I am the more importunate
in the crauing." One is reminded of a greater Poet
who similary marked the flight of his years and
mourned grandly over uneffected purpose and hindering circumstance. Before we turn to this letter we
may pause to read Milton's great sonnet :—

"*On his having arrived at the age of twenty-three..*
How soon hath Time, the subtle thief of youth,
    Stolen on his wing my three-and-twentieth year!
    My hasting days fly on with full career,
    But my late spring no bud or blossom shew'th.
Perhaps my semblance might deceive the truth
    That I to manhood am arrived so near;
    And inward ripeness doth much less appear,
    That some more timely-happy spirits endu'th.
Yet, be it less or more, or soon or slow,
    It shall be still in strictest measure even
    To that same lot, however mean or high,
Toward which Time leads me, and the will of Heaven.
    All is, if I have grace to use it so,
    As ever in my great Task-Master's eye."

I do not think that I do wrong to Herrick when

I judge that in these years there came no such vision of the ' great Task-Master's eye ' to him. It were of the Pleasures of Imagination rather than of the Pleasures of Hope, to think of him as, thus far, more than impulsively ardent in the acquisition of that odd and discursive learning which characterizes his Poems. His fierce Norse blood, I fear, made the ' flesh ' rather than the ' spirit ' master—as the Puritans would have phrased it. There was evidently, as yet, no fixed purpose of studying for ' holy orders ; ' and so, as evidently, he gave full swing to what were accounted lay-liberty to quaff of all cups that might be put to his lips. Even later he had to accuse himself of "wild, unhallowed rhymes," and contemporary with his attendance at the University the manners were gay (in a sorrowful sense), and not a few of the students (so-called) uncleanly. Evidently ' evil reports ' reached the old gentleman—Herrick's uncle—concerning him ; for he deprecates his suspicions (in Letter X). Now for

LETTER III.

From St. Johns in Cambridg.

" Qui timide rogat,
Negare docet."

" Are the minds of men immutable ? and will they rest in only one opinion without the least perspicuous shewe of chaing ? O no, they cannot, for Tempora mutantur et nos mutamur in illis : it is an old but yet young saying in our age, as times chainge, so mens minds are altered : O would . . . .[3] weere seene, for then some pittying Planet would with a dr [op of] deaw refreash my withered hopes, and giue a lyfe to that which [is about ?] to die ; the bodie is preserued by foode, and lyfe by hope, which (but want- ing either of these conseruers) faint, feare, fall, freese, and die. Tis in your power to cure all, to infuse by a pro- fusion a duble lyfe into a single bodie. Homo homini Deus : man should be soe, and he is commanded so ; but, fraile and glass-lik, man proues brittle in many things. How kind Arcisilaus the philosofher was vnto Apelles the painter, Plutark in his Morals will tell you ; which should I heere depaint, the length of my letter would hide the sight of my Labour, which that it may not, I bridle in my Quill, and mildly, and yet I feare too rashly, and too boldly, make knowne and discouer [that] which my modestie would conceale : and this is all : my studie craues but your assistance to furnish hir with bookes, wherein she is most desirous to laboure ; blame not hir modest boldnes, but suffer the aspertions [=sprinklings] of your loue to distill vpon hir, and next to Heauen she will consecrate hir laboures vnto you, and because that Time hath deuoured some yeeres, I am the more importunate in the crauing : suffer not the distance to hinder that which I know your disposition wilI not denie. And now is the time (that *florida ætas*) which promises frutifulness for hir former barrenness, and wisheth

---

[3] The corners of the original are somewhat injured, and hence certain words are illegible.

all to hope : As euery thing will haue in time an end, so
this, which though it would extend it self and ouerflow its
bounds I forceibly withstand it.   Wishing this worlds
happines to follow and attend you in this lyf, and that with
a triumphant crown of glorie you maye be crowned in the
best world to come.   "ROBERT HEARICK."
      [Endorsement :]
          "To the very Worshipf[ul] His
              Vncle Sᵣ W[ill.] Hearicke dwelling
                  at London in Woodstreete. These."

These Letters (I. to III.) belong to 1613-14. So
that 1615, which has hitherto been given as the year of
his going to Cambridge, is proved to be much too late.
The next two Letters—as shown by the receipt at the
foot of the first—belong to January, 1615-6 : another
to February, 1616 : another to April, 1616.   These
have all the same 'burden' of " *mitte pecuniam*," as it
so happens (what must be repeated and remembered)
that this one thing was all that led to correspondence
between nephew and niggard uncle—who gave (of
what was not his own but simply held in trust) as if a
personal bestowment. These four further Letters follow
successively :—

LETTER IV.
                    " Cambridg. [January, 1615-16.
   Sʀ.—Your prosperitie desired and the good success of
your issue, I pronounce my deutie, and wish some felicitie

to my self (as all other creatures do). I entreat you (as
heretofore) so now to paye to Mr. Adrian Morrus, bookseller in the black fryers, the some of tenn pounds, who
hath payd the same some at Cambridg : I cannot meet the
expence for want of primarie consideration; be you but
pleas'd, and I shall iustifie the expectation (which I trust
is religious) of all men. My prayers begin at home, but
end at you their obiect. Bless me with your countenance,
and I shall liue triumphant, and my weake hopes will
receaue vigour. Yf you reflect vpon . . . . I am all yours
and completely yours for euer obsequious,

"ROBIN HARICK."[4]

[Endorsement:]

" To the right Worpfl. his louing Vncle
Sr William Hearick dwelling at
London in great Wood-
street. This."

LETTER V.

"Cambridge, [January, 1616.]

" Before you vnceald my letter (right wor[ll].) it cannot be
doubted but you had perfect knowledg of the essence of my
writing, before you reade it; for custome hath made you
expert in my playne songe (mitte pecuniam) that beeing
the cause sine quâ non, or the power that giues lyfe and
beeing to each matter. I delight not to draw your imagi-

---

[4] The request was granted, and at the foot of the letter appears
Robert Martin's receipt for £10 to be paid to Herrick; this bears
date Jan. 24, 1615-16. The present letter is not in the poet's hand-
writing, but seems to have been written for him, and his name
added playfully.

nation to inextricable perplexities, or knit vp my Love in indissoluable knotts, but make no other exposition but the literall sence, which is to entreat you to paye to Mr. Adrian Morice the some of tenn pounds as customarily, and to take a note of his hand for the receit, which I desire may be effected brefly, because the circumstance of the time must be expressed. I perceaue I must crie with the afflicted *vsquequo, vsquequo, Domine.* Yet I haue confidence that I liue in your memorie, howsoeuer Time brings not the thing hoped for to its iust maturity ; but my beleef is stronge, and I do establish my hopes on rocks, and feare no quick-sands, be you my firme assistant, and good effects (produced from virtuous causes) follow. So shall my wishes pace with yours for the suplement of your owne happiness and the perfection of your owne posterity.

" Euer to be commanded,

" ROBERT HEARICK.

"To paye to Mr. Blunt Bookseller in Paules church yarde the some aboue named.

LETTER VI.

" Chambridge [February, 1616.]

."Because my Commencment is at hand (worthie Sir), I am compeld to write, though it be with a violent reluctation; for what hermonie can be effected when there is diuision 'twixt the hart and hand; want and chardge admit no sympathie, because they are of diffring natures, not conuertibles. Yet volens, nolens, it must be done, and as heretofore so now I desire your worship to paye to this Bearer, Mr. Hotchkin, the dew of tenn pounds for my vse at Chambridge. I haue runn thorough the most of the expense which is not much, but in respect of disabilitie. Yf it may please you to remember me like a trew Maecenas, I shall glory in that my Tale hath raysd me vp a Friend to share in my passions—

'Multorum manibus grande leuatur onus.'

Many hands make light worke ; your healpe can make my burden light. I atend your pleasure, and as I hope such wilbe my hap, I haue fayth in the goodness of your Nature. Attending with patience the complement and consummation of my hopes.

"Euer obseruant

"to your benignant

"fauours, R. HEARIK."[5]

" Bis dat qui cito dat."

[Endorsement :]

" To the right worll. his louing vncle
Sr William Hearick dwelling
at London in Great
Woodstreet.
This."

LETTER VII.

"Camb. [April, 1616.]

"Sir, that which makes my letter to be abortive and borne before maturitie, is and hath been my Commencment, which I haue now ouergonn, though I confess with many a throe and pinches of the purse ; but it was necessarie, and the prize was worthie the hazarde ; which makes me less sensible of the expence, by reason of a titular

---

[5] The acknowledgment of the person who was appointed to receive this sum, is at the foot of the letter as elsewhere.

prerogatiue—& bonum est prodire in bono.   The essence
of my writing is (as heretofore) to entreat you to paye for
my use to Mr. Arthour Johnson bookseller in Paules
church yard the ordinarie sume of ténn pounds, and that
with as much sceleritie as you maye, though I could wish
chardges had leaden wings and Tortice feet to come vpon
me ; sed votis puerilibus opto.   S^r, I fix my hopes on Time
and you ; still gazing for an happie flight of birdes, and
the refreshing blast of a second[6] winde.   Doubtfull as yet
of either Fortunes, I liue, hoarding vp prouision against
the assault of either.   Thus I salute your Vertues.

" Hopefull R. HEARICK."

It has already been stated that there is no trace of
Herrick's matriculation at either St. John's College, or
at Trinity Hall, or at the Registry ; but from the last it is
found that he took his B.A. degree from Trinity Hall in
1616-7, when he signed himself ' Robertus Hearick.'[7]
He must have migrated from St. John's to Trinity Hall
in 1616 ; and thus the letters dated by Mr. Hazlitt[8]
1617, belong to 1615-6 ; for in the last of the next group
he is still a " fellow commoner of St. John's colledg."
As these additional letters are read, be it still borne in

---

[6] The Latin *secundus* ▬favourable, profiting.

[7] Unfortunately only the year-dates are recorded.   Mr. William
Ald. Wright, M.A., Trinity College, Cambridge, was so good as
to favour me with this and another entry at the Registry.

[8] Edition of Herrick, as before, pp. 492-94 *et seqq.*

mind, that their monotonous refrain of 'money' is in consequence of the correspondence being practically so many receipts for (apparently) quarterly payments of the "customarye £10." Again these Letters follow successively :—

LETTER VIII.
" Health from Heauen.

" Chambridg.

" S^r.—I haue long since expected your return in that your long absence hath made me want that which your presence could haue remedied. I trust you are not ignorant what my meaning is; may it therefore please you to send me £10, for my ocasions require so much; and the long time that your Worship hath been absent from London hath compelled me to runne somewhat deepe into my Tailours debt. I entreat your Worship to send me a part of my stipend with all possible sceleritie, for want of which so necessarie helpe, cares greatly posses me, and force me contrarie to my wish, in some sort to neglect my study; whereas yf you would be pleased to furnish me with so much, that I might keepe beforehand with my Tutor, I doubt not but with quicke dispatch to attaine to what I ayme. Thus trusting that you will in some sort be mindfull of me, in sending me that which I haue writ for, with my eternall deutie to your self for euer, togeither with my Ladie, I finish.

" For euer readie
" to be comanded
" during mortallitie
" ROBERT HEARICK."

"I entreate your worship to furnish me with so much as will serue me till the Natiuitie."
[Endorsement :]
"To the right worll. his carefull vncle Sr
William Hearick. These be delivered
at his house in London."

LETTER IX.
"From Cambridg.

"Sr.—I am loath, yet pforce I must, beeing ouerruled by necessitie, trouble you. I haue, before the birth of this letter, sent others which peraduenture haue been stayed by infortunitie; but I trust this will manifest itself. Let it not seeme offensiue, though I exceede a little in length, for your Worships long beeing in the Cuntrie, hath constrained me contrarie to my will to become a debter to my instructr, —wherfore let me entreat your worship to be mindfull of me, and that this weeke I may receaue it; for my extreames be such that vnless I attaine what now I desire, I shalbe constrained to make a iourney to London to satisfie the mind of my Tutour. Good Sr, consider this, and redresse it, and I shall for euer in deutie show my self most abundantly thankfull. I trust this little will suffice to explain my great want, and I hope you will in some sorte bee carefull for my credit, which wilbe weak, except I hear from your worship this weeke. I will not extend too farr, but with my deutie to you and my Ladie, I for this time cease. "Being euer, obsequious to both,

"ROBERT HEARICK."

[Endorsement :]
"To the Right worshipfull his louing vncle
Sr Willia Hearick dwelling at
London in Great Wood-
street, Giue this."

LETTER X.

"Chambridge.

"S[r].—Though my seruice be late, yet better thus then neuer; it is in you to pardon what I haue so long neglected, and I beleeue you will. I will come speadily and personally to attend you at London, and will bring your bond along; to which end (necessitie constrayning me) I entreate you out of my litle possession to deliver to this bearer the customarye £10, without which I cannot meate[9] my ioyrney : I vnderstand it is troublesom to you for the quarterly dispatch, and I am honestly sorrowfull for your disease. Pardon me, and mayntayn some good opinion of me, that what I haue lost heretofore in your estimation, time and my endeuours may redeeme it. Trusting to which I offer vp to them, and to your self, the sacrifice of my vowes.

"ROBERT HEARICKE."

[Endorsement :]

"To his lovinge Vncle Sr William Hearicke
dwellinge at Westminster
this del. del."

LETTER XI.

"Cambridg, 11th of October.

"S[r].—My deutie remembred to your self and La : the cause essentiall is this : That I would entreate you to paye to this bringer (to Mr. Adrian Morrus book seller in the black friers,) the some of £10 the which my Tutor hath receaued, to be payde at London. I have business that drawes me from prolixitie; and I craue pardon for this rudeness, still expecting the sun-shine of youre fauour and

[9] = meet, the expenses of.

the daye of happiness. I end with my prayers for your
preseruation and health, the best terrestriall good. Long lyf
and the aspertions [=sprinklings] of Heauen fall vpon you.

"Yours euer

"obsequious

"R. HEARICK."

[Endorsement :]

"To the right worll., &c."

LETTER XII.

"Cambridg.

"Sir,—I presume againe to present another Embassador,
who, in the best eloquence that was taught him, aboun-
dingly thanks you for the larg extent of your favor and
kindness; which, though present time denies to mak any
ostentation of desert, yet future . . . . crownes the expectation of the hopefull; and because the urgent extreamite
and vnexpected occasion of chamber roome instigats me to
such importunate demands, I am bold to entreat you that
the mony might this week be sent me, for necessitie fer-
vently requires it; and I am sorrie to be the subiect of so
great a molestation to your Worship; but, trusting on
your patience, I am bold to saye that generous minds still
haue the best contentment, and willingly healp where there
is an euidencie of want. Thus hoping to triumph in the
victorie of my wishes, by being not frustraeted in my
expectatiŏ, I take my leaue, and eternally thank you. Liuing
to be comanded by you and yours to the end of mortalitie.

"Euer most

"obsequious

"ROBERT HEARICK."

"Be it known to all, that I Robert Hearick, Fellow com-

moner of St. Johns colledg in Cambridg, acknowledg my
self to stand indebited unto my vncle, Sir Will. Hearick,
of London, in the some of tenn pounds, for so much
receaued of him; to be repayde vnto him a[t] all times : I
saye, receaued tenn pounds by me, Robert Hearick."

[Endorsement :]

" To the right wor^ll. his vncle Sr Willi : Hearicke
dwelling at London in Great Wood
strete giue This."

The wording of the receipt seems to show that
Herrick had either come to the end of his own money
or that the money was a loan over and above his allowance. These importunities for books and necessaries
recall that through the same years, and at the same University, George Herbert was writing in much the same
strain to his good and generous step-father, Sir John
Danvers. It will put the blame on the guardian-uncle,
and lighten the pecuniary-iteration of these letters, to show
that apart from the monies being from his own patrimony,
his requests were really necessities—not forgetting that
Herbert's love of 'gay-dress' probably carried him
further than Herrick. I cull one characteristic letter
from Herbert, as thus :—

Sir,

I dare no longer be silent, lest while I think I am
modest, I wrong both my self and also the confidence my
friends have in me; wherefore I will open my case unto

you, which I think deserves the reading at the least; and
it is this—I want books extremely. You know, sir, how I
am now setting foot into divinity, to lay the platform of my
future life; and shall I then be fain always to borrow
books and build on another's foundation? What trades-
man is there who will set up without his tools? Pardon my
boldness, sir, it is a most serious case, nor can I write coldly
in that wherein consisteth the making good of my former
education, of obeying that Spirit which hath guided me
hitherto, and of atchieving my (I dare say) holy ends. This
also is aggravated in that I apprehend what my friends
would have been forward to say if I had taken ill courses,
'Follow your book, and you shall want nothing.' You
know, sir, it is their ordinary speech, and now let them
make it good; for since I hope I have not deceived their
expectation, let not them deceive mine. But perhaps they
will say, 'You are sulky; you must not study too hard.'
It is true, God knows, I am weak, yet not so but that every
day I may step towards my journey's end; and I love my
friends so well as that if all things proved not well, I had
rather the fault should be on me than on them. But they
will object again, 'What becomes of your annuity?' Sir,
if there be any truth in me, I find it little enough to keep
me in health. You know I was sick last vacation, neither
am I yet recovered, in that I am fain ever and anon to buy
somewhat tending towards my health; for infirmities are
both painful and costly. Now this Lent I am forbid utterly
to eat any fish, so that I am fain to dyet in my chamber at
mine own cost; for in our publick halls you know, is nothing
but fish and white meats; out of Lent also twice a week, on
Fridays and Saturdays, I must do so, which yet sometimes

I fast. Sometimes also I ride to Newmarket, and there lie
a day or two for fresh air; all which tend to avoiding of
costlier matters if I should fall absolutely sick. I protest
and vow I even study thrift, and yet I am scarce able with
much ado to make one half year's allowance shake hands
with the other. And yet if a book of four or five shillings
come in my way, I buy it, though I fast for it; yea sometimes of ten shillings. But, alas, sir, what is that to those
infinite volumes of divinity, which yet every day swell and
grow bigger? Noble sir, pardon my boldness, and consider but these three things : first, the bulk of divinity ;
secondly, the time when I desire this (which is now, when I
must lay the foundation of my whole life); thirdly, what I
desire and to what end—not vain pleasures nor to a vain
end. If then, sir, there be any course, either by engaging
my future annuity, or any other way, I desire you sir, to be
my mediator to them in my behalf.

Now I write to you, Sir, because to you I have ever
opened my heart ; and have reason by the patents of your
perpetual favour to do so still, for I am sure you love your
faithful servant   GEORG HERBÈRT.
"Trin. Coll. March 18. 1617."[1]

Far different was the response to the " sweet Singer "
of " The Temple " from that to the poet of " Hesperides " ; and for my part, across the centuries, I cry,
Beshrew the close-fisted old Knight.

---

[1] Prose of Herbert in Fuller Worthies' Library : Vol. iii. of Complete Works, pp. 485-6.

e

Like Herbert, Robert Herrick had undoubtedly proceeded to the University with a vague intention to study
for the Church ; and, like him, he ought now to have
been "setting foot into divinity." But his next letter
brings him before us as doubtful whether to direct "his
study" to Divinity or to Law. This letter also belongs
to 1616. It follows :—

LETTER XIII.

"After my abundant thanks for your last great loue
(worthie Sir), proud of your fauoure and kindness shewne
by my Ladie to my vnworthy selfe, thus I laye open my
selfe; that, for as much as my continuance will not long
consist in the spheare where I now moue, I make known my
thoughts, and modestly craue your counsell, whether it
were better for me to direct my study towards the lawe or
not; which yf I should (as it will not be impertinent), I
can with facilitie laboure my self into another colledg
appointed for the like end and studyes, where I assure my
self the charge will not be so great as where I now exist;
I make bold freely to acquaint you with my thoughts ; and
I entreat you answeare me : this being most which checks
me, that my time (I trust) beeing short, it may be to a
lesser end and smaller purpose; but that shalbe as you
shall lend direction. Nothing now remaines but my perfect
thankfullness and remembrance of your hopefull promises;
which when Heauen, working with you, shall bring them to
performance, I shall triumph in the victorie of my wishes;
till when, my prayers shall inuocate Heauen to powre vpon

you and your posteritie the utmost of all essentiall happiness.   .   " Yours euer seruicable

"R. HEARICK."

The closing Letter is dated " Trinitie Hall, Cambridge," and is pathetic in its references to his "ebbing
estate"—by which I understand that Sir William had told
him his £400 to £500 was nearly exhausted; nor less
so his resolution in his new College "to liue recluse, till
Time contract me to some other calling, striuing now
with myself (retayning vpright thoughts) both sparingly
to liue and thereby to shun the current of expence."
The yearly amount allowed was (apparently) at most
£40, and had it been from Sir William himself instead of
from his own "little portion," Herrick might have had
no great ground of complaint.   As it was he certainly
had ground of complaint.   It is likewise to be noted
that though Robert (Sir William's elder brother) was
associated with him as 'overseer' of the Will, the
Knight seems practically to have ignored him from the
outset and acted alone.   The last letter thus runs :—

LETTER XIV.

"Trinitie Hall, Camb.

"S^r.—The confidence I haue of your bothe virtuous and
generous disposition makes me (though with some honest
reluctation) the seldomer to solicite you; for I haue so

incorporated beleef into me, that I cannot chuse but per-
swade my self that (though absent) I stand imprinted in
your memorie; and the remembrance of my last beeing at
London serud for an earnest motiue (which I trust liues yet
vnperisht) to the effectuating of my desire, which is not but
in modesty ambitious, and consequently virtuous; but,
where freeness is euident, there needs no feere for forward-
ness; and I doubt not (because fayth giues boldness) but
that Heauen, togeither with your self, will bring my ebbing
estate to an indifferent tyde; meane while I hope I haue
(as I presume you know) changd my colledg for one where
the quan[ti]tie of expence wilbe shortned, by reason of the
priuacie of the house, where I propose to liue recluse, till
Time contract me to some other calling, striuing now with
my self (retayning vpright thoughts) both sparingly to liue,
and thereby to shun the current of expence. This is my desire
(which I entreat may be performd) that Mr. Adrian Morrus,
bookseller of the black fryers, maye be payd ten pounds as
heretofore, and to take his acquittance.   Trusting whereto,
Ile terminate your sight, and end; hoping to see your dayes
many and good; and prosperitie to crown your self and
issue.   " Euer seruiceable

" to your Virtues,

" R. HEARICK."

It rouses one to remember that to the guardian-uncle
to whom these letters were addressed, an additional
quarterly allowance to his nephew would have been as
nothing.   But he was adding broad acre to broad acre,
and ambitious to found a family away down in ances-

tral Leicestershire. That in his land-hunger (of which the greater Sir Walter Scott later spoke so penitently) he was not over scrupulous, appears by this damning record in the MSS. of the House of Lords :

"1640-1, Jan. 15.—Petition of Elizabeth Smyth, the poor distressed widow of Christopher Smyth, deceased, that Sir William Herrick may be called upon to answer for detaining from her a certain estate in the county of Leicester, part of the manor of Beaumanor, to which the Court of Chancery decreed that she is entitled."[2]

From the indefiniteness of the phrase "till Time shall contract me to *some other calling*" in the final letter that remains, it would seem that the proposed change from Divinity to Law was left undetermined. The only further record of him at the University is that he took his M.A degree in 1620, signing himself 'Robert Hearick.' In this year, thereupon, he most probably left Cambridge. As he was not a Fellow, it is not likely that he would continue in residence. Besides, had he remained and 'taught', there must have been some memorials of his teaching and pupils. Certain entries found by Mr. Riley in the Steward's Book, and printed in the *Second Report of the Royal*

---

[2] Fourth Report of the Royal Commission on Historical Manuscripts : Part I. Report and Appendix : p. 40.

Commission on Historical Manuscripts (pp. 121-123) have been too hastily assigned to our Robert Herrick. His nephew—Robert 3rd son of Sir William Herricke, who was " baptized the viii. day of February, 1598," at St. Vedast's Church, Foster Lane, London,[3] was much more probably the person whose indebtedness to his college is therein recorded. Extending as these entries do to 1629-30, or fully nine years after his M.A. degree, it surely bears on the face of it, that it could not be our Robert, and on the other hand, it would be quite in keeping with the Beaumanor Knight's penuriousness and begrudging, so to hamper his own son as to compel him to leave there a small debt, unliquidated.[4]

[3] From the Register by the present Rector, as before. See also Appendix A to this Memorial-Introduction.

[4] I place here Mr. Riley's notes :

"A small memorandum [among Trinity Hall MSS.] without any date, but belonging, no doubt, to the year 1630, bearing reference to Robert Herrick, who had been a member of the College, (the well-known author of the " Hesperides")—The names of those that are to be sued. Will. Wake, 5*l* 18*s*. 6*d*. obol. Thomas Creake, besides ' præ manibus ' [a name apparently given to caution-money] deducted 4*l* 2*s*. 7*d*. Herricke 3*l* ' præ manibus ' being deducted, 7*l* 16*s*. 9*d*. The Steward's accounts of 1629 and 30 follow shortly after, in both of which Herrick's name appears, as debited with 10*l* 16*s*. 9*d*. against it, the largest sum debited against

A study of the facts, leaves the impression that on closing his attendance at the University in 1620 (as *supra*) Herrick—then in his 29th year — came to London, with his future uncertain, but ready to plunge into all the gaieties of ' town.' To these years— 1620-28-9—belong *(meo judicio)* :—

> " Those Lyric feasts
> Made at the Sun,
> The Dog, the Triple Tun,"

any one in the list: reference will again be found made to Herrick's name in the sequel (p. 122) . . . . . " Also a paper book, pamphlet form, entitled—" The Steward his accompt of the whole Commons Booke, the 3rd of October 1623." In this book, col. 2. of page 3, under (tr.),—" Names of those who were in College on the 3rd day of October 1623, and their debts." Herrick is named, as then owing the steward 57s. 7d. (p. 123). I must add to what is said in the text, that had these entries referred to our Herrick, I should have expected that he would be called ' Mr. Herricke.' Walford mistakenly says there is an entry of indebtedness at Trinity Hall in 1617 (p. v). There is no such entry. The earliest is 1623, and the others 1630—at which time he was incumbent of Dean Prior. Anthony a-Wood mistook our Herrick's cousin Robert for him, and so entered him as of Oxford. The cousin may have attended both Universities—as was common—and in such case it was natural that his father would send him to the same College at which his nephew had attended. *Supra*, it was not exactly ' caution,' nor even earnest, but so much being already paid. Be it also noted that the £7 16s. 9d. and £3 make up the same amount and debt as before—viz., £10 16s. 9d.

of which he sang so proudly. To them also belong the still more boastful reminiscences of his "Farewell vnto Poetrie," as thus :—

> —————————"Wee . . . . haue spent our tyme
> Both from the morning to the euening chyme;
> Nay, till the bell-man of the night had tould
> Past noone of night, yett weare the howers not old,
> Nor dull'd with yron sleeps, but haue out-worne
> The fresh and fayrest flourish of the morne
> With flame, and rapture; drincking to the odd
> Number of wyne, which makes vs full with God,
> And yn that misticke frenzie, wee haue hurl'de,
> (As with a tempeste) nature through the worlde,
> And yn a whirl-wynd twirl'd her home, agast
> Att that which in her extasie had past."
>
> (Vol. III. p. 102.)

Nor may we doubt that his "Farewell to Sack" and "Welcome to Sack" find place in the same group.

Be it noted that while the later 'innes' of assembly, "The Sun, the Dog, the Triple Tun" are celebrated, nowhere is the earlier "Mermaid," or "Mitre," or the after-frequented "Windmill" (1605) so much as named. Be it also noted that it would have simply been impossible for Herrick to have met Shakespeare at "The Mermaid" and not have recalled the meeting. As we read his "Apparition of his Mistresse calling him to Elysium"

(Vol. II. pp. 173-4) with its lofty praise of Beaumont and Fletcher and Jonson, we instinctively ask, 'Where is Shakespeare all this time?' But by 1611—at latest— he had gone down to Stratford-on-Avon, and our Poet celebrates only the contemporaries he actually knew. Every one carries in his memory the verse-letter of Beaumont to Ben Jonson of " The Mermaid ":—

——————— " What things have we seen
Done at the Mermaid ! heard words that have been
So nimble and so full of subtle flame,
As if that any one from whence they came
Had meant to put his whole wit in a jest,
And had resolv'd to live a fool the rest
Of his dull life ; then when there hath been thrown
Wit able enough to justify the town
For three days past ; wit that might warrant be
For the whole city to talk foolishly,
Till that were cancell'd ; and when that was gone,
We left an air behind us, which alone
Was able to make the two next companies
(Right witty, though but downright fools) more wise."

But these days were early, when Sir Walter Raleigh founded ' The Club,' and when Herrick was much too young to have joined; and onward, as first 'apprentice' goldsmith, and next at College in (probably) 1612-13, he cannot be supposed to have found his way

within the 'charmed circle.' Accordingly I am not
satisfied that because he refers to the unfavourable
reception of the *Alchemist,* which was brought out in
1610, or because in his lines to John Fletcher he
speaks of the power of his *Maid's Tragedy* (which was
produced in 1611) to make "young men swoon,"
he knew either personally so early as 1610-11.   But
there is abundant evidence that later he did know personally Ben Jonson. It was, however, later—viz., from
1620 forward.   When the Master of Arts, in 1620,
came to town, the purple splendour was still in the air
if not in the sky, though the sun had sunk and only
stars gleamed.   Besides "immortal Ben," if Shakespeare and Francis Beaumont were gone, there still
remained John Fletcher and Philip Massinger, William
Browne and Richard Corbet, James Shirley and William
Cartwright, Thomas Carew and venerable John Selden.
I can very well believe that, bound apprentice to his
goldsmith-uncle on 25th September, 1607, while the
Poet of the "mountain belly and the rocky face" was
bringing out his Volpone, and Epicene, and Alchemist,
and Catiline, and at "Whitehall, and the " Court," his
unapproachable *Masques,* as of the *Masque of Queens*
and Oberon, *the Fairy Prince*—the young apprentice

paid furtive visits to the theatres.[5] His "Fairie Temple," and "Oberon's Feast," and others, were written early ; and therefore, one can understand with what rotund and thundering mouth 'great Ben' would give their conceiver admittance among his sons. But whatever slighter acquaintance there may have been whilst he was passing out of his teens, the likelihoods are that—as above—it was not until 1620 that he "quaffed the mighty bowl" and mingled in those "brave translunary scenes." Perchance in his occasional visits to London while at the University he may have looked in upon the great compotators, and so paved the way for full fellowship on leaving it. By 1620 he had unquestionably composed some, at least, and some of his daintiest Poems (exclusive of the 'Fairy' ones). It was "*in the season*," that is in youth, he sang :—

> "Of brooks, of blossomes, buds and bowers
>   Of April, May, of June and July flowers ;"

and so he could carry proof of his poetic vocation to the august brethren. With Ben Jonson for 'Master,'

---

[5] Volpone, 1605, &c., published 1608—shows a long run: Epicene, 1609 : Alchemist, 1610 : Catiline, 1611 : Bartholomew Fair not till 1614.

there were others subsidiary. I think it is manifest that he elected his subjects and formed his style after CHRISTOPHER MARLOWE (in his sweeter and lowlier vein, and in his epithets), ROBERT GREENE, and JAMES SHIRLEY—exclusive of the Classics. The first in his "Come live with me, and be my love," is echoed in his rural pieces. Then his favourite vocabulary of dews and nard, wine and ambrosia, amber and flames, and spices, white brows, golden hair, cherry lips, eyes that brighten, lily cheeks, 'silver shine,' kisses and clasps, maidens and virgins and 'maidenheads,' favourite flowers as roses, lilies, daisies and daffodils, and out-of-the-way words as 'chequered' and 'diapered' and 'enamell'd' and the like, are all found in Greene. One could imagine it was from the *Hesperides* such things as these have been gathered :—

"Her hair of golden hue doth dim the beames
That proud Apollo giveth from his coach."
                                        (II. 215, Dyce.)

"Her lips are roses over-wash'd with dew
Or like the purple of Narcissus' flower." (*Ib.* p. 228.)

"Her cheeks like ripen'd lilies steep'd in wine

. . . .

When first her fair delicious cheeks were wrought,
Aurora brought her blush, the morn her white ;

Both so combin'd as passèd Nature's thought,
Compil'd those pretty orbs of sweet delight."

(*Ib.* p. 230.)

" Thine eyes are like the glow-worms in the night."

(*Ib.* p. 232.)

————— " Enchanted fits of lunacy." (*Ib.* p. 236.)

" Her haire as Gorgon's foul retorting snakes."

(*Ib.* p. 237.)

"As air perfum'd with amber is her breath."
" Like lilies dipt in Bacchus' choicest wine." (*Ib.* p. 254.)

" Her amber trammels did my heart dismay."

(*Ib.* p. 254.)

[Flora]   " Curld locks of amber hair."   (*Ib.* p. 243.)

—— " Her mantle chequer'd all with gaudy green."

(*Ib.* p. 26.)

" And bade my lambs to feed on daffadil."   (*Ib.* p. 284.)

" Behold my cell, built in a silent shade."   (*Ib.* p. 246.)

Nor is it only in single words and turns that Greene is inevitably recalled.   His " Ode " and " The Palmer's Ode " and the " Penitent Palmer's Ode " have the very touch of Herrick's ' Fairy ' poems :—

> " Down the valley 'gan he track
> Bag and bottle at his back,
> In a surcoat all of gray :
> Such wear palmers on the way,

> When with scrip and staff they see
> Jesus' grave on Calvary."   (*Ib.* p. 243.)

Again, in Francesco's Ode are other characteristics :—

> " Eyes that lighten, and do shine
> Beams of love that are divine,
> Lily cheeks, whereon beside
> Buds of roses show their pride,
> Cherry lips, which did speak,
> Words that made all hearts to break,
> Words most sweet, for breathe was sweet,
> Such perfume for loue is meet,
> Precious words, as hard to tell
> Which more pleasèd, wit or smell."   (*Ib.* p. 249.)

Once more, Infida's Song :—

> " Thy face as fair as Paphos' brooks,—
> Wherein fancy baits her hooks.
> Thy cheeks like cherries that do grow
> Amongst the autumn mounts of snow ;
> Thy lips vermilion full of loue,
> Thy neck of siluer white as doue,
> Thine eyes, like flames of holy fires
> Burn all my thoughts with sweet desires."
>   (*Ib.* pp. 252-3.)

Further :—

> " White her brow, her face was fair
> Amber breath perfum'd the air ;

> Rose and lily both did seek
> To show their glories on her cheek :
> ˙ Love did nestle in her looks
> Baiting there her sharpest hooks ;
> Gold her hair, bright her eyne,
> Like to Phœbus in his shine."   (*Ib.* p. 299.)

And here, as already noticed, is an odd but recurring word of Herrick :—

> " Meads that erst with green were spread
> With choice flowers diap'red."   (*Ib.* p. 302.)

Herrick's " Charon and the Nightingale " (II. 224) and " The New Charon " (III. 110) were certainly inspired by Greene's " Eurymachus' Fancy in the prime of his Affection," and it is only fair to the earlier singer to give here this more complete example of him :—

> " As thus I sat, disdaining of proud love,
>   Have over, ferryman, there cried a boy ;
>   And with him was a paragon for hue,
>   A lovely damsel, beauteous and coy ;
>   And there
>   With her
>   A maiden, cover'd with a tawny veil,
>   Her face unseen for breeding lovers bale.
>   I stirr'd my boat, and when I came to shore,
>   The boy was wing'd ; methought it was a wonder ;
>   The dame had eyes like lightning, or the flash
>   That runs before the hot report of thunder ;

Her smiles
Were sweet,

Lovely her face ; was ne'er so fair a creature,
For earthly carcass had a heavenly feature.
My friend, quoth she, sweet ferryman, behold,
We three must pass, but not a farthing fare ;
But I will give, for I am Queen of Love,
The brightest lass thou lik'st unto thy share ;

Choose where
Thou lov'st,

Be she as fair as Love's sweet lady is,
She shall be thine, if that will be thy bliss.
With that she smil'd with such a pleasing face
As might have made the marble rock relent ;
And I that triumph'd in disdain of love,
Bad fie on him that to fond love was bent,

And then
Said thus,

So light the ferryman, for love doth care,
As Venus pass not, if she pay no fare.
At this a frown sat on her angry brow ;
She winks upon her wanton son hard by,
He from a quiver drew a bolt of fire,
And aim'd so right as that he pierc'd mine eye :

And then
Did she

Draw down the veil that hid the virgin's face,
Whose lovely beauty lighten'd all the place."

(pp. 259-60, as before.)

The closing line is worthy of Spenser, and there is nothing finer in the *Hesperides.*

James Shirley's " Poems " published in 1646 had long
circulated in MS., and I find the original of Herrick's
Julia in his Odelia, and in his " To L. for a Wreath of
Bays sent him," I discern the prototype of his " Welcome to Sack," and ever and anon peculiar ways of
putting things and celebrations of feminine graces,
that Herrick must have seen. Of Shirley I can find
space only for a single quotation. It reminds us in
parts of Herrick's " Welcome to Sack" (I. 133) and
"Farewell to Sack" (I. 76), and also of his Lines " To
Mistresse Katharine Bradshaw, the lovely, that crowned
him with Laurel " (I.163). There is much of their
abandon and ecstatic fancies :

To L. for a Wreath of Bays sent him.

" Soul of my Muse, what active unknown fire
  Already doth thy Delphick wreath inspire !
  O' th' sudden, how my faculties swell high,
  And I am all a powerful prophesy !
  Sleep, ye dull Cæsars, Rome will boast in vain
  Your glorious triumphs ; one is in my brain
  Great as all yours ; and circled with thy bays,
  My thoughts take empire o'er all land and seas :
  Proof against all the planets, and the stroke
  Of thunder, I rise up Augustus' oak,
  Within my guard of laurel, and made free
  From age, look fresh still as my Daphnean tree.

f

My fancy's narrow yet, till I create
For thee another world, and in a state
As free as innocence, shame all poets and wit,
To climb no higher than Elysium yet,
Where the pale lovers meet, and teach the groves
To sigh, and sing vain legends of their loves;
We will have other flights, and taste such things
Are only fit for sainted queens and kings.
Musaeus, Homer and ye sacred rest
Long since believ'd in y^r own ashes blest,
Awake, and live again ! and having wrote
One story, wish your songs forgot,
And yourselves too : but one high subject must
In spite of death and time, new soul y^r dust.
What cannot I command ? what can a thought
Be now ambitious of, but still be brought
By virtue of my charm ? I will undo
The year, and at my pleasure make one new,
All spring, whose blooming paradise but when
I list, shall with one frown wither again.
Astrologers, leave searching the vast skies :
Teach them all fate, O Delia, from thine eyes ;
All that was earth resolves my spirits free,
I have nothing left now but my soul and thee."
(Works by Gifford & Dyce, vi., pp. 413-14.)

I cannot doubt that besides those named, he had studied Barnabe Barnes and Richard Barnfield and other of the early Singers. With an absolute and unique originality Herrick, nevertheless, reveals that, Bee-like, he gathered his honey from many flowers. Yet was it his boast that anything he took was 'adopted, not stolen,' as thus :—

Upon his Verses.

" What off-spring other men have got,
The how, where, when, I question not.
These are the Children I have left ;
Adopted some; none got by theft.
But all are toucht (like lawfull plate)
And no Verse illegitimate." (Vol. II. p. 223.)

He had been a Poet at Cambridge, and came to ' town' all ringing with his poetic readings and his own fine imaginings. It was something that there were still surviving so many who could appreciate his rare gift.[6]

During the year 1620 onward, it is just possible that

---

[6] I wish here to express my admiration for a brilliant paper on Robert Herrick, by Mr. Edmund W. Gosse, which appeared in *Cornhill* (August, 1875). I am unlucky enough to be compelled to express and vindicate differences (as above and onward) in several important points of fact, and likewise in criticism; but none the less do I appreciate the fine spirit of the paper, and its finished workmanship. Besides, Mr. Gosse was really the first to write in full sympathy with Herrick's genius, and to try to indicate (if not always accurately) his reading. See II. Critical. for remarks on Mr. Gosse's conception (eheu! misconception) of Herrick in relation to the events and circumstances of the period, and other matters.

through his uncle he was received at Court.   His later royal poems " sung at Whitehall " and his usual language to the King and Queen, suggest that he had been for years known to them, if certain also suggest that he met with inevitable courtly disappointments—as George Herbert too had to confess.   The only really dated poem is his rendering of the " Dialogue betwixt Horace and Lydia," which is inscribed " Translated anno 1627," and " set by Mr. Ro. Ramsey."   To have found such a distinguished composer as Ramsey to ' set' his verses, is surely declarative of a position already gained ; for Ramsey, and Laniere, and Wilson, and the Lawes'—all of whom ' set' his poems—moved in the Court and among the " Upper Ten."

In 1629 two important events in Herrick's life took place.   The first—hitherto unascertained — was the death of his mother.   I am able to give here, *for the first time*, her Will, which is again *literatim*, as follows :—

"In the name of God, Amen, I, Julian Hirricke of Brantā, in the Countie of Suff., Gent., being in perfect memorie, (thankes bee vnto God) yet remembringe the vncertainty of this life, doe make my last will and Testament in forme following, ffirst I bequeath my soule vnto God my mercifull ffather, And my bodie to to bee buried at the place of my departure.   Imp^r. I will & bequeath to my daughter Wingfeild one hundred pounds. Item to my sonne Wingfield, Twenty pounds. It. to my Grandchild Mercy Wingfield, fiftie pounds. It. to theire sonne, Humphrey Wingfeld, Twentie pounds. It. to their sonne, John, Tenne pounds, and to theire sonne, Willm, ten pounds. It. to my sonne, Willm Herricke, one hundred pounds ; and to his two children, ten pounds apeece. To my Goddaughter, Ellis, my lesser Cutt worke handkerchiefe. To his wife, a Ringe of Twenty shillings. To my two sonnes, Nicholas and *Robert*, either of them a Ringe of Twenty shillings apeece. To my sonne Willm, his wife, a Ringe of Twenty shillings. It. to Dr. Jones, fortie shillings. It. to Mr. Herdson, three pounds ; to his wife, my saddle and cloth. Item to Mr. Cauldred, a Ringe of Twenty shillings. Item to Charls Cutler, Twenty shillings. To Laurence Crick, Twenty shillings. To mine owne maide, Twenty shillings, besides her wages. It. to An Tomson, twenty shillings. To Humph : Huggins, Twenty shillings. It. to Nurse Lawter, Twenty shillings. To the Coachmã, tenne shillings. It. to the boye in the Kitchin, Ten shillings. To the maides now in the house, ten shillings apeece. To the poore of Brantã, fortie shillings. All the rest of my goods now at Brantã I bequeath to my daughter Wingfeld, the siluer skillet and plate, after her decease, to Mercy, her daughter. And I doe appoint my sonne Willm and my daughter Wingfeld my Executors, and my sonne Wingfeld supra-uisor of this my last Will. In witnes whereof I haue here-vnto set my seale the fower and Twentieth of August, One thousand six hundred twenty nine, Julian Hirricke.

" Sealed and deliuered in the presence of Ro : Grimble,

John Rand.—Nowe Lord letst thie Servant depart in peace."[7]

Recorded in Book " Ridley " at folio 97.

This Will was proved in the Prerogative Court of Canterbury 5th November, 1629, by William Herricke (not Hirricke or Hiricke as the mother spelled) the son and Mary Wingfield the daughter of the testatrix, the executors named by her. So that she probably died shortly after making these arrangements. That she came to be resident at Brantham in Suffolk, is explained by her daughter ' Mercie ' having married there. Unfortunately the Register of Brantham does not commence until 1634 ; but until comparatively recent years Wingfields are found in the register and Parish. All that Robert and his elder brother Nicholas received was " a ringe of twenty shillings " apiece. Sir William Herrick does not get even a ' ringe '—a suggestive omission in the remembrance that he had been one of the two "chief overseers." The solitary reference to his mother does not indicate any very warm regard ; and it is noticeable that he who wrote Epitaphs so incomparably for so many, left none for her, neither aught of memorial-verse.

[7] Obtained through Colonel Chester, as before.

The second event of the year 1629 is his taking
orders, and his presentation to the 'living' of Dean
Prior in Devon. I know not on what authority it has
been stated that it was through the (then) Earl of Exeter
the 'presentation' was obtained. The fact is that the
vicar of Dean Prior,—Potter—several of whose family
find a place in *Hesperides* — being promoted to the
bishopric of Carlisle, he was admitted thereto on 2nd
October, 1629. What bishop gave him 'orders' has
not been transmitted. From his Lines to Williams
Bishop of Lincoln on his imprisonment, one might
suspect that he had thrown obstacles in the way of
his ordination. But it may be that the felt injury was
neglect or even flouting by that most astute but unpo-
etical dignitary, of the earlier " Charoll," which the Poet
had sent him. Nor have we any light on the long
delay from 1620 to (apparently) 1629, that is until
nearly his 40th year, in seeking, or at least being made
' priest.' His *motif* for seeking ordination was at any
rate not mercenary, or for "a piece of bread." He
asserts this unmistakably in his impassioned " Farewell
vnto Poetrie," as thus :—

—————————" *'Tis not need*
(The skarcrow vnto mankinde) *that doth breed*

Wiser conclusions in mee, since I knowe
I've more to beare my chardges, then way to goe ;
Or had I not, I'de stopp the spreading itch
Off craueing more : soe yn conceipt bee ritch ;
But tis the god of nature who yntends,
And shaps my function for more glorious ends : "

To-day a more charming portion of the great Vine-
yard (to fitly appropriate Bible language) than Dean
Prior is scarcely conceivable.   Leaving Brent—a
station on the South Devon Railway, about 16 miles
from Plymouth,—you take the road in a north-easterly
direction, passing just below the edge of the moor.
The road is not particularly beautiful or interesting, but
you get glimpses of the hills sometimes on your left,
and a mile and a half from Brent there are a few old
cottages, and then the road passes through a fordable
stream by a clump of trees, and from a little stone
bridge for foot passengers that they call in Devonshire
a *clam*, you look over the hedge to your right upon
rich meadows, well backed with wood.   Another mile
and you come to the narrow lane on the right which
leads down to Dean Church, *i.e.* the Church and vicarage
and a small farm-house and a few cottages clustered
round them.   The Church town as it is called in Devon
and Cornwall, lies in a small but deep valley.   Look-

ing down upon them from the high road, the church
and houses seem sunk among the trees. The trees
now standing are all of recent growth, but from the
sheltered situation of the little valley, it was probably
always well wooded. About a mile further on is Dean
Prior, another little hamlet, close to which stands Dean
Court, now a farm, but anciently a great manor-house.
In Herrick's time it was beautified by Sir Edward
Giles, the lord of the manor, who left his family-seat at
Bowden near Totness, and came thither to reside a few
years before his death in 1637. Close to this hamlet
of Dean Prior—(which *en passant* gets its name from
the manor having been, up to the Reformation, the
property of the Priory of Plympton) the little river
Dean flows down to join the Dart near Buckfastleigh,
a market-town a mile further on the road to Ashburton.
The stream flows from the moor through one of the
coombs, or deep and wooded valleys which abound on
the borders of Dartmoor. Like all Devonshire streams
it has a rocky bed. The wood through which it
bickers is called Deany Wood, and just above the wood
is another little hamlet called Dean Combe. These
three hamlets, Dean Combe, Dean Prior and Dean
Church, all within the parish of Dean, form as it were
the points of a triangle, of which each side is about

three-quarters of a mile in length.   The parish contains
4,165 acres, and in 1871 the population was 400, the
number of people having diminished since the beginning of the present century, and being probably less
than it was in Herrick's time.   According to the Clergy
List the tythe-rent charge is now about £230 a year
with 93 acres of glebe.   The old manor-house—Dean
Court—was the only great house in the parish.   From
Sir Edward Giles, who enlarged the house and made a
park, and apparently kept up some state there, it
passed into the family of Yarde, and from them—long
after Herrick's death—by marriage, to the Bullers.
Lord Churston, the present head of the Buller family,
is now lord of the manor, but Dean Court is shorn of
its grandeur, and is now an ordinary farm-house, with
but few remains of its ancient dignity.

Two centuries and a half ago Dean Prior was remote
from literary society, and its parishioners not very
capable of giving intellectual sympathy to their Vicar.
The change from London to " dull Devonshire " and
the " loathèd West " to such a sociable and erewhile
pleasure-taking nature must have been in Dominie
Sampson's exclamation—prodigious ! The links that
bound him to the great Metropolis were not easily
severed.   From his " loopholes of retreat" he looked

thitherward. Within a few months of his settlement
he wrote " A Pastoral upon the Birth of Prince
Charles," afterwards Charles II., and it is headed,
" Presented to the King," (Charles I.) " and set by
Mr. Nic. Laniere." Three years onward—1633—he
similarly greeted another royal birth, entitling his poem,
" The Poet's Good Wishes for the most hopeful and
handsome prince, the Duke of York," afterwards
James II. Later still, sick-at-heart, through hope long
deferred (I fear) he thus addressed his Muse on sending (as seems likely) a copy of *Hesperides* :

> " Go wooe young Charles, no more to looke
> Then but to read this in my booke :
> How Herrick beggs, if that he can-
> Not like the Muse, to loue the man
> Who by the shepherds, *sung long since*
> The starre-led birth of Charles the Prince."

namely his " Pastorall."

Thus was it continuously, on through the troublous
and dolorous years of conflict between Kingdom and
King. That he cultivated his gift as a Poet in Devonshire is certain, albeit *Hesperides* in its order or disorder violates all chronology and makes it impossible
to date earlier and later except occasionally. So far as
I have been able to trace, his first appearance in print

was the anonymous publication of fragments of his " Fairy " poems—so imperfect as to suggest that they had been surreptitiously obtained.   This was in 1635, in a delicious little booklet called, " A Description of the King and Queene of Fayries, their habit, fare, their abode, pompe and state.   Beeing very delightfull to the sense, and full of mirth."[8]   Ben Jonson's death took place on 6th of August, 1637[9]; but Herrick did not contribute to " Ionsonus Virbivs " (1638).   Within the next few years he must have been well known as a Poet ; for when in 1640 there came out " Wit's Recreations " there were included in it no fewer than 62 of the poems contained in *Hesperides* afterwards, and one (" Description of a Woman ") not reprinted therein. In common with the entire collection, these are all without name or even initials ; but they establish their authoritative publication by the author's own most careful revision and reproduction of them subsequently.[1] It is noticeable that so much from him should have found place in a book that was the first to bring to-

[8] This will likely be reproduced as one of my " Occasional Issues."

[9] It is usually said to have been 16th August.   Whether it was old or new style I am not aware.   If new style it would be ▬ 18th August.

[1] See II. Critical for more on " Wit's Recreations."

gether—sadly intermixed, no doubt—some of the most choice pieces of the greater poets and a few originals, as of Richard Crashaw's immortal " Wishes," if somewhat poorly given.   The probabilities are that he came and went between Devonshire and London.   The provincial Winters could not but be dull and lonely; and for the elder generation of his poetic contemporaries there were rising into notice Carew and Lovelace, Denham and Suckling, and Charles Cotton, with all of whom he formed friendships apparently.

Of his life as a clergyman—except in the lights and shadows of touching memorial and ' epitaph ' verses beyond all Greek and Roman exquisiteness, and marriage greetings comparable with Catullus at his best, and stinging and rough epigrams hitting off his parishioners emulative of Martial at his worst, in *Hesperides*—we know very little.   That he entered on his office with a real sense of new responsibilities, and that he was resolved to be delivered from all that would hinder his consecration to its manifold duties, is certain. This indeed is made to stand out very definitely, in a sense, awfully—though, strange to say, it has escaped all his Biographers.   Among the Ashmolean MSS. a little poem—complete in itself, and not a fragment—is informed with a passion and has over it a shadow of

solemnity most unusual to Herrick, and declarative of a
resolute breaking off from earlier entanglements and
self-indulgences, and a profound sense of being now a
' priest of the Most High God,' and so set apart for
holy and celestial work.   We know that he remained
unmarried ; and hence there was reality in the " Farewell " of this remarkable poem.   Let us study it,
meditatively :—

> " *Vpon Parting.*
>
> Goe hence away, and in thy parting know
> 'Tis not my voice, but heauens that bidds thee goe ;
> Spring hence thy faith, nor thinke it ill desart
> I finde in thee, that makes me thus to part.
> But voice of fame, and voice of heauen haue thunderd
> We both were lost, if both of us not sunderd :
> Fould now thine armes, and in thy last looke reare
> One Sighe of loue, and coole it with a teare :
> Since part we must, let's kisse ; that done, retire
> With as cold frost, as erst we mett with fire;
> With such white vowes as fate can nere dissever,
> But truth knitt fast ; and so farewell for euer."
>
> Vol. III. p. 109.

It needs no italicizing or capitals to arrest attention to
the significance of these words :—

> " Voice of fame and voice of heauen have thunderd
> We both were lost, if both of us not sunderd :
>
> .   .   .   .
>
> .   .   .   and so farewell for euer."

There was probably folded up in this " Parting" such unsuspected struggle and conquest as similarly unsuspected, went on with Phineas Fletcher.[2]   Even his Muse was to be forsaken, as his equally striking and memorable " Farwell vnto Poetrie " remains to attest— although it proved a mere mood, not an irreversible or unreversed decision ; or rather, henceforward he would ' sing ' his " Noble Numbers " rather than add to " Hesperides."   Will the Reader tarry at this point to read and re-read this " Farwell " (Vol. III., pp. 101-6), or at least the italicized lines in these two brief quotations from it :—

——— " Vnto mee, bee onlye hoarse, *since now*
(Heauen and my soule beare record of my vowe)
I, my desires screw from thee, and directe
Them and my thoughts to that sublim'd respecte
And conscience vnto priesthood."   (p. 104.)

Then thus of higher aims in his after-verse :—

" Thus with a kisse of warmth, and loue, I parte
Not soe, *but that some relique yn my harte*
Shall stand for euer, though I doe addresse
Chiefelye my selfe to what I must proffess :
Knowe yet (rare soule) when my diuiner muse
Shall want a hand-mayde (as she ofte will vse)

---

[2] See my Memoir of Phineas Fletcher, F. W. Library edition of his Works.

Bee readye, thou for mee, to wayte vppon her,
Thoughe as a seruant, yet a mayde of honor.
The crowne of dutye is our dutye : well
Doing's, the fruite of doinge well.   Farewell."

(P. 106.)

Swift's and Sterne's Sermons remain to witness how
they could and actually did preach—to the confusion of
all theories and preconceptions about them, for where
do you find of their kind, better? We have not this
advantage in the case of Herrick. Anthony a-Wood
characterizes his Sermons as " florid and witty [=wise]
discourses," but he shews himself ill-informed on him
in several ways. He states, too, that he was much
" beloved by the neighbouring gentry." A late
tradition, from the mouth of the "oldest inhabitant,"
aged 99, one Dorothy King, informs us that " he
one day threw his sermon at his congregation, cursing
them for their inattention."[3]   It has been said of
Sterne's portrait that it looks as if he were going to
fling his wig at his auditors. He had too keen a
sense of the ridiculous to have run such a grotesque
risk ; but somehow one does not feel it incongruous if
Herrick did what venerable Dorothy recalled. She
shewed that her old Vicar's memory was dear to her

---

[3] Quarterly Review : Mr. Barron Field, as before.

by regularly using stray verses of his " Letanie " in bed o' nights and preserving in her memory other lines.[4] I suspect that not in the pulpit, but as a free and easy associate with the " neighbouring gentry," and his humblest parishioners in their joys and sorrows, amusements and superstitions, did the Vicar exercise influence. From his repeated self-portraitures and descriptions of his ' cell ' (as he called his Vicarage) it is abundantly manifest that if there were high thinking, his ordinary living was homely. His one house-keeper and servant, ' Prue,' or Prudence Baldwin, lives " for all time " in *Hesperides.* His spaniel ' Tracy' takes its place beside Cowper's and Scott's. One other pet he has not celebrated. Dame Dorothy King distinctly remembered that he had a " favourite pig, which he amused himself by teaching to drink out of a tankard." This latter ' favourite' has been repeated in our own day in a ' parson ' of equal uniqueness of character and almost equal poetic genius—the Vicar of Morwenstow, the Rev. Robert Stephen Hawker, M.A., of whom his Biographer (the Rev. S. Baring-Gould, M.A.) states : " He had a favourite rough pony which he rode, and a black pig of Berk-

[4] *Ibid.*

shire breed, well cared for, washed and curry-combed, which ran beside him when he went out for walks and paid visits.   Indeed, the pig followed him into ladies' drawing-rooms, not always to their satisfaction.   The pig was called ' Gyp,' and was intelligent and obedient. If Mr. Hawker saw that those whom he visited were annoyed at the intrusion of the pig, he would order it out, and the black creature shrunk out of the door, with its tail out of curl."[5]   Elsewhere (II. Critical) it will be amply shown that the Vicar of Dean Prior had a deeper vein of Christian thoughtfulness than *Hesperides*, or even *Noble Numbers* hastily read, would lead us to suppose.   There will be found also a striking undertone of melancholy.   Fundamentally, it will appear that no misconception is more absolute than that he went on singing his jovial lyrics and throwing off his light fantastiques of verse and broad epigrams while the most disastrous events were occurring in the nation.   A thoughtful study of *Hesperides* reveals him as moved in the deepest of him by every element of the sorrowful national conflict, and that his gay ' singing' was long prior to these years.   There was gravity all along in combination with his jesting, aye, even when what was " not convenient " fell from him.

[5] Page 20.

From 1629 to 1647 he continued Vicar of Dean
Prior.   Then came thundering " The Revolution,"
with Oliver Cromwell's truncheon as " Lord Protector,"
more potential than kingly sceptre gripped by Charleses.
John Selden was Herrick's friend " next to idolatry ; "
but Herrick was an avowed Royalist and ' Loyalist '—
that is to the King, rather than to the Kingdom.   His
' Loyal ' poems are open-mouthed in his avowal of the
' divine right' of kings to ' govern,' wrongly or rightly.
There are memorable *bits* that go to prove he saw with
tear-wet eyes, the madness of Charles I. and his advisers—saw the glory paling in his ideal sovereignty—
the rainbow vanishing in a drizzle of bodiless rain ;
but substantially he held fast by the old anchor
of hereditary monarchy as such.   As a consequence he
was disloyal to the Commonwealth and its ' government'
—a government built up, if as augustly, also against as
great odds as was the second Temple on Mount Zion.
One can understand the chivalry of such loyalty ;
especially as nowhere is there a ribald or even tart
word against the Roundheads or Cromwell personally ;
but we must equally comprehend the inevitableness of
the Vicar's removal.   " Sober and learned " he might
or might not be—as John Walker in his folio of " Sufferings of the Clergy " [6] names him ; but then one true

* Page 253.

to the powers that were, in every parish, was a neces-
sity. And so Robert Herrick stepped out, and good
and brave and venerable JOHN SYMS stepped in. That
it was unreluctantly he gave way is loudly proclaimed
in his " Return to London "—all palpitating as the
poem is with gladfulness in once more being back in
his native country (as he designates it) and free from
his banishment. We must tarry to read this poem:

His returne to London.

From the dull confines of the drooping West,
To see the day spring from the pregnant East,
Ravisht in spirit, I come, nay more, I flie
To thee, blest place of my Nativitie !
Thus, thus with hallowed foot I touch the ground,
With thousand blessings by thy Fortune crown'd.
O fruitful Genius ! that bestowest here
An everlasting plenty, yeere by yeere.
O Place ! O People ! Manners ! fram'd to please
All Nations, Customes, Kindreds, Languages !
I am a free-born *Roman ;* suffer then,
That I amongst you live a Citizen.
London my home is : though by hard fate sent
Into a long and irksome banishment ;
Yet since cal'd back ; henceforward let me be,
O native countrey, repossest by thee !
For, rather then I'le to the West return,
I'le beg of thee first here to have mine Urn.
Weak I am grown, and must in short time fall ;
Give thou my sacred Reliques Buriall.

It is evident that the 'outed' Vicar's return to London was as of a Jew's from captivity and exile. Walker (as before) states that "after his Ejectment he returned to *London*, and having no fifths paid him, was subsisted by Charity, until the Restoration." This needs sifting—and shall now have it. First of all, Mr. Walford, in sheer ignorance of the facts, sneers at his "godly successor," repeatedly putting 'godly' within inverted commas. Now had he deigned to inquire, instead of sneering, he would have superabundantly discovered that John Syms was a man of men—an humble, devoted, learned, conscience-ruled servant of the 'great Taskmaster'—a man whose memory bore fragrance in it across a century and more, as well for the multitude of his 'sufferings' on account of his heroic Nonconformity, as for the meekness and modesty and unclamorousness with which he bore them. Next, in like ignorance of the facts, the non-payment of 'Fifths' is turned not only into a sneer, but an accusation. If, again, Wood and Mr. Walford and your ultra-Churchmen had inquired, it would have been made clear to them that in the case of such slender 'livings' to give 'Fifths' was an impossibility, if body and soul were to be kept together, and that it was only in such cases, naturally, as warranted the deduc-

tion, or in special circumstances, that 'Fifths' were due
to the 'outed' clergyman.   Then one is compelled to
remind your Mr. Walfords that when the later Ejection
of 24th August, 1662, was enforced, those who
returned' in not a solitary instance paid 'Fifths,' or
paid one sixpence to the then 'outed'; and yet these
" Two Thousand " were as learned, as cultured, as
'godly,' as consecrate (to say the least), and as lawfully
and 'divinely' appointed as they were.   More than
that : they were 'ejected' not for disloyalty to an
earthly sovereign, but as being loyal to the King of
Kings as their consciences instructed them.   I cry
shame on the 'restored,' who while 'out' had regularly drawn their 'Fifths' and more—and yet forgot
the good men and true who beyond the letter had kept
the law toward them.   I protest with indignation
against such traducing of honourable and illustrious
men.

Further : the alleged poverty and 'subsisting by
charity' is sheer nonsense.   For, unlike most, Herrick
had innumerable wealthy relatives of the nearest, and
many open doors of welcome in brothers and sisters
well-married.   It is out of the question to accredit
that all these resources were dried up.   As a Royalist
in the Commonwealth, he doubtless had his hardships

and vexations; but there is not one iota to warrant the alleged abject poverty. We are the more disposed to argue this from the numerous indications of the most friendly relations being sustained by the Poet with his family on both sides. The Stones and Soames and Wingfields, and the other Herricks, and their sons and daughters—all kindly remembered as ' kinsmen ' —have prominent and heart-full celebration all through *Hesperides.* Probably the origin of the whole misrepresentation is to be looked for in ' gossip ' concerning gifts bestowed on him by noble and other friends, as was the *mode.* That, like others, he received such gifts, is evident by his acknowledgments to the Earl of Pembroke, as thus :—

> " You, my lord, are one, whose hand along
> Goes with your mouth, or do's outrun your tongue,
> *Paying before you praise,* and cockring wit,
> Give both the gold and garland unto it."
>
> (Vol. II. p. 63.)

So " To the Patron of Poets, M. End. Porter ":—

> —— " Let there be Patrons; Patrons llke to thee,
> Brave Porter ! Poets ne'r will wanting be :
> Fabius, and Cotta, Lentulus, all live
> In thee, thou man of men ! who here dos't give
> Not onely subject-matter for our wit,
> *But likewise oyle of maintenance to it.*

Fcr which, before thy threshold, we'll lay downe
Our Thyrse, for Scepter, and our Baies for Crown."

(Vol. I. p. 70.)

: A brother of Endymion Porter may also have been a 'patron'; but it must be remembered that the two introductory stanzas of " An Ode to Master Endymion Porter, upon his Brother's Death " are put into the mouth of Endymion and express his loss, not Herrick's own. Otherwise the second stanza would have suggested weighty obligation, if not dependence, *e.g.* :—

" Alas for me ! that I have lost
E'en all almost :
Sunk is my sight ; set is my Sun ;
And all the loome of life undone :
The staffe, the Elme, the prop, the shelt'ring wall,
Whereon my vine did crawle,
Now, now, blowne downe ; needs must the old stock fall."

(Vol. I. p. 124.)

The opening precludes the application of this to Herrick :—

" Not all thy flushing sunnes are set,
Herrick, as yet."

Such 'gifts' partook not at all of the nature of eleemosynary payments ; and yet I feel persuaded that Anthony a-Wood had merely caught up a perverted rumour concerning them, and so wrote of his " subsisting by charity."

In 1647-8 he published his " Hesperides : Works Humane and Divine," with his portrait—of which more in the sequel—prefixed. He describes himself as " Robert Herrick, Esq." ; so assuming the lay character, as was possibly expedient, alike from the circumstances and from the matter-of-fact that in so far as the bulk of the poems went, they had been composed by him while a layman. Elsewhere again (II. Critical) I examine his matterful and marvellous double-volume. Here it is sufficient to remark that never had the Cavaliers so congenial a gift in a book—redolent as it was of that type of wit with which they set " the table in a roar."

A tradition lingered in Devonshire that Herrick was the originator of " Poor Robin's Almanac " that ultimately became renowned and held a long lease of life, if indeed it do not still in humble guise circulate. Nichols in his Leicestershire accepts the tradition as possible, as he also accepts his (impossible) poverty while in London. Others recalling that the Almanac was first published in 1661 regard it as impossible. I have disposed of the poverty in any pauper-sense ; but I am inclined to accredit the tradition. For (1) The

Restoration of "our most religious king" Charles II. came with sudden unexpectedness; so that such a literary scheme might be extremely timely to Herrick, and while all ready, years before, he may have simply postponed publication until 1661.   (2) It was not until the 'Ejection' of 24th August, 1662, that John Syms was 'outed' from Dean Prior; and so Herrick might still up to 1662 be gladly occupied in such a venture.   (3) Such a tradition could scarcely be invented—for it was not a thing at all likely to be ascribed to their Vicar by his Parishioners unless he himself had told and owned it.   (4) It is specially to be remembered (albeit from Chaucer onward 'Robin' was the accepted name for a simple rustic) that both in his Poems, and in at least one letter, " Robin " and " Robin Herrick " was his self-chosen playful way of describing himself. An examination of the earlier ' Poor Robin's' Almanacs and of later, gives things that in my judgment might have been written by Herrick.[7] If only we had the key—and a chance turning out of old MSS.

---

[7] I regret that space cannot be found for specimens. Had one known absolutely that they were his, space must have been taken. As it is, we must wait confirmation. The verses, sooth to say, are not of high quality. Certes they are not equal to *Hesperides*, though they must have come after.

may any day put it into our hands—I imagine it would be discovered that the Poet of the *Hesperides* and *Noble Numbers* took part in the fecund literature of the period. It seems inconceivable that he could give the world " Hesperides " and " Noble Numbers," and then cease production. And yet this must be believed if we set aside anonymous writing ; for outside of his books, all that persistent research has recovered is the tomb-inscription of his neighbours, Sir Edward and Lady Giles. This, and the Poems from the Ashmolean and B. Museum MSS. are the whole that have been added to his ' Works.' Here and there poems of the *Hesperides* were inserted in after-books, e.g. in the ' Musarum̄ Deliciæ ' (1656) and the continuous editions of " Wit's Recreations " and the like. How strangely even *Hesperides* had fallen out of sight so early as 1657 is evidenced by Henry Bold's " Wit a sporting in a pleasant Grove of New Fancies," wherein various of its Poems were undetectedly appropriated bodily, and others disguisedly.

Returned to Dean Prior after 24th August, 1662— John Syms. still ' preaching' with splendid devotedness and fearlessness of penalties in neighbouring villages— Herrick was then in his 71st-72d year ; but, in all likelihood beneath his grey hairs carried as clear an intel-

lect and joyous a spirit as of old. He had vowed that
nothing should ever take him back to loathed Devonshire :—

> " A people currish ; churlish as the seas ;
> And rude (almost) as rudest Salvages ;
> With whom I did, and may re-sojourne when
> Rockes turn to Rivers, Rivers turn to Men."
> (Vol. I., p. 48.)

but mellowed and softened by the intervening years of
national and personal trial, he no doubt went back
gratefully and graciously.   He was destined to reach
the "four score years" and upwards.   There is an
inexplicable absence of contemporary notices of him.
How he bore himself in his white-headed old age there
is no light to see.   At last the "lean fellow" who
beats all conquerors paid the ultimate call.   He died
in October, 1674, in his 83d year.   As with George
Herbert, the exact day of his death cannot be fixed ;
but in the church-register at Dean-Prior is still preserved this entry :

" Robert Herrick, vicker, was buried ye 15th day of
October 1674."

His grave is unknown, or at least uncertain.   There
is a characteristic introduction of himself in his epitaph
lines for Sir Edward and Lady Giles ; and if composed
long after their decease for a late-raised monument, the

expectant attitude of the words I venture to italicise, is significant and pathetic :

> " Here's the Sun-set of a Tedious day :
> These two asleep are : *I'le but be Vndrest*
> *And so to Bed :* Pray wish us all Good Rest."

A collateral descendant (W. Perry-Herrick, Esq., of Beaumanor Park, Leicestershire) erected a costly monument to his memory in Dean Church.   It is cut out of a great block of Caen stone, and carven in fruit and foliage.   The inscription is on a brass plate and runs as follows :

IN THIS CHURCHYARD LIE THE REMAINS OF
ROBERT HERRICK,
AUTHOR OF THE HESPERIDES AND OTHER POEMS,

OF AN ANCIENT FAMILY IN LIECESTERSHIRE, AND BORN IN THE YEAR 1591. HE WAS EDUCATED AT ST. JOHN'S COLLEGE AND TRINITY HALL, CAMBRIDGE.   PRESENTED TO THIS LIVING BY KING CHARLES I., IN THE YEAR 1629. EJECTED DURING THE COMMONWEALTH AND REINSTATED SOON AFTER THE RESTORATION.

HE DIED VICAR OF THIS PARISH IN THE YEAR 1674.

This Tablet was Erected

TO HIS MEMORY BY HIS KINSMAN, WILLIAM PERRY HERRICK OF BEAUMANOR PARK, LEICESTERSHIRE, A.D. 1857.
" OUR MORTAL PARTS MAY WRAPT IN SEARE-CLOTHES LYE,
GREAT SPIRITS NEVER WITH THEIR BODIES DIE."

HESPERIDES.
VIRTUS OMNIA NOBILITAT.[3]

---

[3] Works : Fuller Worthies' Library, Vol. II. p. 70.

And so I leave my little Biography with the Reader, asking him, if so he please, to turn next to II. Critical. If in both I have sought to revive the 'fame' of Herrick it has been with a recollection of the axiom of Fulke Greville, Lord Brooke, in his "Inquisition vpon Fame and Honour":—

" Thus see we, both the force and use of Fame ;
How States and men have honour by her stile,
And ecchoes that enuiron in Order's frame,
Which disproportion waiteth to beguile :
    Fame walks in truth, and cherisheth her end,
    Knowes neither why, nor how, yet is her friend."
                    (Works in F. W. L., ii. p. 70.)

II. CRITICAL.

THE outward Facts in the life of Herrick, even as
more matterfully told by us (I. Biographical) are
few and simple. None the less has he secured that
'eternity of fame' of which again and again he prophe-
sied in his *Hesperides*. It is as Singer he is remembered; and if his memory thus endure through relatively humble and fragile verse, it is only the old old
story of the fern in its little nook out-during the stately
Manor-house. Flowers bloom across the centuries,
while the rock crumbles and moulders. The merest
lilts and playthings of Poetry keep green and fragrant
the name of their Maker, when (so-called) 'great' works
are benignantly covered with the fine small dust of
oblivion. And yet there is more, infinitely, than
flower-beauty or bird-like singing in *Hesperides*. Apollo
was still Apollo when he played his oaten reed; but Apollo
who played his oaten reed was the 'unshorn' sun-god.
Similarly, if you look and listen whilst you read the Poetry
of Robert Herrick, you will discover that you have genius
of a unique and masterful sort—no mere dainty weaver
of words into rhyme. Greatness is not a synonym for

bulk.   Perfectness, on however small a scale, is the signet of the one man in ten thousand, whatever be his material, and whatever his art.   Keeping all this in mind, I ask the Reader to accompany me in an examination of the Works of Herrick so as to bring out their and his characteristics—the latter the more necessary because if not the Poet at least the Man has not been adequately estimated ; contrariwise, has been mis-estimated.   These six things I propose to look at successively :—

I.   The Book in its arrangement or disarrangement : of what it consists, and wherefore.

II.   Evidences of patient and genuine workmanship.

III.   What the Book tells of the Man and his relation to his times.

IV.   The specialities of his Poetry.

V.   His assurance of fame.

VI.   His Portrait.

I. *The Book in its arrangement or disarrangement : of what it consists, and wherefore.*   In " The Argument of his Book," (I. p. 7-8) the 'argument' is sweetly and alluringly put.   As one is thankful to turn the leaf of our (Authorised) English Bible, and pass from the pious profanities and lying of the Epistle-dedicatory " to the most high and mighty prince, James," so one inhales

with sense of relief from mephitic air the freshness of the outburst that succeeds the verse-dedication
"To the most illustrious and most hopefull Prince,
Charles, Prince of Wales." One cannot read it too
often ; and so here it is :—

> I sing of *Brooks*, of *Blossomes*, Birds, and *Bowers* :
> Of *April, May*, of *June*, and *July*-Flowers.
> I sing of *May-poles, Hock-carts, Wassails, Wakes*,
> Of *Bride-grooms, Brides*, and of their *Bridall-cakes*.
> I write of *Youth*, of *Love*, and have Accesse
> By these, to sing of cleanly-*Wantonnesse*.
> I sing of *Dewes*, of *Raines*, and piece by piece
> Of *Balme*, of *Oyle*, of *Spice*, and *Amber-Greece*.
> I sing of *Times trans-shifting ;* and I write
> How *Roses* first came *Red*, and *Lillies White*.
> I write of *Groves*, of *Twilights*, and I sing
> The Court of *Mab*, and of the *Fairie-King*.
> I write of *Hell;* I sing (and ever shall)
> Of *Heaven*, and hope to have it after all.
>
> (Vol. I., pp. 7-8.)

With this 'argument' for guide, it is not difficult to find
it fulfilled (filled full)—for, as in *Noble Numbers*, he
says of God :—

> He gives not poorly, taking some
> Between the finger, and the thumb ;
> But, for our glut, and for our store,
> Fine flowre prest down, and running o're.
>
> (III. p. 146.)

h

But there is a great deal more in *Hesperides* than the
'argument' promises. You come first of all on celebrations of eminent contemporaries and near relatives and
others, and then all-too-often on what are designated
'Epigrams.' Neither of these are in any way so much
as hinted at in the 'argument.' I notice this in the
outset because it gives a solution of different problems
that start themselves as you study the Book, and perchance lightens, if it do^{es} not absolutely relieve, the
blame of those offences against good manners, and
even good breeding, that stain the pages.

The verse-celebrations addressed to friends and eminent contemporaries were evidently designed to form a
separate work from *Hesperides*. They are these—Upon
his Sister-in-Law, Mistresse Elizab : Herrick (I. p. 39).
To the reverend shade of his religious Father (I. pp.
45-6)—To the Earle of Westmerland (I. p. 67)—To
the Patron of Poets, M. End. Porter (I. p. 70)—His
parting from Mrs. Dorothy Keneday (I. p. 72)—Upon
Mrs. Eliz: Wheeler, under the name of Amarillis (I. p.
78-9)—To his dying brother, Master William Herrick
(I. p. 125-6)—To Mistresse Katherine Bradshaw, the
lovely, that crowned him with Laurel (I. pp. 163-4)—
To the most vertuous Mistresse Pot, who many times
entertained him (I. p. 165)—To the High and Noble

Prince, George, Duke, Marquesse, and Earle of Buckingham (I. 173)—Mrs. Eliz. Wheeler, under the name
of the lost Shepardesse (II. pp. 3-4)—To the most
accomplisht Gentleman Master Edward Norgate (II. p.
29—To his honoured kinsman Sir William Soame (II.
p. 45)—To the Lady Mary Villars, Governesse to the
Princesse Henrietta (II. p. 56)—The meddow verse or
Aniversary to Mistris Bridget Lowman (II. pp. 60-1)—
To the right honourable Philip, Earle of Pembroke,
and Montgomery (II. pp. 62-3)—To the most learned,
wise, and Arch-Antiquary, M. John Selden (II. p. 65)
—To the most fair and lovely Mistris, Anne Soame,
now Lady Abdie (II. pp. 69-70)—Upon his Kinswoman-
Mistris Elizabeth Herrick (II. pp. 70-1)—Upon M.
Ben Johnson—Another (II. pp. 78-9)—To his Nephew,
to be prosperous in his art of Painting (II. p. 79)—To
his Maid Prew (II. pp. 80-1)—To his peculiar friend,
Sir Edward Fish, Knight Baronet (II. p. 82)—To his
peculiar friend, Master Thomas Shapcott, Lawyer (II.
p. 110)—To the right gratious Prince, Lodwick, Duke
of Richmond and Lenox (II. pp. 113-4)—To the Right
Honourable Mildmay, Earle of Westmoreland (II. p.
118)—To his Kinsman, Sir Tho. Soame (II. p. 124)—
To his worthy Friend, M. Tho. Falconbridge (II. p.
132)—To Sir Clisebie Crew (II. p. 134)—To his Hon-

oured Kinsman, Sir Richard Stone (II. pp. 139-40)—
To the right Honourable Edward Earle of Dorset
(II. p. 143)—To his Kinswoman, Mrs. Penelope
Wheeler (II. p. 145)—Another upon her *(ibid)*—To
Mistresse Mary Willand (II. p. 148)—To his Kins-
woman, Mistresse Susanna Herrick (II. p. 152)—Upon
Mistresse Susanna Southwell her cheeks (II. p. 153)—
To his honoured friend, Sir John Myntz (II. p. 154)—
To his worthy Kinsman, Mr. Stephen Soame (II. p.
162)—To his Honoured friend, M. John Weare,
Councellour (II. p. 166)—Upon his Kinswoman, Mis-
tresse Bridget Herrick (II. p. 169)—To his Brother in
Law, Master John Wingfield (II. p. 181)—His Prayer
to Ben Johnson (II. p. 185)—To his worthy friend, M.
Arthur Bartly (II. p. 216)—To M. Denham, on his
Prospective Poem (II. p. 220)—To Doctor Alablaster,
(II. pp. 258-59)—Upon his Kinswoman Mrs. M. S. (II.
pp. 259-60)—To his deare Valentine, Mistresse Margaret
Falconbrige (II. p. 272)—To his faithfull friend, Master
John Crofts, Cup-bearer to the King (II. pp. 276-7)—
To my dearest Sister M. Mercie Herrick (II. pp. 180-1)
—To Mistresse Amie Potter (II. 288)—To M. Henry
Lawes, the excellent Composer of his Lyricks (II. p.
293)—To his Friend, Master J. Jincks (II. p. 295)—
To his Honour'd Friend, Sir Thomas Heale (II. pp.

298-9)—Vpon Ben Johnson and An Ode for him (III. pp. 11-12)—To M. Kellam (III. pp. 14-15)—To his honoured and most ingenious friend Mr. Charles Cotton (III. p. 24)—To M. Leonard Willan his peculiar friend (III. p. 27)—To his worthy friend M. John Hall, Student of Grayes-Inne (III. 27-8)—To the most comely and proper M. Elizabeth Finch (III. pp. 28-9) —Ultimus Heroum, or to the most learned, and to the right Honourable Henry, Marquesse of Dorchester (III. p. 31)—To his learned friend M. Jo. Harmar, Phisitian to the Colledge of Westminster (III. pp. 32-3)—To his Sister in Law, M. Susanna Herrick (III. p. 37)—Upon the Lady Crew (III. p. 37)—Of Tomasin Parsons (III. p. 38)—To his Kinsman, M. Tho: Herrick, who desired to be in his Book (III. p. 39)—To the handsome Mistresse Grace Potter (III. p. 43)—To his peculiar friend M. Jo: Wicks (III. p. 65)—To Sir George Parrie, Doctor of the Civill Law (III. p. 66)—A Dialogue betwixt himselfe and Mistresse Eliza: Wheeler, under the name of Amarillis (III. p. 69)—To the Honoured, Master Endimion Porter (III. pp. 70-1)—The School or Perl of Putney, the Mistress of all singular manners, Mistresse Portman (III. pp. 73-4)—To M. Laurence Swetnaham (III. p. 76)—To the most accomplisht Gentleman Master Michael Oulsworth (III. pp. 77-8) —To his Brother Nicolas Herrick (III. p. 80).

As the most of these 'celebrations,' compared with the majority of the others, are of considerable extent, it will be seen that their proportion to the whole is large. Now turning to certain of them, there appear various titles for the Book within which he was writing the several tributes. Thus to Sir Edward Fish (1) :—

> Since for thy full deserts (with all the rest
> Of these chaste spirits, that are here possest
> Of Life eternall) Time has made thee one,
> For growth in this my rich Plantation.   (II. p. 82.)

Again, to Sir Richard Stone (2) :—

> To this white Temple of my Heroes, here
> Beset with stately Figures (every where)
> . . . .
> Come, thou."   (II. p. 139.)

Once more, to Mrs. Penelope Wheeler (3) :—

> Next is your lot (Faire) to be number'd one,
> Here, in my Book's Canonization :
> Late you come in ; but you a Saint shall be,
> In Chiefe, in this Poetick Liturgie.   (II. p. 145.)

Further, to Mr. Stephen Soame (4) :—

> Nor is my Number full, till I inscribe
> Thee sprightly *Soame,* one of my righteous Tribe
> . . . .

Among which Holies, be Thou ever known,
Brave Kinsman, markt out with the whiter stone :
Which seals Thy Glorie; since I doe prefer
Thee here in my eternall Calender.   (II. p. 162.)

Again, to Dr. Alablaster (5) :—

Nor art thou lesse esteem'd, that I have plac'd
(Amongst mine honour'd) Thee (almost) the last.
                                    (II. p. 258.)

Once more, to Susanna Herrick (6) :—

The Person crowns the Place ; your lot doth fall
Last, yet to be with These a Principall.
How ere it fortuned ; know for Truth, I meant
You a fore-leader in this Testament. (III. p. 37.)

Finally, to his kinsman, M. Tho. Herrick, who desired
to be in his Book (7) :—

Welcome to this my Colledge, and though late
Th'ast got a place here (standing candidate)
It matters not, since thou art chosen one
Here of my great and good foundation.
                                    (III. p. 39.)

. The first, by the use of " Plantation," might have
been interpreted as applicable to *Hesperides*, as such ;
but all the others point out definitely a Book of Friends,
a Book dedicated to their honour and poetic immortality.
Then the third to Mrs. Penelope Wheeler, while called

"Late," is early in *Hesperides*, though well-advanced in the list of those separately renowned ; and so of Dr. Alablaster, "almost the last" does not at all hold of his place in Hesperides, neither is the sixth tó Mrs. Susanna Herrick "last." Besides, finally, the seventh to M. Tho. Herrick recalls the first-announced purpose of that Book in which he had "desired to be." Hence I think most will agree with me that Herrick had a manuscript book wherein he copied out his Verses to the inner circle of his friends and compeers, and which he pleasantly thought of, as a Gallery of Portraits, or a Hall of Statues, or a College of good and great. Their repeated annunciation of 'immortality' would lead us to conclude that they were meant one day to be published. Add to these the royal and loyal poems— of which anon—and the brilliant Epithalamiums and tender Epitaphs and rural poems to his Brother, and Crewe, and Pemberton, and sunny self-portraits—which all more or less partake of the same character,—and we can understand the Poet's lofty estimate of such a book when it should be given to the world.

The Epigrams, in relation to the 'argument' are also and likewise made conspicuous by its absolute silence on them. Taken as a whole they were evidently written off after a laugh over Martial, or at some odd or offend-

ing parishioners. With very rare exceptions they lack the
keenness of the classical Epigram. With as rare exceptions they are just so many 'spots' of putridity placed
among the good things of the banquet. I cannot
suppose that their Author designed them for publication, or at least, as part of *Hesperides*. A friend suggests
that the Vicar of Dean Prior answered his parishioners
as Solomon says the fool ought to be answered, that
is, descended to their low level and versified in their
own rough and coarse fashion the every-day subjects of
their unlicensed wit and mirth. It may have been so
—may be conceded that refinement would have been
cast away on such " currish " natives. None the less is
it to be lamented that their Vicar descended rather than
sought to elevate them. Yet must it be added that
among old clergymen, even down to our own day, an
extraordinary freedom of speech was common. A very
small grain of salt gave circulation to exceedingly broad
stories ; and notwithstanding, one could not doubt of
the reality of the worth of such ancient and jocund
clerics. The sorrow is that in Herrick's case *his* Epigrams were printed and published—only let after-con-
siderations thereon be weighed.

Had those poems announced in the 'argument'
alone been published, *Hesperides* had been such a gift

to our finest poetical literature, as should have remained to-day unapproached for etherealness and delicacy, for brightness and whiteness, for colour and fragrance and melody.   But self-evidently the Publisher had an eye to the sale, and his own remuneration ; and on the plea of slenderness if only such Poems composed the volume, over-persuaded Herrick to entrust him with his " Book of the Just" and his miscellaneous Manuscript of Epigrams and the like, and his marked copy of "Wit's Recreations."   Whereupon he or some unskilled subordinate proceeded to intermix these additions with the others.   That the Poet himself had nothing to do with the arrangement or disarrangement lies on the surface.   Thus " The Fairie Temple " of which the last line is

" Goe's to the Feast that's now provided "

is separated from the Feast by nearly fifty pages, and then after fully nine pages comes " Oberon's Palace," which begins " After the Feast."   These three poems were most certainly intended to form one, or to be set together.   Then " The Beggar to Mab " would naturally have followed the others.   It may be presumed that the beggar saw the fairy banquet, and asked for a share of the crumbs.   Similarly one is constantly coming on poems in *Hesperides* utterly incongruous, yet associated. You have such a blossoming of flowers, or such an incense of scents, or such a healthy breath of vernal wind, or such a vivid word-landscape as the setting of some fine old English country usage, as thrills one ; and lo ! on the same or next leaf you have an Epigram without one grain of salt of wit, or some *hit* at a luckless parishioner, or some outrage on common decency that might have done for " Wit's Recreations " or the " Musarum Deliciæ," but which in *Hesperides* is a sorrow and a scandal. I should very gladly have re-arranged the whole, shovelling away the Epigrams bodily into an appendix that might not be read, and as one removes a snail from a lily's heart, occasional lines throughout. But as the Book was published during the Author's own life-time, it is too late, in an edition of his Works, to venture on this. I have before noted that there appeared in " Wit's Recreations " (1640), sixty-two poems afterwards included in *Hesperides.* Mr. Hazlitt has a section of his edition of Herrick which he entitles " Poems Attributed to Herrick." They are the following :—

1. King Oberon's Apparell.
2. The Fairy King.
3. The Fairy Queen, or the Fairies Fegaries.

4. Another Copy.

5. The Fayrie Kings Diet and Apparrell.

6. A Description of the Fairies' Revel and Feast.

7. To a Gentlewoman with one eye.

8. Domina Margarita Sandis : Anagramma.

9. On Chloris Walking in the Snow.

10. On Julia's Weeping.

11. On a Beautifull Virgin.

12. A Loving Bargain.

13. To Celia Weeping.

14. The Wake.

Except No. 10—a couplet—which belongs to *Hesperides* (Vol. II., p. 250) and appears in its place in Mr. Hazlitt's own edition — there is not a shadow of authority for assigning any one of these to Herrick. Nos. 7, 8, 9, 11, 12, 13, and 14 were published in "Wit's Recreations" (1640) and seeing that Herrick reclaimed no fewer than sixty-two Poems from "Wit's Recreations" for *Hesperides*, and did not these, this is decisive that they were not his; while internally no student of the *Hesperides* could for a moment imagine them to belong to our Poet. Nos. 1, 2, 3, 4, 5, and 6 are expressly assigned in three public MSS. and in several others to their actual Authors. Thus "King Oberon's Apparell" appeared in "Musarum

Deliciæ " (1655) and faultily in Poole's " English Parnassus ." (1657)—in both anonymously ; but in the Rawlinson MS. Poet 147, p. 102, under the heading of " The Faery King," it is signed Sr. S. St., and who was meant thereby is ascertained from—among others —the additional MSS. B. Museum 11,811, fol. 18, where the name is written in full, S[ir] Simeon Steward, which again agrees with MS. Malone, 17, and various other MSS. known to me in private hands. To Sir Simeon Steward therefore belongs " King Oberon's Apparell," and so too, of course, the variant of it (No. 2) " The Fairy King." In *Hesperides* there is a verse-Letter to Sir Simeon Steward (Vol. II. pp. 36-39) which prepares us to find him a writer of verse imitative or reflective of Herrick. Had " King Oberon's Apparell " or " The Fairy King " been Herrick's own, there was no reason whatever that when he published his Fairy poems he should not have included it. Nos. 3 and 4, " The Fairy Queen, or the Fairies Fegaries," and " Another copy " exists in a number of MSS., public and private, but in none is Herrick's name found. It was printed fragmentarily in a little volume already noticed, viz, " A Description of the Queen of Fayries," etc., etc., (1635) and like all therein, anonymously ; but in MS. Ashmole 36, there is an endorsement, " To the right wo^{ll}. his moste deare and much respected Father James Pagitt at Battersey, present these." This may or may not mean that Pagitt (filius) was the author. Mr. Hazlitt is disposed to regard him as the transcriber only. Be this as it may —but for myself it is just such a juvenile writing after Herrick as one might expect in a young friend of his— that Herrick is not its composer is again made sure by his not reclaiming it for *Hesperides*, while he did so in the case of another fragment which appeared in the same volume—as will be seen immediately. Internally there is the faint echo, but not at all the real voice of Herrick. No. 5, " The Fayrie King's Diet and Apparrell," occurs in the Rawlinson MS. Poet 142 (near the middle of the volume). It is a somewhat stupid adumbration, of Nos. 1 and 2, and Herrick's " Feast." The two parts in the MS. are separated by a line. Mr. Hazlitt states that " the writer of this collection evidently supposed them to be portions of the same poem." This alleged 'supposition' is not quite certain. The second part was probably derived from an early MS. of Herrick's—as in the sequel will appear. Nowhere is the first part ascribed to him, and nobody worth considering will agree with Mr. Hazlitt's haphazard ascription of it to him. Still more emphatically must every one reject the possibility of Herrick perpetrating such rubbish as No. 6, "A Description of the Fairies Revel and Feast." In the Ashmole MS. 36, fol. 47, *recto* (not 45, as Mr. Hazlitt) whence Mr. Hazlitt fetched it, has no author's name attached. It is an outrage to make Herrick responsible for such inartistic rhymes—our word re-reminding that Mr. Hazlitt in st. 2d, l. 3, misreads ' artistically ' for ' artificially ' and otherwise mangles what can hardly be made worse than the original. No. 7, " To a Gentlewoman with One Eye," is found in Rawlinson MS. 147, p. 13 (not 142, as Mr. Hazlitt) and is signed " Henry Molle." In place of seeing with Mr. Hazlitt that this is "unmistakeably" Herrick's, no capable reader will discern anything in the lines that could not have been written by Henry Molle or any other, not excluding Mr. W. C. Hazlitt himself. Nos. 8, 9, 11, 12, 13, and 14, having all been published in "Wit's Recreations" (1640) whence Herrick re-claimed sixty-two poems for *Hesperides* (as before) they are set aside as not his, by the fact of his not claiming them. This is additionally confirmed by his having, on the other part, re-claimed No. 10—as already pointed out. Were it worth while, it might be shown to whom these belong; but not being Herrick's, there seems no call to think more about them. It is with a sense of infinite relief that I have rescued Herrick from the imputation of the authorship of so much additional trash.   The Publisher's unhappy mixture and intermixture of all the Herrick MSS., good-naturedly entrusted to him by their Writer, has wrought sufficient damage, without more being contributed to the weeds and thorns and nettles and pestilential growths of *Hesperides.*   Our section yclept ' Golden Apples ' it had been pity to lose—the last, ' Epitaph on Sir Edward and Lady Giles' being very fine—but these "Poems attributed to Herrick," with the slight exception of the fragment from an early MS. of the " Feast," are to be summarily and gratefully rejected.

Let the student of *Hesperides* keep in his forgiving recollection that for a great deal at any rate of the incongruous arrangement or disarrangement of his book, not Herrick, but JOHN WILLIAMS and FRANCIS EGLESFIELD, his publishers, must be held answerable. It would have been a ' gainfull loss ' had they not been allowed access to the Epigrams.   By their indiscriminate insertion the Author's lines concerning the Errata were additionally illustrated :

" For these Transgressions which thou here dost see,
    Condemne the Printer, Reader, and not me ;
    Who gave him forth good Grain, though he mistook
    The Seed ; so sow'd these Tares throughout my Book."

II. *Evidence of patient and genuine workmanship.*
Differing from SIR PHILIP SIDNEY earlier, and GEORGE
HERBERT later, the Works " humane and divine " of
Herrick had the advantage that none were posthumous
—every " clause and word " having passed under his
own eye, although—as shewn—he allowed himself to
be over-persuaded by his Publishers to let them print
everything put into their hands in his MSS.   But on
the other hand—especially in the light of the intermixture and disarrangement that have been demon-
strated—it is a disadvantage that *Hesperides* and *Noble
Numbers* remained in the one edition, without revision,
without revelation of the Poet's mind about his volume,
and besides, an absolute after-silence (except possible
anonymous writing) of upwards of a quarter of a
century.   There are not consequently those printed
VARIOUS READINGS and Author's changes that so
often (as in Spenser, and Shakespeare, and Daniel,
and in modern days, Shelley, and Wordsworth, and
Tennyson) reveal to us the crystallization of thought
and the gradual perfection of the ultimate poem—
though, alas ! all too-often revealing strange and
almost incredible deterioration, e.g. even Spenser, and
Daniel, and Wordsworth, and Tennyson, are found to
spoil the very bloom, and to remove the fine powder

i

of many of their most exquisite fancies. When therefore I propose to give evidence of patient and genuine
workmanship, my meaning is not to bring forth from
Hesperides or *Noble Numbers* examples of supreme and
consummate workmanship.   This I shall do in stating
the specialities of his Poetry.   Here and now, through
Manuscripts that remain to us—none, unhappily, autograph—and through prior publication, as in "Wit's
Recreations" (1640), I wish to look in upon the
Poet at his fine work, and shew, in so far as within
these limits can be done, that Herrick's genius was
too substantive and non-accidental to have given us his
Lyrics and rural-breathed Poems off-hand (so-to-say).
That is, admitting the apopthegm, *Ars est celare artem*,
therein as throughout, there was art as well as genius—
genius kindling and inspiring the flame, but art giving
it lustre, and setting it in its 'golden candlestick.'   I
should stand in doubt of the reality of genius of any type
that was sundered from the long and ever-aspiring patience of nicest and devoutest workmanship.   Turning to
"Wit's Recreations," as might almost have been antici-
pated, material for the evidence now sought is relatively
scanty.   The likelihoods are that Herrick simply marked
his own Poems in a copy of the book and allowed his
Publishers to transfer them from "Wit's Recreations"

to *Hesperides* and *Noble Numbers.* Yet are there
noticeable. variants that are declarative of the
Author's revision. The following are the sixty-two
pieces that originally appeared in "Wit's Recreations "
—taken in the order in which they are found therein,
and on the left-hand side the places in our edition of
the Poems :

Hesperides.				Wit's Recreations.
1.	Vol. 1. pp.	- —Cherry Pit .	.	p. 457.
2.	„	„ 47-8—Upon Love .	.	p. 465.
3.	„	„ 51-2—The Bag of the Bee		pp. 413-4.
4.	„	„ 72-4—The Teare sent to		
		her from Stanes.	.	pp. 339-40.
5.	„	„ 76-78—His Farewell to		
		Sack. . .	.	pp. 432-3.
6.	„	„ 103-4—The Cruell Maid		pp. 342-3.
7.	„	„ 106-7—His Misery in a		
		Mistresse . .	.	pp. 344-5.
8.	„	„ 112-13—A Ring presen-		
		ted to Julia	.	pp. 321-2.
9.	„	„ 138—Upon Gubbs. Epig.		p. 89.
10.	„	„ 144-5—To the Virgins,		
		to make much of time		pp. 474-5.
11.	„	„ 170—Upon Himselfe	.	p. 465.

Looking now more closely at the Poems and Epigrams, No. 1 in "Wit's Recreations," is in the indirect
form thus :—

Cherry-pit.

" *Nicholas* and *Nell* did lately sit
Playing for sport at Cherry-pit ;
They both did throw, and having thrown,
He got the pit, and she the stone."

In *Hesperides* it is direct, as thus :—

" Julia and I did lately sit,
Playing for sport, at cherry-pit :
She threw ; I cast ; and having thrown,
I got the pit, and she the stone."

In No. 2, which is headed 'On Love,' for l. 3 in *Hesperides*, "To signifie, in love my share," the original reads, "To tell me that in love my share " : l. 7, carelessly as losing a rhyme with ' he ' reads, " That joynt to ashes should be burnt," for " That joynt to ashes burnt should be,"—which ought perhaps to have been adopted as our text. In No. 3, l. 1, in " Wit's Recreations " has " To have the sweet Bag of the Bee," for " About the sweet bag of a bee ; " and ll. 7-8 :

" And taking from them each his flame,
With myrtle rods she whipt them."

for

" And taking thence from each his flame,
With rods of mirtle whipt them."

The ' About ' in L 1 is an after change.

In No. 4 in *Hesperides* the more definite inscription is " The Teare sent to her from Stanes," that is from the royal residence there, is in " Wit's Recreations," simply " A Tear sent to his Mistresse."   Otherwise only the orthography and punctuation differ. In No. 5 " His Farewell to Sack " of *Hesperides* is entitled " A Farewell to Sack," and is enlarged from 36 lines to 54 lines, but with four remarkable lines, in turn, omitted. So important a poem in every way as this " Farewell " calls for a full record of all the variants. Lines 1-2 for those in *Hesperides :*—

> " Farewell, thou thing time-past so knowne, so deare
>   To me, as blood to life and spirit : Neare "

in " Wit's Recreations " read :—

> " Farewell . . . . so true and dear
>   To me . . . . and near."

Line 3, " . . . . Kindred, friend or wife," for " Kindred, friend, man, wife ;" l. 4, " . . . . Soul to the body " for " Soule to body ;" l. 6, " Of the yet chast, and undefilèd Bride " is transfigured in *Hesperides* into " Of the resigning yet resisting bride."   The Master's touch ! Ll. 7-8 are added :—

> " The blisse of virgins ; foot-prints of the bed ;
>   Soft speech, smooth touch, the lips, the maiden-head."

Ll. 9-10 for the original :—

> " These and a thousand more could never be
> More near, more dear, than thou wert once to me "

are altered to :—

> " These, and a thousand sweets, co'd never be
> So neare or deare as thou wast once to me."

Ll. 11-22 are additions in *Hesperides* to which the critical Student will do well to turn. They begin, "O thou the drink of Gods and Angels ! wine," and end, " Vexation of the mind and damn'd despaire." Line 23 of *Hesperides*, " 'Tis thou alone, who, with thy mystick fan," at first read " 'Tis thou above, that . . . ." L. 25, " To rouse the sacred madnesse, and awake," was originally " To raise the holy madnesse." L. 27 for the later " flashing " had " sketching," and l. 28 " souls " for " soule." Lines 29-36 are another noticeable addition in *Hesperides*. Line 37 as now reads " But why? why longer do I gaze upon" for " But why? why longer do I gaze afar." L. 39 read "when " "sure." Ll. 42-3 now :—

> " Then know that Nature bids thee goe, not I :
> 'Tis her erroneous self has made a braine "

originally ran :—

> " Know then 'tis Nature bids thee hence, not I ;
> 'Tis her erroneous self hath form'd my brain."

L. 45-6 in *Hesperides* read :—

> " Prethee, not smile,
> Or smile more inly, lest thy looks beguile."

Originally they were as follows, along with four other lines cancelled in *Hesperides :*—

> " I prethee draw in
> Thy gazing fires, lest at their sight the sin
> Of fierce Idolatry shoot unto me, and
> I turn Apostate to the strict command
> Of Nature ; bid me now farewell, or smile
> More ugly, lest thy tempting looks beguile."

L. 47, for " denounc'd " read originally " pronounc't ;" l. 49, "boldly" for "freely ;" l. 51 originally read " And love, but not taste thee" for " And love thee, but not taste thee ;" l. 53, for "inadult'rate " read " inadulterate ;" and, finally, l. 54, " Hereafter shall smell . . . " originally read " Shall smell hereafter." These various readings, insertions and the omission, show how cunningly the Poet wrought out this Donne-like poem—the omission, perhaps, the most suggestive thing of the whole. No. 6, " The Cruell Maid," except in orthography and punctuation, as always, in "Wit's Recreations " only drops the needed " has " in l. 7 of *Hesperides.* No. 7 is identical in

both, save that in " Wit's Recreations " the heading is
"His misery" and in *Hesperides* "His misery in a Mis-
tresse." No. 8 in both is again identical, but in
" Wit's Recreations " the heading is as follows :—

With a ◯ to Julia.

No. 9 is the same in both. No. 10 in "Wit's Recreations" is inscribed "To make much of Time ;" in
Hesperides, " To the Virgins, to make much of Time ;"
and originally thus read in 1st and 2nd :—

> " Gather your Rose-buds whilst you may,
> Old Time is still a-flying;
> And that same flower which smiles to-day
> Too morrow may be dying.
> The glorious Lamp of Heaven, the Sun,
> The higher he is getting,
> The sooner will his race be run,
> And nearer to his setting."

The text of *Hesperides* reveals dainty improving
touches (Vol. I., p. 144-5); the remaining stanzas agree
in both. No. 11 in " Wit's Recreations " is headed
"On an old Batchelour" instead of " Upon himselfe ;"
and in l. 3 reads "married" for "wedded," in l. 4
" one " for " a jot," and l. 6 " Rather than mend me,

blind me quite," instead of the later " Rather than
mend, put out the light."   No. 12, " To the Rose," in
st. 1st, l. 5, originally has " hath " for " has ;" st. 2d,
l. 1, " If she frets, that " for " If she's fretfull, I ;" l. 3,
" struggles " for " struggle ;" and l. 5, " although not
kill " for " though not to kill." Nos. 13 and 14 agree,
only for " Gentlewoman " in *Hesperides* there was originally " Madam." No. 15, " How Violets came blew,"
is of a class that must have been a favourite with
Herrick.   They are anything but admirable.   Originally
this runs :—

How the Violets came blew.

The Violets, as poets tell,
  With *Venus* wrangling went
Whether the Violets did excell
  Or she in sweetest scent ;
But *Venus* having lost the day,
  Poor Girle, she fell on you,
And beat you so, as some do say,
  Her Blowes did make you blew."
(Vol. II. p. 2.)

Besides the correction of " Girles " for " Girle " in
l. 6, even this trifle shows revision. (Vol. II., p. 2.) Nos.
16 and 17 are the same in both, but the latter is originally
headed " A Foolish Querie " instead of " Gold before

Goodnesse." No. 18 in "Wit's Recreations" is inscribed
" A vow to Cupid," and in *Hesperides* " A short hymne
to Venus ;" and so originally in l. 1 reads " Cupids "
for " Goddesse," l. 2 " like Pearl " for " with," l. 3
" that I may " for " I may but," l. 5 " I do " for " I
will." No. 19 is alike in both, but originally is headed
" A Check to her delay " for " Upon a delaying
Lady." Nos. 20 and 21 are nearly identical ; but I
can suppose that it was with a chuckle that in the latter
the Author removed the hyphen from " be-long " that
your stupid reader might not catch the equivoque.
No. 22 is headed originally " To a stale Lady," and
in l. 1 reads " Thy wrinkles are no more." Nos. 23,
24, and 25 are the same. No. 26 curiously enough in
l. 5 of *Hesperides*, " He to work, or pray," read originally " or play." Nos. 27, 28, and 29 agree. No. 30,
" To Oenone," is inscribed originally " The Farewell
to Love and to his Mistresse." It is singular that in
both in st. 1st, l. 2, " won " should be mis-spelled
" one," and so remain, certes by inadvertence in my
own text. In st. 3d, l. 1, mis-reads " Court not both
or" for " Covet not both, but." No. 31 is originally
headed simply " Change," but in both are alike.
No. 32, " To Electra," is originally addressed " To
Julia," but otherwise both agree. Nos. 33 and 34

are the same, save that in the latter for " woman's " it
is originally " women's." No. 35, " To the Maids to
walke abroade," is originally inscribed " Abroad with
the Maids," but otherwise is alike in both. No. 36,
" Upon a child," is also left untouched in its pathetic
simpleness. To have changed a syllable would have
been as risky as trying to pluck a dewy flower with any
hope of preserving the dew. Abstention from alteration is in such instances truer insight than alteration. I
have not found anywhere that Herrick changed his
wording in his accepted perfect work. No. 37, " Upon
an Old Man, a Residenciarie," and Nos. 38, 39, 40,
41, 42, 43, 44, and 45 are nearly identical in both.
No. 39 substitutes " Lucie " in *Hesperides* for " Betty "
in " Wit's Recreations," and in No. 40 an obvious slip
of " and blast " for " one blast " is corrected in
Hesperides. It is satisfying that only to a slight extent
did Herrick bestow an after-look on his *Epigrams.*
No. 46 is the couplet that, though it did appear in
Hesperides, Mr. Hazlitt printed from " Wit's Recreations " as a new poem. No. 47, " The Wake," is in
" Wits' Recreations " headed " Alvar and Anthea ;"
otherwise is identical in both. There follows " The
Wake " in " Wit's Recreations," and Herrick probably
gave the new name of " The Wake " to the other

expressly to disown " The Wake " that so follows ; and
yet Mr. Hazlitt has "attributed" it to him ! No. 48
in *Hesperides* removes an unneeded "a " in l. 4 of the
penultimate stanza. Nos. 49, 50, 51, 52, and 53 are
the same in both, except in *Hesperides* a lacking "the "
is supplied in No. 52. No. 54, " Upon a Maide," is
again characteristically left untouched. Nos. 55 and 56
are once more identical, only the latter was originally
inscribed "Satisfaction." Nos. 57, 58, 59, 60, 61, and
62 are alike in both ; but in No. 62 the heading is
" Of this Booke." It is surely declarative of perfunctory study of Herrick that the present edition is the
first to bring to light these various readings. Mr.
Hazlitt contented himself with lazily remarking : " Six
or eight other poems [*i.e.*, in addition to those which
we have seen are not Herrick's at all] also occur, but
the text presents no noticeable variations from that given
in the common printed collection " (I. vi.) and noting
a few of the altered headings.

Passing now to those Poems that are preserved in
MSS.—public and private—it is of the deepest interest
to read these earlier texts in the light of that adopted
and published in *Hesperides.* Mr. Hazlitt has a section
in his edition called " Different Versions of Poems
already Printed," and there is one other somewhat

noticeable. I am not aware that any of these have been submitted to critical examination or comparison.

The first is in Harleian MS., 6917, fol. 10, and is an early version of the brilliant " Nuptiall Song, or Epithalamie on Sir Clipseby Crew and his Lady " (Vol. II. pp. 12-20). The opening of this poem has been cited to show that Milton had read it and remembered it in his choruses in "Samson Agonistes." I cannot say that I discern such remembrance or use of this " Epithalamie ;" but it has all Milton's early luscious-ness and stateliness. In l. 3 " faire injewel'd May " was originally written " faire enamell'd May," and l. 10 for "emergent" reads "emerging." In l. 14 for "Tread-ing upon vermilion " there was " Throwing about ver-milion." The following entire stanza was rejected in *Hesperides* just after the preceding :—

" Lead on faire paranymphs, the while her eyes
    Guilty of somewhat, ripe the strawberries
        And cherries in her cheekes ; there's creame
        Already spillt, her rayes must gleame
            Gently Thereon,
    And soe begett lust and temptation,
        To surfeit and to hunger;
    Helpe on her pace, and, though she lagg, yet stirre
        Her homewards ; well she knowes
        Her heart's at home howere she goes."

In the next stanza, l. 4, for the original, perhaps more realistic "*Spirting forth* pounded cinnamon," *Hesperides* gave 'perspiring,' and in l. 7, "Who would not then consume" for the later "Who therein wo'd not consume." In the succeeding stanza the MS. mis-spells 'margerum' for 'marjoram' (l. 2); and in l. 4, reads 'thy' for 'the bridegroom,' and l. 6 'besparckling' for 'disparkling;' and in the last line "Or like a firebrand he will waste," for "Or else to ashes he will waste." Then comes in this fragmentary stanza, which again is omitted in *Hesperides* :—

> "See how he waves his hand, and though his eyes
>   Shootes forth his iealous soule, for to surprize
>   And ravish you, his bride : do you
>   Not now perceiue the soule of C. C.   =Clipseby
>   Your mayden knight   [Crew.
>   . . . .
>   . . . .
>   With kisses to inspire
>   You with his iust and holy ire."

The next stanza in the MS. begins, "If so glide through the ranks of virgins, passe," for "Slide by the bankes of virgins then, and passe,"—the latter giving her the motion of a stream. In l. 10 *Hesperides* substitutes "as doth a fish," for "as doe the fish." Once more an omitted stanza succeeds :—

k

> "Why then goe forward sweet auspicious bride,
> And come upon your bridegroome like a tyde,
> Bearing downe time before you, hye
> Swell, mixe, and loose your sailes ; implye
> Like streames which flow
> Encurlld together, and noe difference show
> In their silver waters ; runne
> Into your selues like wooll together spunne ;
> Or blend so as the sight
> Of two makes one hermaphrodite."

In the following stanza l. 1 has originally "confesse
you wise," for "confesse y'are wise," and the change
gives that ripple in the flow of his rhythm, which
Herrick loved and affected.   In l. 2 for the later, " In
dealing forth those," he had written, " In drawing
forth those."   The felicitous close of this stanza was
worked out, not struck out as at a heat.   The MS. has

> "On then, and though y'are slow
> In going, yet however goe."

In *Hesperides* with cunning imitativeness of the linger-
ing yet wistful motion, it reads :—

> "On then, and though you slow-
> Ly go, yet, howsoever, go."

The divided word here and elsewhere is a trick caught

from his favorite Catullus.   Two omitted stanzas come
next :—

" How long soft bride shall your deare [Brides'-maids]
        make
  Loue to your welcome with the mistick cake,
    How long, oh pardon, shall the house
    And the smooth handmaids pay their vowes,
        With oyle and wine,
    For your approach, yet see their altars pine ?
        How long shall the page, to please
    You, stand for to surrender up the keyes
        Of the glad house ? come, come,
        Or Lar will freeze to death at home.

  Welcome at last unto the threshold, Time
  Throaned in a saffron euening, seemes to chyme
      All in ; kisse, and so enter ; if
      A prayer must be said, be brief ;
        The easy gods
  For such neglect, haue only myrtle rodds
      To stroake not strike ; feare you
  Not more, milde nymph, then they would haue you doe ;
      But dread that you doe more offend
      In that you doe beginne, then end."

In stanza 7th, l. 6 originally read :—

      " Us (and God shield her) " . . . .

changed into " The house (love shield her) " . . . . ; in
l. 10, ' has ' for ' your.'   Again two omitted stanzas are
here in the MS. :—

"What though your laden altar now has wonne
The creditt from the table of the sunne
    For earth and sea ; this cost
    On you is altogether lost,
        Because you feede
    Not on the flesh of beasts, but on the seede
        Of contemplation, your
    Your eyes are they, wherewith you draw the pure
        Elixar to the minde,
        Which sees the body fedd, yet pined.

  If you must needs for ceremonies sake
  Blesse a sacke possett, lucke goe with you, take
    The night charme quickly, you have spells
    And magick for to ende, and hells
        To passe, but such,
    And of such torture, as noe God would grudge
        To liue therein for euer, frye,
    I, and consume, and grow againe, to dye
        And liue, and in that case
        Love the damnation of that place."

In the succeeding stanza, l. 1, for 'kind truths' the MS. writes 'sweet': l. 2 drops in MS. 'and,' and in l. 3 begins 'And' for 'But': l. 6, 'Hearing' for 'Telling.' In the next stanza, l. 2 originally reads "noe" for "no strife," and l. 3, "Further then vertue lends" for "Further then gentlenes tends": l. 4, 'catching at' for 'striving for': l. 8, 'gentle' and 'fragrous' for

' youthfull '. and ' fragrant.'   In stanza 11th, ll. 5-6, which originally read

> " List, oh how
> Euen heauen giues up his soule betweene you now "

are changed into :—

> " O marke yee how
> The soule of Nature melts in numbers ; now " :

l. 7, " Marke how " for " See a."   In the next stanza, l. 2 originally has ' rising ' for the later ' swelling,' and in line 3,

> " Tempting thee too too modest "

for *Hesperides*

> " Tempting the two too modest " :

l. 7, ' hugge you ' for ' hugge it ' : ll. 8-9,

> " Your selues unto that mayne, in the full flow /
> Of the white pride "

> for

> " Your selues into the mighty over-flow /
> Of that white pride " :

l. 10, ' The starrs ' for ' The night.'   Stanza 13th, l. 1 in MS. reads " You see 'tis ready " for " The bed is ready " : l. 7, " And doe it in the full reach " for " And do it to the full ; reach " : l. 8, " High in your owne

conceipts, and rather teach " for " High in your conceipt, and some way teach " : l. 10, ' Sport ' for ' Play.'
In *Hesperides* there follows next the second of the last
two omitted stanzas before " If you must needs," &c.,
with only one noticeable reading in the last line of ' confusion ' for ' damnation '—not an improvement if it be a
softening of the passionate thought.   In the MS. is
here another omitted stanza :

> " And now y'haue wept enough, depart, yon starres
>   Begin to pinke, as weary that the warres   =*grow small*
>   Know so long treaties ; beate the drumme
>   Aloft, and like two armies, come
>   And guild the field ;
>   Fight brauely for the flame of mankinde, yeeld
>   Not to this, or that assault,
>   For that would proue more heresy then fault,
>   In combatants to flye,
>   Fore this or that hath gott the victory."

In stanza 15, l. 3, originally, it reads " with ribbe of
rocke and brasse " for the later " with rock or walles of
brasse ": and in the last line ' sheetes ' for ' sheet '
oblivious of line 2d.   In the closing stanza, line 28, for
the *Hesperides* misprint of ' that, that ' the MS. reads
' that the.'   In the place I corrected it preferably with
' two ' as in the next line.   The MS. is signed " R.
Herrick."   It will reward the Student to ponder and

compare these abundant various readings, and to consider the opulence that could dispense with the omissions. There are *bits* in the omissions that one is
grateful to have from the MS., although as a whole the
Poet showed nicety of taste, as well as sound judgment
in erasing them. The next Poem, " Herrick's Sack,"
in the Rawlinson MS. poet. 142, is an imperfect copy
of his " Welcome to Sack." I have recorded its very
unimportant variants in my examination of the text in
" Wit's Recreations," compared with the fuller version
in *Hesperides*.[8] A third MS., viz. Ashmole 38, p. 90,
Art. 110, is a similar inaccurate copy of his great poem
to his brother, Thomas Herrick. It is headed, " In
praise of the Country Life." Most of the various
readings are the Scribe's blunders, and call for no
detailed notice ; but here and there, certain enable
us to follow the shaping of the final text, e.g. l. 3,
" Canst leave the cittie, with exchange, to see," for
" Couldst leave the city, for exchange, to see ": l. 10,
" Wayes not to liue but to liue well," for " Wayes
lesse to live then to live well ": l. 22, " That mange,"
for " That plague ": l. 23, " sparing," for " warie " :
l. 26, " quench," for " coole." In the MS., ll. 28-30
do not appear, and instead this couplet :—

[8] See pages cxxxvi-viii.

> "The first is Naturs end : this doth imparte
>   Least thankes to Nature, most to art " :

Line 31 reads, " But that which next creates thy
happye life," for " But that which most makes sweet
thy country life " : and there follow in these MSS. two
omitted lines :—

> " And in thy sense her chaster thoughtes commend
>   Not halfe soe much the act, as end " :

—a wise omission certainly. Line 43 reads in the MS.,
' crawling ' for ' feebly ' : l. 46, ' bediapered ' for
' enameled ' : l. 51, ' vowes ' for ' comes ' : l. 52,
" rau'nous wolfe the wolly sheep," for " rav'ning wolves
the fleecie sheep ": l. 55, ' selfe ' [not ' sleepe,' as in
Mr. Hazlitt's] for ' rest ' : l. 57, ' Crowes ' for ' Warnes ' :
l. 60, ' crackling ' for ' spirting ' : l. 61, ' thumb thus '
for ' thumb this sentence ' : l. 61, ' Jove ' for ' God ' :
l. 65, ' farthest Inde ' for ' Western Inde ' : l. 66, ' lye '
for ' fly ' : l. 68, ' securer ' for ' securest ' : l. 70, ' better '
for ' whiter ' : l. 78, ' Viewing ' for ' Seeing ' : l. 79,
" By their shadowes, their substances," for " By those
fine shades, their substances ": l. 80, ' borrowing ' for
' taking small ' : l. 81, ' seal'd ' for ' deafe ' : l. 85,
' Fame tells the states ' [not ' of,' as in Mr. Hazlitt's]
for ' Fame tell of states ': l. 90, " Vice is vicegerent

at the courte," for "Vice rules the most, or all at
court ": l. 91, 'godly' for 'pious': l. 92, 'Vertue had
mouèd jn her sphere' for 'Vertue had, and mov'd her
sphere.' Here follow these omitted lines in the MS:—

> " Nor knowe thy happye and vn-enuey'd state
>   Owes more to vertue then too fate,   = to
>   Or fortune too ; for what the first secures,
>   That as herselfe, or Heauen, indures.
>   The two last fayle, and by experience make
>   Knowne, not they giue againe, they take " :

Then l. 93 reads, " But thou not fearest them," for
" But thou liv'st fearlesse": l. 95, 'hopes stronge built,'
for 'thoughts prepar'd': l. 96, 'For to salute her,' for
' To take her by': l. 99, 'sturdye' for 'surly'—the latter
a mistaken reading certainly: l. 101, 'braue' for
'bold': l. 109, 'toothe' for 'mouth': l. 111, 'cheer'
for 'fare': and l. 112, 'deare' for 'rare.' Here next
comes (after l. 116) in the MS. this omitted couplet :—

> " Canst drinke in earthen cuppes which ne're contayne
>   Colde hemlocke, or the lizzards bane '' :

l. 117, "Nor is ytt fitt thou keep'st, " for "Nor is it
that thou keep'st": l. 128, 'build' for 'make': l. 132,
'flye' for 'shun': l. 135, "neate, firme, close, and
true," for "and close, and wisely true": l. 145, "Till

then, lett faith soe prompt your liues yee may," for
" Till when, in such assurance, live ye may."

The next MS., viz. Ashmole 38, p. 93, Art. 111, is
headed, " Mr. Herricke his Charge to his Wife."   Had
this not been included in *Hesperides*, we should
naturally have concluded that it was by that cousin
Robert Herrick whose marriage Mr. J Payne Collier
having stumbled on, he at once set down as the Poet's,
forgetful of all the facts.[9]   Besides the Ashmole MS.,
the Kingsborough-Hazelwood MS. of my friend W. F.
Cosens, Esq., London, has another version.   Both
pretty closely follow the same text. Neither offers much
worthy of special record ; but the following may interest from Mr. Cosens MS. :—l. 4, ' woers by thy
haire ' for ' thousands with a haire ' : l. 10, ' things ' for
' that ' : l. 18, ' beauty ' for ' feature ' : l. 24, " emblems
which express the itch " for " are the expressions of
that itch " : ll. 27-8 :

---

[9] Bibliographical Account I. 370.   Mr. Collier's record is : " As
a small, but new contribution to the biography of Herrick, we may
add here the registration of his marriage at St. Clement's Danes,
Westminster : — ' 5 June, 1632.   Robert Herrick and Jane
Gibbons.'   All that we have hitherto known, we believe, is that
the Christian name of his wife was Jane."   Contrariwise, all that
we have hitherto known, and still know, is that Herrick lived and
died a bachelor.

" For that once lost thou needs must fall
To one, then prostitute to all "

for

" For that once lost, thou't fall to one
Then prostrate to a million " :

Lines 11-16 of *Hesperides* that follow the last couplet
in the MS., and closing thus :—

" And thinke, each man thou seest doth dome
Thy thoughts to say I backe am come " :

Lines 38-9,

" Let them call thee wondrous faire
Crowne of woeman, yett despaire "

for

" Let them enstile thee fairest faire
The pearle of princes, yet despair " :

l. 47, ' vertuous ' for ' gentle ' : ll. 55-6 :

" Thy fortres, and must needs prevaile
Gainst thee and force "

for

" Thy fortress, and will needs prevaile :
And wildly force " :

l. 65, ' Creates ' for ' That makes ' : l. 67, ' Glory ' for

'Triumph': l. 70, 'Take my last regret' for 'Take this compression': l. 79, 'Sharp' for 'Lean': l. 80, " In my full triumph " for "its one triumphant ": l. 81, " In thee, the height," for " In thee all faith."

In Harleian MS. 6917, fol. 48 (*verso*) is an early copy of the supreme " Mad Maid's Song," than which nothing out of the snatches put in the mouth of Ophelia is more conquering in its simple pathos. The variants are slight, e.g. st. 1, l. 2, 'morrow' for 'morning' (repeated): l. 4, ' All dabbled ' for ' Bedabled ': st. 2, l. 3, 'teares' for ' flowers ': l. 4, ' was ' for ' is ': st. 5, l. 1, ' I hope ' for ' I know ': st. 7, L 2, ' balsome ' for ' cow-slips.' Perhaps the substitution of 'morning ' in *Hesperides* for ' morrow' was a mistake : and ' tears ' for ' flowers ': and at least 'balsome' for ' cow-slips' had been preferable.

The next MS., " Charon and the Nightingale," from Rawlinson MS., poet 65, fol. 32, is a fuller copy of "Charon and Phylomel, a Dialogue sung," of *Hesperides* (Vol. II., pp. 244-5). Only ll. 1—26 are in *Hesperides*—the remainder is additional. Before giving the additions, these variants between the MS. and *Hesperides* text of the opening portion, call for record, passing over others of trivial moment :—l. 5, ' voice' for 'sound ': l. 6, ' what' for ' where ': l. 7, 'shade'

for 'bird': l. 11, 'warbling' for 'watching': l. 12,
'made me hoist up sail' for 'made me thus hoist
saile': l. 13, 'I'le be gone' for 'I'le returne': l. 18,
'praise' for 'pray': l. 19, 'sighs' for 'vowes': l. 22,
'in' for 'with': l. 24, 'Our passage' for ' Our 'sloth-
full passage.' The new MS. commences after l. 26,
" Who els with tears wo'd doubtless drown my ferry"
(in MS. " our wherry ")—as thus :—

> " A boat, a boat, hast to the ferry,
>   For we goe over to be merry,
>   To laugh & quaff and drink old sherry.
> [*Phil.*] Charon, O Charon, the wafter of all soules to bliss
>   or bain,
> [*Char.*] Who calls the ferryman of Hell ?
> [*Phil.*] Come neer & say who lives in bliss & who in pain :
> [*Char.*] Those that dye well eternall bliss shall follow,
>   Those that dye ill, their own black deeds shall
>   swallow.
> [*Phil.*] Shall thy black barg those guilty spirits row
>   That kill themselves for love ? [*Char.*] Oh no, oh
>   no,
>   My cordage cracks when such foule sins draw neer,
>   No winde blows fair nor I my boat can steer.
> [*Phil.*] What spirits pass & in elizium reign ?
> [*Char.*] Those harmless soules that love & are belovd again.
> [*Phil.*] That soule that lives in love & faign would dye to
>   win
>   Shall he goe free ? [*Char.*] Oh no, it is too foul a
>   sin.

> He must not come aboard, I dare not row,
> Storms of dispair my boat will over-blow.
> But when thy m⁷ shall close up thine eys then come
>   aboard   =misery
> Then come aboard & pass; till then be wise &
>   synge."

It will be observed by the critical reader that there is a resemblance in thought in this MS. portion to the " New Charon " (Vol. III., p. 110). But whether it be or be not Herrick's, it does not agree with the former part ; for in it she is a shade, and in this she is not dead. Perhaps the explanation is that this portion may have been a first sketch, and the other an expansion ; and that afterwards the thought in the later was used in the " New Charon." I ask if the inserted song, " A boat, a boat," &c., be not a catch that does not belong to Herrick? and I note that the unfinished character of the MS. is shown by the last couplet not rhyming.

Rawlinson MS. 147 Poet. p. 14, gives us an interesting variant of " To a Gentlewoman objecting to him his Grey Haires " (Vol. I. p. 107) as thus :—

> "*An old Man to his yonge Mrs.*
> Am I despis'd because you say
> And I beleiue that I am gray ?
> Know lady you haue but your day,

And night will come when man will sweare
Time hath spitt now upon your hayre.
Then when in your glasse you seeke,
And find no roses on your cheeke,
No, nor the bud at least to show,
Where such a fayre carnation grew,
And such a smiling tulippe too.
Ah ! then too late close in your chamber keeping,
It will be told
That you are old,
By those true teares y'are weepinge."

We have now reached the "Fairy" Poems, and it
is of rarest interest to mark the fine and subtle working
on these most dainty and delicate-fancied productions
of Herrick's imaginative vein. The first is "King
Oberon's Pallace." Mr. Hazlitt prints it in his Appendix (Vol. II. pp. 466-470), but has neglected to state
whence he derived it. It is found in Ashmole MS. 38,
p. 101 and 118. This MS. omits the opening (ll. 1-8).
Thereafter, l. 9, reads "Of peltish waspes, well knowne
his guarde " for the less accurate "we'l know his
guard " of *Hesperides*; ll. 20-1, "the grass of Lemster
ore, soberlye sparkling," for "the finest Lemster ore
mildly desparkling," l. 29, "girdle" for "ceston":
l. 30, "The eyes of all doth straight bewitch " for "All
with temptation doth bewitch." After l. 37 the MS.
inserts these twenty-seven singular enumerative lines :—

" And further of, some sorte of peare,
   Apple or plume is neatly layde   =plum
   (As yf yt were a tribute payde)
   By the round vrchin ; [1] some mixt wheat
   The which the ant did taste, not eate :
   Deafe nutts,[2] softe Iewes-eares, and some thinne
   Chipping, the mice filcht from the binn
   Of the graye farmer: and to theis
   The scrappes of lentells, chitted pease,
   Dryed hony-combes, browne acorne cupps,
   Out of the which hee sometymes sups
   His hearby-broath ; and theis close by
   Are puckered bullas, cankers, and dry
   Kernells and withered hawes; the rest
   Are trinketts falne from the kytes neast,
   As buttered bread, the which the wilde
   Birde snatcht away from the crying childe ;
   Blew pynes, taggs, sepcus, beades and things
   Of higher price, as halfe jett rings,
   Ribands, and then some silken shreakes
   To virgines lost att barlye breakes ;
   Many a purse-stringe, manye a threade
   Of gould and silver there is spread.

     .   .   .   .
     .   .   .   .

   Lyes here about ; and as wee ghesse,
   Some bitte of thymbles seeme to dresse
   The braue cheafe worke; and for to faue
   The easie excellence of the caue
   Squirrells, &c."

    [1] = hedge-hog rolled up.   [2] = hollow nuts.

Then comes substantially the same as in *Hesperides*,
but with certain variations—*e.g.*, l. 47 in the MS. reads
" Serue here, bothe which in-chequered " for " Are
neatly here enchequerèd," and then the continuation
runs :—

> " With castors doucettes (which poore thay
>   Bitt off themselues, to scape away)
>   Browne toade-stones, ferrettes eyes, the gumm " :

l. 51, " Hand enchasing here those wartes " for " With
hand enchasing here those warts": l. 55, 'slye' badly for
'shie': l. 62, 'richly' for 'neatly': l. 64, 'roche' for 'fish':
l. 69, 'caue' for 'roome': l. 70, " Can gett reflection
from their jemmes " for " Can make reflected "——:
l. 73, 'Candle-masse' for 'taper-light': l. 80, 'con-
uenient' for 'obedient': l. 84, 'whiter' for 'luckie':
l. 88, 'spungie' for 'spunge-like': l. 98, " Wee call
the files of mayden-heades " for " Broke at the losse of
maiden-heads ": l. 99, 'soft' for 'pure': l. 100,
'Which' for 'Dropt': l. 101, 'are shed when' for
'when panting': l. 112, 'yearne' for 'flax.'

The next 'Fairy' poem is " Kinge Oberon's Feast,"
from Ashmole MS. 38, p. 100, Art. 117. As in the
former, the MS. omits the opening, (ll. 1-6) and begins

l

> "A little mushromp table spread
> After the dance " :—

for

> "A little mushroome table spred,
> After short prayers" :—

ll. 3-4 :—

> "A yeallowe corne of heckey wheate
> With some small sandye greets; to eate"   =grits

for

> "A moon-parcht grain of purest wheat
> With some small glitt'ring gritt, to eate " :

l. 8, "Wee dare not thinke" for "We must not think":
l. 10, "His fier, the pittering grasshopper" for "His
spleen, the chirring grasshopper ": l. 11, 'prussing' for
'puling.'   After l. 12 comes an omitted couplet:

> "The humming dor, the dyinge swann,
> And each a choyse musitian " :

l. 16, 'besweeted' for 'besweetned': ll. 21-2 :

> ————————"but with a little
> Neate cole alaye of cvckoes spittle,"

for "Of that we call": l. 25-8 :—

> ——————— "but hee not spares
> To feed vppon the candide hayres

> Of a dryed canker, with a sagg
> And well bee-strutted bee's sweet bagg "

for

> ――――――"but then forthwith
> He ventures boldly on the pith
> Of sugred rush, and eates the sagge," &c.

l. 29, "Shocking" for "Gladding." Then come these five lines that are in part inserted a little onward in *Hesperides :*—

> "A pickled magget and a drye
> Hipp, with a red-cappt worme that's shutt
> Within the carcasse of a nutt,
> Browne as his tooth : and with the fatt
> And well broyl'd inch-pin of a batt" :

ll. 32-3 read

> "A bloated eare-wigg, with the pythe
> Of sugred rush, he gladds hym with "

for

> "A bloated earewig, and a flie;
> With the red-capt worme," &c.,

and then follow these lines (in the MS) :—

> "But most of all the glow-worme's fier
> (As much bewitching his desire
> To knowe his queene) must with the farr
> Fetcht binding ielley of a starr,
> The silke wormes seed "

l. 42, 'fruittfull' for 'flattering'—the latter used repeatedly by Herrick (in III. "Golden Apples"): l. 45,
'a daysy challice' for 'a dainty daizie.' This Poem
appeared originally in a small volume more than once
mentioned by us, viz., "A Description of the King and
Queene of Fayries," &c. (1635); and this probably was
Herrick's first printed production.   The first form was
very imperfect, and I deem it expedient to reprint it
here *literatim* for comparison—as thus :—

> *"A Description of his Dyet.*
>
> Now they the Elves within a trice,
> Prepar'd a feast lesse great than nice.
> Where you may imagine first,
> The Elves prepare to quench his thirst,
> In pure seed Pearle of Infant dew
> Brought and sweetned with a blew
> And pregnant Violet; which done
> His killing eies begin to runne
> Quite ore the table, where he spyes
> The hornes of water'd Butter-flies.
> Of which he eats, but with a little
> Neat coole allay of Cuckowe spittle.
> Next this the red cap worme thats shut
> Within the concave of a nut.
> Moles eyes he tastes, then Adders eares;
> To these for sauce the slaine stagges teares,
> A bloated earewig, and the pith
> Of sugred rush he glads him with.

> Then he takes a little Mothe,
> Late fatted in a scarlet cloth,
> A Spinners ham, the beards of mice,
> Nits carbonado'd, a device
> Before unknowne; the blood of fleas
> Which gave his Elveships stomacke ease.
> The unctuous dew tops of a Snaile,
> The broke heart of a Nightingale,
> Orecome in musicke, with the sagge
> And well bestrutted Bees sweet bagge.
> Conserves of Atomes, and the mites,
> The silke wormes sperme, and the delights
> Of all that ever yet hath blest
> Fayrie land : so ends his feast."

If it were needful it would not be difficult to extend these various readings from other MSS., public and private. A number have been kindly sent to me and otherwise pointed out ; but enough have been adduced to convince that, in common with the greatest and most spontaneous of our Poets, Herrick worked with a fine artistic patience and genuine concentration and consecration on his Verse. What is accidentally revealed in those thus minutely examined and reported on by us, warrants the conclusion that thus was it throughout. The student of our language and literature will be thankful for this additional evidence of highest art in combination with highest genius (of its kind), and will

(I hope) be helped to discern with what admirable insight and ear our Poet changed and omitted. To him equally with Ben Jonson may be applied William Cartwright's inestimable praise :—

> " Where are they now that cry thy Lamp did drink
>   More Oyl than th' Author Wine, while he did think ?
>   We do embrace their slander; thou hast writ
>   Not for Dispatch but Fame; no Market Wit;
>   'Twas not thy Care that it might pass and sel
>   But that it might endure, and be done well;
>   Nor wouldst thou venture it unto the Ear
>   Until the File would not make smooth, but wear."
>
> (Poems, as before, p. 314.)

That Herrick did use the ' File ' cunningly and patiently is everywhere apparent; and in anticipation of apparently an early death and before he should be ' in print ' be appealed to Julia :—

> " Julia, if I chance to die
>   Ere I print my poetry,
>   I most humbly thee desire
>   To commit it to the fire :
>   *Better 'twere my Book were dead*
>   *Then to live not perfected.*" (Vol. I. p. 35.)

and elsewhere :

> " *Parcell-gilt Poetry.*
>   *Let's strive to be* THE BEST; the Gods, we know it,
>   Pillars and men, hate an indifferent poet."
>
> (Vol. III. p. 46.)

III. *What the Book tells of the Man and his relation to his times.*—The merest glance over the manifold headings of the Poems, longer and shorter, of *Hesperides* and *Noble Numbers*, reveals that Herrick was not at all reluctant to tell the world of himself. Even in cases wherein he might have concealed his own personality he prefers revelation of it to concealment, silvern speech to golden silence—*e.g.*, in "Wit's Recreations" certain quaint lines had been inscribed " Of an old batchelor," but when they were transferred to *Hesperides* he bravely substitutes " Upon Himself " (Vol. I. p. 170); and so, too, with " Cherry Pit " in " Wit's Recreations " indirect, while in *Hesperides* direct "Julia and I."[1] This is typical. If it were harsh to allege that he " wore his heart upon his sleeve for daws to peck at," one must recognize a frank volubility and a fearless confidentialness about Robert Herrick by Robert Herrick, that are extremely noticeable. No more than Cromwell does he seek to tone down either the coppery hue of that feature which was so prominent

---

[1] I refer here simply to the change to " Julia and I." Of course it is clear he had other motives for the alteration, e.g. the first form shows he wrote for the sake of the equivoque, and then he altered it for the sake of better effect. The equivoque and meaning conveyed in his equivoque was also too gross for him to speak it really as of himself.

in Bardolph, or to remove his warts.   This suggests
another element—his fundamental truthfulness.   It is
not simply that there is realism of description and utter
nakedness of discovery, but that, whether grave or gay,
you have a sense of absolute integrity of confession and
profession.   Both may mainly relate to moods and
swift-coming and as swift-going thought and emotion;
but then it is so because the man was a phenomenal
man, a man of sudden moods, as changeful and as unexpected as the patterns made by a kaleidoscope.   Forsooth there is often and often the same wonder over
the verse-record, touched with imaginative splendours,
as over the strange beauty shapened and coloured
therein out of bits of broken glass and other valueless
scraps.   You turn to a poem headed " Of Himself,"
and lo ! the starting-point is a mere nothing, but before
the close you are startled with something that lifts you
up and ennobles the common-place.   To take a repre-
sentative example.—Like Thomas Randolph, he had
lost a finger, and so he must ' sing ' of the loss—not for
Noble Numbers, but for *Hesperides*—and here is the
result, one which the Reader might do worse than
meditate on a little :—

" *Upon the losse of his Finger.*
One of the five straight branches of my hand
Is lopt already; and the rest but stand

Expecting when to fall : which soon will be;
First dyes the Leafe, the Bough next, next the Tree."

(Vol. II. p. 170.)

Compare this with the volatile Randolph's apostrophe
to his finger lost in a scuffle :—

——————— " deare finger, though thou be
Cut from those muscles govern'd thee.
And had thy motion at command ;
Yet still as in a margent stand
To point my thoughts to fix upon
The hope of Resurrection :
And since thou canst no finger be,
Be a death's-head to humble me,
Till death doth threat her sting in vain,
And we in heaven shake hands again."

(Poems : 1652 pp. 121-2.)

How much truer and simpler and right from the
heart is the pathos of Herrick over against the mere
'trick' of Randolph.   One accepts as real the one :
as in reading *his* George Herbert-like " Necessary
Observations," the tongue in cheek is inevitably called
up in the other.   I say this as judging by the ultimate
impression left on the student of Herrick and of *blazè*
Randolph.   Herrick 'convinces' you of his truthfulness, whether he aspire or grovel.   It were easy to
multiply similar engrandeuring and entendering of very

ordinary things; but all along I wish rather to lead the way than to exhaust those characteristics that have suggested themselves to me.

Springing out of these unlooked for touches of gravity and art of the Poet as distinguished from the mere rhymer, is another element still more largely present in *Hesperides* and *Noble Numbers* when you are vigilant in looking for it. I refer to an unlifted shadow of melancholy that must have lain broad and black over Herrick. Joyousness is not at all in contradiction with this, any more than is the shadow with the real brightness of the light whose shadow it is. Your 'merry' nature—merry toward others, through keen self-repression and self-denial—has often a dark thread interwoven in it. I find this melancholy (the 'Melancholia' of Robert Burton) in the perpetually-recurring thought of death in the Poetry of Herrick. The intermixture of the Poems—before accounted for—is apt to hide this; but when you read pencil in hand, you are struck with the fascinating frequency of allusion to 'the end' of all; your ear, once open, catches tones and semi-tones of an unmoving sense of mortality and uncertainty; you see the gleam of tears in the very sunbeams of laughter. His " Gather ye rosebuds " is only a lighter setting to music of an habitual thought in this so blithe and whole-hearted Singer. This is the more remarkable as a recollection of the facts of his Life (I. Biographical) makes it certain that the largest proportion of his Poems must have been written when he was comparatively young. Nevertheless, his ' gray hairs' and death come in with a peculiar iteration among the earliest.[2] As we have already seen, the very remarkable Lines from the Ashmolean MS. entitled "Vpon Parting" ("Golden Apples," Vol. III. p. 109) mark his disentanglement from all his " Mistresses " (in the poetic, and only subsidiarily actual sense of ' sweethearts') on his assuming 'holy orders.' The other poem, " The Farewell vnto Poetrie " (*Ibid* pp. 101-6), is kindredly serious. About to be made ' priest,' he means to do his duty. Now all this was in or before 1629, when he was ' ordained ' and installed as Vicar of Dean Prior. By 1629, consequently, or in his 38th year, his ' Antheas,' and ' Perillas,' and ' Julias,' and

---

[2] Herrick's melancholy and thoughts of death are abiding, not transient, much less mere phrases. An unpublished autograph note of Voltaire to Lord Chesterfield gives an example of the mere jesting-phrase reference to death—as follows :—

" Si je ne suis pas mort, je Serai a vos ordres, si je suis mort, je vous en demande pardon d'avance.   V."

    A my lord.

        Comte Chesterfield : 1772 or 1773 : MSS. at Bretby Park.

'Silvias,' and all the bevy of fair girls and women were
of the Past—earlier in his 'wild, unhallowed' youth-
hood and later after leaving the University and being
resident in town, prior to ordination, and when he was
of the 'Sun,' and the 'Dog,' and the 'Triple Tun,'
and other great gatherings, social and literary ; and
yet it is in these relatively early poems the deepest
and saddest notes are found.   Let us glance over the
Book to briefly indicate (by italics) and illustrate this,
—going from the opening pages onward.   Thus " To
Perilla " he writes,—the last line (italicized) being very ·
fine in another aspect than what is now being looked
at :—

> "Ah, my Perilla ! do'st thou grieve to see
>   Me, day by day, to steale away from thee ?
>   Age cals me hence, *and my gray haires bid come,*
>   *And haste away to mine eternal home ;*
>   *'Twill not be long* (Perilla) after this,
>   *That I must give thee the supremest kisse :*
>   *Dead when I am* . . . .
>   Follow me weeping to my Turfe, and there
>   Let fall a Primrose, and with it a teare :
>   Then lastly, let some weekly-strewings be
>   Devoted to the memory of me :
>   Then shall my Ghost not walk about, but keep
>   Still *in the coole, and silent shades of sleep.*"
>   (Vol. I. pp. 14-15.)

Again, in his "To Robin Red-brest" how touch-
ingly does he go away back as when a little child on
the child's legend in all lands of the "Babes in the
Wood," and seek a friend in the 'house-hold' bird of
"the red stomacher":—

> "*To Robin Red-brest.*
> Laid out for dead, *let thy last kindnesse be*
> With leaves and mosse-work for to cover me :
> And while the Wood-nimphs my cold corps inter,
> Sing thou my Dirge, sweet-warbling Chorister !
> For Epitaph, in Foliage, next write this,
> Here, here the Tomb of Robin Herrick is !"
>   (Vol. I. p. 32.)

Once more, "To Anthea," as to "Perilla," we
have this ; and, as in I. Biographical I have re-
marked, it is surely very clear that under these fanciful
names a real love-story of his youth is concealed,
making us think of his bachelorhood as constrained by
some disappointment in a first love :—

> "*To* Anthea.
> *Now is the time, when all the lights wax dim :*
> *And thou (Anthea) must withdraw from him*
> *Who was thy servant.* Dearest, *bury me*
> *Under that Holy-oke, or Gospel-tree :*
> *Where (though thou see'st not) thou may'st think upon*
> *Me,* when thou yeerly go'st Procession :

> Or, for mine honour, *lay me in that Tombe*
> *In which thy sacred Reliques shall have roome.*
> For my Embalming (Sweetest) there will be
> No Spices wanting, when I'm laid by thee."
>
> (Vol. I. p. 34.)

Yet again, how unforced, how inevitable, how soft
and tender is his :—

> " *Divination by a Daffadill.*
>
> When a Daffadill I see,
> Hanging down his head t'wards me;
> Guesse I may, what I must be :
> First, I shall decline my head;
> Secondly, I shall be dead ;
> Lastly, safely buryèd.   (Vol. I. p. 64.)

Tenderer still is this :—

> " *Upon his eye-sight failing him.*
>
> I beginne to waine in sight;
> Shortly I shall bid goodnight :
> Then no gazing more about,
> When the Tapers once are out."
>
> (Vol. II. p. 131.)

Even when he is wearing, if not motley, at least the
vine-wreath of Anacreon or the violets of Catullus, he
semi-unconsciously deepens his raillery of " The cruell
maid " into passionate entreaty, as thus :—

> · —" *I'le trouble you no more ; but goe*
> *My way, where you shall never know*
> *What is become of me : there I*
> *Will find me out a path to die ;*
> Or learne some way how to forget
> You, and your name, for ever " :

and again :

> ———————" *yet this thing doe,*
> *That my last Vow commends to you :*
> *When you shall see that I am dead,*
> *For pitty let a teare be shed ;*
> And (with your Mantle o're me cast)
> *Give my cold lips a kisse at last :*
> If twice you kisse, you need not feare,
> That I shall stir, or live more here."
>
> (Vol. I. pp. 103-104.)

Still more interpenetrated and penetratively, is

> " *The Olive Branch.*
>
> *Sadly I walk't within the field,*
> *To see what comfort it wo'd yeeld ;*
> *And as I went my private way,*
> An Olive-branch before me lay :
> And seeing it, I made a stay.
> And took it up, and view'd it ; then
> Kissing the Omen, said Amen :
> Be, be it so, and let this be
> A Divination unto me :
> *That in short time my woes shall cease ;*
> *And Love shall crown my End with Peace."*
>
> (Vol. I. pp. 126-7.)

Very striking is the working in of himself and his antici-
pated early death in the else gay rather than sombre
" Meditation for his Mistresse."   He has likened her
to 'Tulip,' and 'July-flower,' and ' Rose,' and 'faire-set
Vine,' and 'Balme,' and 'dainty Violet'! Then, like
one of Mozart's marvellous notes in his Choruses, there
is this close :

> " You are the Queen all flowers among,
>   But die you must (faire Maide) ere long,
>   *As He, the maker of this Song.*" (Vol. I. p. 152.)

Similarly in " The Changes.   To Corinna "—

> " Time, ere long, will come and plow
>   Loathèd Furrowes in your brow :
>   And the dimnesse of your eye
>   Will no other thing imply,
>   But you must die
>   *As well as I.*"   (Vol. I. p. 169.)

These will suffice to satisfy the Reader that not only
was there beneath Herrick's moods of mirth and boist-
erousness an abiding element of melancholy, but besides,
a deeper vein of thinking and feeling than is commonly
suspected.   This leads me to speak of another element
in the make of the man that demands statement and
insistence, seeing that inattention to it does him no ordinary injustice—his love of country, his Shakespeare-like

proudness of being an Englishman. This comes out very delightfully in the fulness and fine credulity of his celebration of English ways and habits, and even superstitions. For where will you find such pictures of England's flowers and herbage, the freshness and brightness of her sunshine, and rains, and dews, the fragrance of her blossoms, and buds, and leafage, and fruits; the deliciousness of her bird-filled woodland and lanes, and twilights, the daintiness of her Christmas, and other home and harvest ordinances and customs, as Hock-cart, May-pole Morris dance, Wake, Quintell, Trentall, Twelfth Night, the heartiness and opulence of her firesides, gentle and simple, the exquisiteness and delicate fancies of her 'Fairy' lore, the peerless loveliness of her 'fair women,' and the imperial brains of her 'brave men,' the thorough gladness of the brown lads and ruddy lasses in the comely country round, or quaffing their nut-brown ale. So that his own appeal and request when he would have his verses read must be remembered by those who would drink in their finest inspiration—as thus :—

" In sober mornings, doe not thou reherse
  The holy incantation of a verse ;
  But when that men have both well drunke, and fed,
  Let my Enchantments then be sung, or read.

m

When Laurell spirts 'ith' fire, and when the Hearth
Smiles to it selfe, and guilds the roofe with mirth ;
When up the *Thyrse* is rais'd, and when the sound
Of sacred *Orgies* flyes, A round, A round ;
When the Rose raignes, and locks with ointments shine,
Let rigid Cato read these Lines of mine."

(Vol. I. pp. 11-12.)

But if more occult not a whit less pervading is the
further evidence that Herrick, more than most of his
contemporaries, felt keenly all through the tragedy of
the Civil War, the vastness of the issues and the mourn-
fulness of the conflict.   When—as with his melancholy
—you study *Hesperides* and *Noble Numbers* with this in
mind, you are surprised and touched by the depth
and strength of emotion as he writes of the men and
the events of his age.   In I. Biographical, I have
stated that he was a Royalist, and 'loyal' to the
King as against the Kingdom.   In his case, as in many
others, I have recognised the chivalry of his loyalty.
If I must side with Cromwell not Charles, or with the
Nation and not the Court, I none the less honour such
as sacrificed everything in fealty to their convictions
and principles.   But underlying Herrick's Royalism and
loyalty, there was open-eyed and sad-hearted insight
into the high-handed procedure of his sovereign and
his advisers, and a yearning for a way of escape and

reconciliation. To those consequently who have turned to *Hesperides* as a mere Garden of Flowers, and Fruit, and Birds, and rural sights and fragrancies, and colours, and sounds, it is necessary to assert that his Poems, when adequately studied, give us unmistakable evidence that in him all the lights and shadows, the successes and disasters, the angers and estrangements, the wisdom and unwisdom of thick-coming occurrences were reflected. The evidence here is so universal that I must content myself with typical examples. At a chance opening of his Book take this to begin with :—

To his Friend on the untunable Times.

"Play I co'd once; but (gentle friend) you see
My Harp hung up, here on the Willow tree.
Sing I co'd once; and bravely too enspire,
(With luscious Numbers) my melodious Lyre.
Draw I co'd once (although not stocks or stones,
Amphion-like) men made of flesh and bones,
Whether I wo'd; but (ah!) I know not how,
I feele in me, this transmutation now.
Griefe, (my deare friend) has first my Harp unstrung;
Wither'd my hand, and palsie-struck my tongue."

(Vol. I. p. 146.)

Again:—

On Himselfe.

"Aske me, why I do not sing
To the tension of the string,

As I did, not long ago,
When my numbers full did flow?
Griefe (ay me!) hath struck my Lute,
And my tongue at one time mute."

(Vol. II. pp. 45-6.)

Once more:—

The Poet hath lost his pipe.

"I cannot pipe as I was wont to do,
  Broke is my Reed, hoarse is my singing too :
  My wearied Oat Ile hang upon the Tree,
  And give it to the Silvan deitie."   (Vol. II. p. 172.)

Again:—

His wish to privacie.

"Give me a Cell
      To dwell,
  Where no foot hath
      A path :
  There will I spend,
      And end
  My wearied yeares
      In teares."·   (Vol. II. p. 262.)

Again:—

His Answer to a friend.

"You aske me what I doe, and how I live?
  And (Noble friend) this answer I must give :
  Drooping, I draw on to the vaults of death,
  O're which you'l walk, when I am laid beneath."

(Vol. III. pp. 50-51.)

Further :—

His change.

" My many cares and much distress,
  Has made me like a wilderness :
  Or (discompos'd) I'm like a rude,
  And all-confusèd multitude :
  Out of my comely manners worne ;
  And as in meanes, in minde all torne."

(Vol. III. p. 51.)

There are many such personal plaints ; but there are more than these. His expressly 'royal' poems directly addressed to the King and his followers were natural enough from him. Their ' loyalty' lies on the surface. It needs not that I should quote from them. But with all his ' royalism ' and 'loyalty,' how deep was his lamentation over kingly and courtly vengeances, and how burning his shame over incompetence among high-advisers. Take this :—

Clemency.

" For punishment in warre, it will suffice,
  If the chiefe author of the faction dyes ;
  Let but few smart, but strike a feare through all :
  Where the fault springs, there let the judgement fall."

(Vol. II. p. 47.)

So, too, in his " Pitie to the Prostrate " :—

> " 'Tis worse then barbarous cruelty to show
>   No part of pitie on a conquer'd foe."
> > (Vol. II. p. 163.)

This latter may have been a groan for the beaten King
—and this also :—

> *Change common to all.*
> " All things subjected are to Fate;
>   Whom this Morne sees most fortunate,
>   The Ev'ning sees in poor estate."
> > (Vol. II. p. 179.)

How pathetic his verses to Wicks :—

> " W'ave seen the past-best Times, and these
>   Will nere return."   (Vol. II. p. 48.)

Similarly, in his " Parting Verse " :—

> " As for myself, since time a thousand cares
>   And griefs hath fil'de upon my silver hairs."
> > (Vol. II. p. 61.)

Again, in his "Lachrimæ, or Mirth turn'd to Mourning":

> " Call me no more,
>   As heretofore,
> The musick of a Feast;
>   Since now (alas)
>   The mirth that was
> In me, is dead or ceast."   (Vol. II. p. 67.)

Once more, " To his Booke " :—

> " He's greedie of his life, who will not fall,
> Whenas a publick ruine bears down All."
> (Vol. II. p. 87.)

So in his " Pastorall sung to the King " :

> " Bad are the times.   And wors then they are we :
> Troth, bad are both; worse fruit, and ill the tree."

and the close :—

> " The shades grow great; but greater grows our sorrow,
> But lets go steepe
> Our eyes in sleepe;
> And meet to weepe
> To morrow."   (Vol. II. pp. 93-96.

He could see the evil of ' royal ' favouritism to the un-
worthy, as thus :—

Pollicie in Princes.

> " That Princes may possesse a surer seat,
> 'Tis fit they make no One with them too great."
> (Vol. II. p. 101.)

I think this must refer to Edgehill :—

Haste hurtfull.

> " Haste is unhappy : what we rashly do
> Is both unluckie ; I, and foolish too.

Where War with rashnesse is attempted, there
The soldiers leave the Field with equall feare."
(Vol. II. p. 279.)

There returns his own personal grief : —

His weaknesse in woes.
" I cannot suffer ; and in this, my part
Of Patience wants. Grief breaks the stoutest Heart."
(Vol. II. p. 111.)

Here is the cry of a pathetic heart pierced to the core :—

Upon the troublesome times.
" O ! Times most bad,
Without the scope
Of hope
Of better to be had !

Where shall I goe,
Or whither run
To shun
This publique overthrow ?

No places are
(This I am sure)
Secure
In this our wasting Warre.

Some storms w'ave past ;
Yet we must all
Down fall,
And perish at the last."
(Vol. II. pp. 183-4.)

It was a mistaking of the coming down of a palace-
ceiling (so to say) for the ruin of the ever-enduring
dome of the sky (when *it* was only beclouded) ; none
the less real were the pain and the trial.   How curiously
intermixed is his " Bad season makes the Poet sad," as
thus :—

> " Dull to my selfe, and almost dead to these
> My many fresh and fragrant Mistresses :
> Lost to all Musick now ; since every thing
> Puts on the semblance here of sorrowing.
> Sick is the Land to'th' heart ; and doth endure
> More dangerous faintings by her desp'rate cure.
> But if that golden Age wo'd come again,
> And *Charles* here Rule, as he before did Raign ;
> If smooth and unperplext the Seasons were,
> As when the *Sweet Maria* livèd here :
> I sho'd delight to have my Curles halfe drown'd
> In *Tyrian Dewes*, and Head with Roses crown'd.
> And once more yet (ere I am laid out dead)
> Knock at a Starre with my exalted Head."
>
> (Vol. II. pp. 187-8.)

As shewn by the absence of the Queen, these lines must
have been written after July, 1644.   The facts give a
keener edge to the couplet entitled " Love' :—

> " This Axiom I have often heard,
> *Kings ought to be more lov'd then fear'd."*
>
> (Vol. II. p. 220.)

and again :—

True safety.

" 'Tis not the Walls, or purple that defends
 A Prince from Foes; but 'tis his Fort of Friends."

(Vol. II. p. 237.)

and once more :—

Clemency in Kings.

" Kings must not only cherish up the good,
 But must be niggards of the meanest bloud."

(Vol. II. p. 266.)

and yet again, very articulately :—

Moderation.

" In things a moderation keepe,
 Kings ought to sheare, not skin their sheepe."

(Vol. II. p. 267.)

Further :—

Bad Princes pill their People.

" Like those infernall Deities which eate
 The best of all the sacrificèd meate;
 And leave their servants, but the smoak & sweat :
 So many *Kings*, and *Primates* too there are,
 Who claim the Fat, and Fleshie for their share,
 And leave their subjects but the starvèd ware."

(Vol. II. p. 284.)

' Primates ' is peculiarly significant—Laud being intended, doubtless.   Again :—

Kings and Tyrants.

" 'Twixt Kings & Tyrants there's this difference known,
Kings seek their Subjects' good : Tyrants their owne."

(Vol. II. p. 296.)

Again, indignant over the shorn ears and slit nostrils of
Prynne, and Burton, and Bastwicke, and which we
have Dean Hook telling us to-day Laud did not
sanction—"except perhaps by his vote"!!!—is this :—

Cruelty.

" Tis but a dog-like madnesse in bad Kings,
For to delight in wounds and murderings.
As some plants prosper best by cuts and blowes ;
So Kings by killing doe encrease their foes."

(Vol. III. p. 18.)

Once more :—

Patience in Princes.

" Kings must not use the Axe for each offence :
Princes cure some faults by their patience."

(Vol. III. p. 46.)

Significant is this :—

Examples, or like Prince, like people.

" Examples lead us, and wee likely see,
Such as the Prince is, will his People be."

(Vol. II. p. 256.)

Further, boldly, and yet with a sad pensiveness :—

" We two (as Reliques left) will have
    One Rest, one Grave.
And, hugging close, we will not feare
    Lust entring here :
Where all Desires are dead, or cold
    As is the mould :
And all Affections are forgot,
    Or Trouble not.
Here, here the Slaves and Pris'ners be
    From Shackles free :
And Weeping Widowes long opprest
    Doe here find rest.
The wrongèd Client ends his Lawes
    Here, and his Cause.
Here those long suits of Chancery lie
    Quiet, or die :
And all Star-Chamber-Bils doe cease,
    Or hold their peace.
Here needs no Court for our Request,
    Where all are best ;
All wise ; all equall ; and all just
    Alike i'th' dust.
Nor need we here to feare the frowne
    Of Court, or Crown.
Where Fortune bears no sway o're things,
    There all are Kings."   (Vol. II. p. 147.)

Again :—

Gentlenesse.

" That Prince must govern with a gentle hand,
Who will have love comply with his command."

                    (Vol. III. p. 68.)

Finally, I know nothing more affecting than his address " To his angrie God," with himself wounded in and out, and his outlook ominous and spectral :—

> " Through all the night
> Thou dost me fright,
> And hold'st mine eyes from sleeping ;
> And day, by day,
> My Cup can say,
> My wine is mixt with weeping.
> Thou dost my bread
> With ashes knead,
> Each evening and each morrow :
> Mine eye and eare
> Do see, and heare
> The coming in of sorrow.
> Thy scourge of steele,
> (Ay me !) I feele,
> Upon me beating ever :
> While my sick heart
> With dismall smart
> Is disacquainted never.
> Long, long, I'm sure,
> This can't endure ;
> But in short time 'twill please Thee,
> My gentle God,
> To burn the rod,
> Or strike so as to ease me." (Vol. III. p. 141.)

I venture to assume that now it has been made good

that Herrick was no heathen Anacreon or Catullus 'singing' jocundly his own mirthfulness, and singing heedless of the mighty ongoings that contemporaneously through long years reverberated over the land. I therefore quote, if in sorrow and wonder, yet also thankfully—because it puts effectively a long-prevalent misunderstanding and misconception of our Poet— from MR. EDMUND W. GOSSE's paper in *Cornhill* (August, 1875). "This period was one of great lyrical ability; the drama was declining under Massinger [?] and Shirley, and all the young generation of poets, brought up at the feet of Jonson and Fletcher, were much more capable of writing songs than plays. Indeed no one can at this time determine what degree of technical perfection English literature might not have attained if the Royalist lyrists had been allowed to sun themselves unmolested about the fountains of Whitehall, and, untroubled by the grave question of national welfare, had been able to give their whole attention to the polishing of their verses. In fact, however, it will be noticed that only one of the whole school was undisturbed by the political crisis. The weaker ones, like Lovelace, were completely broken by it; the stronger, like Suckling, threw themselves into public affairs with a zeal and intensity that supplied

the place of the artificial excitement of poetry so completely as to put a stop to their writing altogether.
Herrick alone, with unfashionable serenity, continued
to pipe out his pastoral ditties, and crown his head
with daffodils, when England was torn to pieces with
the most momentous struggle for liberty that her annals
can present.   To the poetic student he is, therefore, of
special interest, as a genuine specimen of an artist,
pure and simple.   Herrick brought out the *Hesperides*
a few weeks before the King was beheaded, and people
were invited to listen to little madrigals upon Julia's
stomacher at the singularly inopportune moment when
the eyes of the whole nation were bent on the unprece-
dented phenomenon of the proclamation of an English
republic.   To find a parallel to such unconsciousness
we must come down to our own time, and recollect
that Theophile Gautier took occasion of the siege of
Paris to revise and republish Emaux et Camèes " (pp.
176-7).   I feel sure that no one will be more eager
than Mr. Gosse to recall his hard and utterly erroneous
judgment of Herrick.   I must iterate and re-iterate,
that in no contemporary do you find such multiplied,
poignant, over-mastering, and nevertheless unclamorous
' consciousness ' of these ' troublous times.' The imagi-
nary coincidence of the publication of *Hesperides* with

the beheading of the King is singularly unfortunate.
The title-page of *Noble Numbers* is 1647, and that of
Hesperides 1648. The Book came out early in 1648.
The King was beheaded January 30th, 1649. Equally
mistaken is the notion that " the little madrigals upon
Julia's stomacher " and the like belong to the period of
the nation's throes for liberty. They were certainly of
his earliest, many probably of 1610-12, and assuredly
all, or nearly all, prior to 1629 ; or well-nigh, even in
the latter, a good quarter of a century before the Civil
War and its mournful strife and dolour. I would recall that even his ' flower ' verses were all early ; for
thus "To Flowers " does he ' sing ' :—

> " *In time of life*, I grac't ye with my Verse."
>
> (Vol. I. p. 57.)

and when he thinks of his imperishable Lyrics, he
exclaims :—

> " *Before I went*
> To banishment
> Into the loathèd West ;
> I co'd rehearse
> A Lyrick verse,
> And speak it with the best."
>
> (Vol. II. p. 67-8.)

that is before 1629.

Going on from his undoubted patriotism, I wish to put stress on this thing of the chronology of the Poems of Herrick, for another reason. There no doubt still remains in the *Epigrams*, inexplicable contradiction to *Noble Numbers*, and to much of deepest and greatest in *Hesperides*. There must have been a streak of animalism to the last in him as in Rabelais, and Swift, and Sterne; for I dare not conceal, if I might, his portraits of parishioners, and loathsome allusions to corns, and toes, and sweat, and stinks, and "raw eyes," and "gum of the eyes," and "running ears," such as a Satyr given pen and ink might have written. But it does lift off a weight of blame and incongruity to keep fast hold of the simple matter-of-fact that his love-lays, and endless flaming after 'Mistresses,' and riot of self-indulgence in sack, and 'winking wine,' and such hilariousness and abandon as are not for an instant to be associated with a clergyman, WERE ALL THE PRO-DUCT OF HIS 'LAY' YEARS, AND SOCIAL MEETINGS WITH JONSON AND HIS COMPEERS. I would re-affirm that " Robert Herrick, *Esq.*," on his title-page was intended, as it was fitted, to disassociate his Poems—as a whole —from his 'clerical' years. It was long before even 1629 he sang :—

" I feare no Earthly Powers,
But care for crowns of flowers ;
And love to have my Beard
With Wine and Oil besmear'd.
This day Ile drowne all sorrow ;
Who knowes to live to-morrow ? "

(Vol. I. p. 111.)

Here spoke the young man 'about town,' with his bones full of marrow, and his blood of fire, and his entire temperament pleasure-loving and sensuous. I quote again from Mr. Gosse that again the reader may be forewarned and forearmed against his further fundamental misconception of Herrick, through forgetfulness that the one set or class of Poems was sundered by a quarter-of-a-century at least from the other. Not in his " dreary Devonshire vicarage," but when his 'fine frenzy' was kindled by the guests of " The Dog," and " The Sun," and " The Triple Tun," was he so 'outspoken' in his " half-classical dreams about Favonius and Iris, and in flowery mazes of sweet thoughts about fair, half-imaginary women." With these preliminary words, here is our further quotation, after above lines, " I fear no earthly powers " :—
" This was his philosophy, and it is not to be distinguished from that of Anacreon or Horace. One knows not how the old pagan dared be so outspoken

in his dreary Devonshire vicarage, with no wild friends
to egg him on, or to applaud his fine frenzy. His
Epicureanism was plainly a matter of conviction, and
though he wrote *Noble Numbers*, preached sermons,
and went through all the perfunctory duties of his
office [Not a shadow of proof of the ' duties of his
office ' having been ' perfunctory'], it is not in these
that he lives and has his pleasure, but in half-classical
dreams about Favonius and Iris, and in flowery
mazes of sweet thoughts about fair, half-imaginary
women. It matters little to him what divinity he
worships, if he may work daffodils into the god's bright
hair. In one hand he brings a garland of yellow
flowers for the amorous head of Bacchus, with the
other he decks the osier-cradle of Jesus with roses and
Lent-lilies. He has no sense of irreverence in this
rococo devotion. It is the attribute, and not the
Deity he worships. There is an airy frivolity, an easy-
going callousness of soul that makes it impossible for
him to feel very deeply " (p. 180)· A thousand and a
thousand times ' No.' My gifted friend is oblivious of
dates, and imposed on by the intermixture of earlier
and later, light and serious, through the Publishers',
not the Author's, arrangement or disarrangement of
Hesperides. I am beyond measure astounded that a

critic of the *calibre* and the weight of Mr. Gosse could
deliberately write such a paradox of Herrick, as that
his was " an easy-going callousness of soul that makes
it impossible for him to feel very deeply " ! Contrariwise, ' callousness ' is the very antipodes of his nature
in its surcharge of the emotional, and ' depth,' the one
word to express his ' feeling,' in what of truest and
noblest he has given us. I must add that there was
no simulation, but intense fervour and sincerity in his
passion at the moment, and for the moment, if it is to
be conceded that it was also as changeable as Robert
Burns's in the eighteenth century. Hence, as criticism,
it is bewilderingly the reverse of the fact when Mr.
Gosse thus further writes :—" There is a total want of
passion in his language about women—the nearest
approach to it, perhaps, is in the wonderful song ' To
Anthea,' when the lark-like freshness of the ascending
melody closely simulates intense emotion—with all his
warmth of fancy and luxurious animalism, he thinks
more of the pretty eccentricities of dress than the
charms the garments curtain. He is enraptured with
the way in which the Countess of Carlisle wears a
riband of black silk twisted round her arm ; he palpitates
with pleasure when Mistress Katherine Bradshaw puts a
crown of laurel on his head, falling on one knee, we

may believe, and clasping his hands as he receives it. He sees his loves through the medium of shoe-strings and pomander bracelets, and is alive, as no poet has been before or since, to the picturesqueness of dress. Everybody knows his exquisite lines about the " tempestuous petticoat," and his poems are full of little touches no less delicate than this " (p. 180). Read *cum grano salis* there is truth in his eye to " the picturesqueness of dress " ; but a very little study of the poems referred to will satisfy that the Wearers, not the ' dress,' inspired him to sing, and that his fault was not lack, but exuberance and wildness of ' passion.'

Within these wider relations of Herrick to his times, and the insight which they give us into his bearing through periods of national peril and sorrow, there was his every-day life at Dean Prior. Looked at broadly, Mr. Gosse has well sketched it for us, as follows :— " In many sweet and sincere verses he gives us a charming picture of the quiet life he led in the Devonshire parsonage, that he affected to loathe so much. The village had its rural and semi-pagan customs, that pleased him thoroughly. He loved to see the brown lads and lovely girls, crowned with daffodils and daisies, dancing in the summer evenings in a comely country round ; he delighted in the may-pole, ribanded and

garlanded like a thyrsus, reminding his florid fancy of
Bacchus and· the garden-god.   There were morris-
dances at Dean Prior, wakes and quintels ; mummers,
too, at Christmas, and quaint revellings at Twelfth
Night, with wassail bowls and nut-brown mirth; and
we can imagine with what zeal the good old pagan
would encourage these rites against the objections of
any round-head Puritan who might come down with
his new-fangled Methodistical notions to trouble the
sylvan quiet of Dean Prior.   For Herrick the dignity
of episcopal authorship had no charm, and thunders
of Nonconformity no terror.   Busier minds were at
this moment occupied with *Holy Living and Holy
Dying*, and thrilled with the *Sermons of Calamy*.   It is
delightful to think of Herrick, blissfully unconscious of
the tumult of tongues and all the windy war, more
occupied with morris-dances and barley-breaks than with
prayer-book or Psalter.   The Revolution must indeed
have come upon him unaware " (p. 181).   Bating the
reference to the illustrious and venerable Calamy,
whose matterful· sermons had Mr. Gosse read, he
would have spared his (I fear intended) sneer, and the
already pointed out mistake that in his seclusion the
Vicar was ' unaware ' of the march of events to ' The
Revolution,'—this vivifies to us the long-past ' resi-

dence.' I feel disposed to acquiesce in the phrase of
the " Devonshire parsonage, that he *affected* to loath."
I suspect his objurgations and ' parish ' *Epigrams*,
were written during Winter, when the air was chill, and
the roads miry, and society gone to town.   One
cannot credit that Poems so informed with the breath
of the country, and so pulsating with love for everything rural and primitive, were not inspired by true
enjoyment.   It could only have been in a fit of bile,
or when the old rhyme of ' rainy Devonshire ' was
being monotonously accomplished, that he thus wrote :

Upon himself.

" Come, leave this loathèd Country-life, and then
   Grow up to be a Roman *Citizen.*
   Those mites of Time, which yet remain unspent,
   Waste thou in that most Civill Government.
   Get their comportment, and the gliding Tongue
   Of those mild Men, thou art to live among :
   Then being seated in that smoother *Sphere,*
   Decree thy everlasting *Topick* there.   =abode
   And to the Farm-house nere return at all,
   Though Granges do not love thee, Cities shall."
                  (Vol. II. p. 116-7.) [1]

---

[1] It may be noted here, *en passant*, that in Randolph's finest
poem, "An Ode to M. Anthony Stafford to hasten him into the

Let us read the ancient rhyme as the key to such
irate loathing :—

> " The West wind comes and brings us rain,
> The East wind blows it back again ;
> The South wind brings us rainy weather,
> The North wind cold and rain together.
> When the sun in red doth set,
> The next day surely will be wet.
> But if the sun should set in gray
> The next will be a rainy day !
> When buds the ash before the oak,
> Then, that year, there'll be a soak,
> But should the oak precede the ash,
> Then expect a rainy splash."

Country " you have the obverse of the medal. The opening will
illustrate :—

> " Come spurre away,
> I have no patience for a longer stay ;
> But must go down,
> And leave the changeable noise of this great Town.
> I will the Countreye see,
> Where all simplicity,
> Though hid in gray,
> Doth look more gay
> Than fopery in plush and scarlet clad.
> Farewell you Citty-wits that are
> Almost at Civill-warre :
> 'Tis time that I grow wise when all the world grows mad."

(Poems 1652, pp. 61-64.)

If the ' Western Wind,' like North, and South, and East, brought rain, and rain, and rain, it got other messages from the Poet too, as thus :—

> " Sweet western wind, whose luck it is,
>   (Made rivall with the aire,)
> To give Perenna's lip a kisse,
>   And fan her wanton haire.
> Bring me but one, I'le promise thee,
>   Instead of common showers,
> Thy wings shall be embalm'd by me,
>   And all beset with flowers."
>
> (Vol. I. p. 179.)

Nay, more, his " Noble Numbers " at least were the product of "dull Devonshire"; and so he gratefully sums up his " Discontents in Devon " :

> " More discontents I never had,
>   Since I was born, then here ;
> Where I have bee'n, and still am sad,
>   In this dull *Devon-shire.*
> Yet, justly too, I must confesse,
>   I ne'r invented such
> Ennobled numbers for the Presse,
>   Then where I loath'd so much."
>
> (Vol. I. p. 32.)

Then there is the title of his Book, *Hesperides,* which, if with a sly reminder of ' dragons,' also tells of

---

"Golden Apples" from the West. There are home-
Poems, that transparently assure us of real contentment
and happiness. It will do us all good to read "His
Grange, or private wealth," thus :—

>   " Though Clock,
> To tell how night drawes hence, I've none,
>   A Cock,
> I have, to sing how day drawes on.
>   I have
> A maid (my *Prew*) by good luck sent,
>   To save
> That little, Fates me gave or lent.
>   A Hen
> I keep, which creeking day by day,
>   Tells when
> She goes her long white egg to lay.
>   A Goose
> I have, which, with a jealous eare,
>   Lets loose
> Her tongue, to tell what danger's neare.
>   A Lamb
> I keep (tame) with my morsells fed,
>   Whose Dam
> An Orphan left him (lately dead).
>   A Cat
> I keep, that playes about my House,
>   Grown fat,
> With eating many a miching Mouse.
>   To these

A *Trasy* I do keep, whereby
      I please
The more my rurall privacie :
      Which are
But toyes, to give my heart some ease :
      Where care
None is, slight things do lightly please."
               (Vol. II. pp. 240-1.)

Other Poems—homelier and in a lower key—give equal testimony; and his actual return in 1662 is still more consolatory. It was inevitable, that, buried in ' the country '—he went to Dean Prior in October—he would yearn after old days and the old associates in London ; but from 1646 to 1662 would suffice for town, especially with the grand men of his youth all gone. And so he would ' travel West,' not grudgingly or sadly, but thankfully. His *Epigrams* on obnoxious parishioners would be long forgotten ; but there is proof that his *Noble Numbers* and his rural pieces were ' learned by heart ' *(Scotice)*, and long lingered in aged memories. Then Devonshire had still its old-mannered usages and ' characters,' its feminine loveliness, its ' tors,' and vales, and shadowy lanes ; its primroses and violets, wild roses, wild strawberries and honeysuckle, cowslips and daffodils; and the lark, and nightingale, and robin, and thrush. April and May, and June, and

July, would bring the old games, and the old mirth in the old gatherings. Even the slighted months then as now would yield him their own profuse beauty of ivy, and fern, and hedgerow. I like to picture the mellowed septuagenarian giving a kiss, glowing as thirty years before, to the 'maiden' whom he had baptized, and whose parents he had married. His hair might be white, but his heart was as young as ever. Broad of jest, perchance, and laughter-loving still, —loud, not low,—abhorrent of pretence, keen-eyed to sanctimoniousness taking the guise of saintliness, but soft-hearted and generous to the last; not " an old Pagan," but a hale, old-fashioned Churchman, who loved the ancient forms and ancient prayers, and ancient usages altogether, and who, not brazenly and merely orthodoxally, had with stooped head said in 1648 :—

——————"I sing, and ever shall
Of *Heaven,* and hope to have it after all."*
(Vol. I. p. 8.)

His relation to his Contemporaries I have already indicated in I. Biographical. Too early for knowing Shakespeare—away down in Stratford, not in London, unless on a chance-visit—we have found him

couched at the feet of 'Rare Ben,' and a welcome guest
among the immortals.   It is pleasant to read his generous praise of his younger brethren—as DENHAM and
CHARLES COTTON.   They in turn, doubtless, looked
up to him.   Two of his poems got among the posthu-
mously-published Poems of Thomas Carew, viz, " The
Enquiry " (Vol. II., p. 3), and " The Primrose "
(Vol. II., p. 177).   Both appeared in " Wit's Recreations" (1640), and both were reclaimed from thence for
Hesperides.   It is most likely in tacit reference to these
and possibly others, that he affirmed his express pro-
prietorship of all, as thus :—

> *" Upon his Verses.*
> What off-spring other men have got,
> The how, where, when, I question not.
> These are the Children I have left ;
> Adopted some ; none got by theft.
> But all are toucht (like lawfull plate)
> And no Verse illegitimate."   (Vol. II. p. 223.)

It is more than satisfying that the great and good
John Selden, though no Royalist, won his reverence
and affection.   It is characteristic of the spacious-
hearted man that he had words of praise and recognition for merit wherever met.   His judgments
are invariably sound.   It surprised me, I own, to come

on his estimate of Mildmay, Earl of Westmoreland, as
a Poet ; but, guided by his estimate, to his privately-
printed " *Otia Sacra* ", I was more than rewarded.
Until the whole is given (in my " Occasional Issues ")
let this little poem gain for itself a reading, as warranting
Herrick's counsel to ' print ' :—

Quid amabilius.

If I must needs Discover
I am in Love : be Christ again my Lover,
And let His Passion bring
My actions to their touch and censuring :
Who in this world was born,
Liv'd in it, and was put to death with scorn,
That I to Sin might die,
Being born again to live eternally :
Thus I'l no longer make
Addresses to my Glass for this curles sake,
Or that quaint garb, whereby
I may enchanted be with flattery :
Nor on luxurious vow,
Becircling Rosebuds seek to gird my brow ;
But with a melting thought
Bring home that Ransom whereat twas bought,
In Contemplation
Of that same Platted Crown He once had on.
And when my Glove or Shoo
Want Ribbond, call for th' Nails that pierced Him too :
Else farther to be drest,
Borrow the Tincture of His naked brest :

Nor wash, but in Soul Pride,
'Then use no other Bason but His Side :
So, up and ready, think
How He, for Me, low in the grave did sink,
That I again might rise
With Him, who was both Priest and Sacrifice,
To make atonement in
The Difference 'twixt his Father's wrath, Mans' sin ;
Whereto it must remain,
That I through Faith requite this love again.

(Otia Sacra, p. 70.)

IV. *The specialities of his Poetry.*—I do not say that
' specialities ' is the best possible word to express my
purpose in the present observations ; but I wanted
to mark out something more definite than ' characteristics '—all the more that I have already stated and
illustrated his ' characteristics ' as Man and Poet in
working out a higher object.   These five things include
what I wish to note for the Reader :—

1. *His imaginative realism.*
2. *His realistic imaginativeness.*
3. *His exquisiteness and brightness of fancies.*
4. *His allusive reading*
5. *His sacred verse.*

1. *His imaginative realism.* I am thinking now of the
fidelity with which he puts before you what he elects to

' sing ' of.   He can be as coarsely and offensively realistic as any be-praised Dutch ' interior ' painter ; and he is by no means fastidious in his choice of sight or theme.   But *at his best* his realism is touched like the opal-edge of clouds just after sunset, with imagination.   Look at his Primroses.   They are not mere ' yellow primroses,' not even Wordsworth's interpenetrated with matter of direct ethical and spiritual teaching, but himself ageing, what a light of glory lies on them as ' fill'd with dew' they interpret the changefulness of human experiences.   Let us read :—

" *To Primroses fill'd with morning-dew.*

1. Why doe ye weep, sweet Babes ? can Tears
        Speak griefe in you,
        Who were but borne
    Just as the modest Morne
    Teem'd her refreshing dew ?
Alas, you have not known that shower,
        That marres a flower ;
        Nor felt th'unkind
    Breath of a blasting wind ;
    Nor are ye worne with years ;
        Or warpt, as we,
    Who think it strange to see,
Such pretty flowers, (like to Orphans young,)
To speak by Teares, before ye have a Tongue.

2. Speak, whimp'ring Younglings, and make known
 .   The reason, why
       Ye droop, and weep ;
  Is it for want of sleep ?
  Or Childish Lullabie ?
  Or that ye have not seen as yet
       The *Violet ?*
       Or brought a kisse
  From that Sweet-heart, to this ?
  No, no, this sorrow shown
       By your teares shed,
       Wo'd have this Lecture read,
  That things of greatest, so of meanest worth, `
  Conceiv'd with grief are, and with teares brought forth."
                          (Vol. I. pp. 181-2.)

Of the same type, but though worn through quotation, not nearly so fine as the ' Primroses ' nor so original, is his " Gather ye Rose-buds while ye may."[1] This imaginativeness is absent from none of those Poems that give Herrick his peculiar place among the Poets of England ; and I call attention to it, because it is so common to take him at his lowly self-estimate, and look no deeper, e. g. thus, Mr. Gosse writes of *Hesperides,* as

[1] Mr. Robert Roberts, of Boston, has recently issued a delightful booklet yclept " Poesies of Roses " (8vo. pp. 22) wherein he has brought together several interesting variants on "Gather ye Roses." In Forbes' Cantus a poor answer to Herrick is found.

o

" songs, children of the West, brought forth in the soft, sweet air of Devonshire."   " The Poet," says he, " strikes a key-note with wonderful sureness in the opening couplets of the opening poem :—

> ' I sing of brookes, of blossoms, birds and bowers,
> Of April, May, of June, and July flowers.
> I sing of maypoles, hock-carts, wassails, wakes,
> Of bridegrooms, brides, and of their bridal cakes.'

It would not have been easy to describe more correctly what he does sing of. The book is full of all those pleasant things of spring and summer, full of young love, happy nature, and the joy of mere existence. As far as flowers are concerned, the atmosphere is full of them. One is pelted with roses and daffodils from every page, and no one dares enter the sacred precincts without a crown of blossoms on his hair. Herrick's sun might be that stray Venus of Botticelli's, which rises, rosy and dewy, from a sparkling sea, blown at by the little laughing winds, and showered upon with violets and lilies of no earthly growth. He tells us that for years and years his muse was content to stay at home, or, straying from village to village, to pipe to handsome young shepherds and girls of flower-sweet breath, but that at last she became ambitious to try her skill at

Court, and so came into print in London. In other words, these little poems circulated widely in manuscript long before they were published " (p. 182). All true so far as it goes ; but beyond the ' simple sights ' and transfiguring the humblest 'flowers,' there is a subtle light, sometimes pure as the white light, sometimes purpled; and pensive thoughtfulness and tender meditativeness born of imagination—not an imagination grand as Dante's or Milton's, but of kin with Spenser in his ' gentle ' mood, and infinitely above your modern wordpainter whose realism is a bootless effort to transform the pen into a brush. It matters not what Herrick describes—he gives you its very " form and pressure," and over it, as the seven-fold rainbow breaking into ineffable fragments under its load of rain, or before the blast of the wind ; and better than saint's nimbus, you have the ' final touch ' in epithet or in break of music, that differentiates the Poet from the Versifier. Even when it is the artificial—not nature—he sings of, there is this presence of the Poet's imaginativeness. Thus in his " Bracelet of Pearls : to Silvia," you have not only nicest and daintiest, not coarse workmanship, but the suggestion of a whole sphere of living romance, and that by one name linking on to the great Past. Again let us read :

" I Brake thy Bracelet 'gainst my will ;
   And, wretched, I did see
Thee discomposèd then, and still
   Art discontent with me.

One jemme was lost ; and I will get
 ⸜ A richer pearle for thee,
Then ever, dearest *Silvia*, yet
   Was drunk to *Antonie*.

Or, for revenge, I'le tell thee what
   Thou for the breach shalt do ;
First, crack the strings, and after that,
   Cleave thou my heart in two."

                              (Vol. II. pp. 230-1.)

I do not deem it expedient to enlarge on this ; but
if the Reader will turn to " A Country Life : to his
Brother, M. Tho: Herrick " (Vol. I. pp. 57-64), and to
" The Hock-Cart or Harvest-home, to the Earl of
Westmoreland " (Vol. I. pp. 175-8), the former being
on Horatian wings—one of Herrick's best-sustained
and noblest flights, and the latter deliciously fresh and
vivid, and with a matchless flavour of dear old England
—he will discover abundant evidence of that imaginativeness that suffuses his realism which I am now
insisting upon.   Then in his " Panegerick to Sir Lewis
Pemberton " (Vol. II. p. 71) he will find the same
speciality, and humour and vigour besides.

Finally here, " No one has ever known better than
Herrick how to seize, without effort, and yet to absolute
perfection, the pretty points of modern pastoral life.
Of all these poems of his, none surpasses ' Corinna's
going a-Maying,' which has something of Wordsworth's
faultless instinct and delicate perception.[1] The picture
given here of the slim boys and the girls in green
gowns going out singing into the corridors of blossoming whitethorn, when the morning sky is radiant in all
its 'fresh-quilted colours,' is ravishing, and can only
be compared for its peculiar charm with that other
where the maidens are seen at sunset, with silvery
naked feet and dishevelled hair crowned with honeysuckle, bearing cowslips home in wicker baskets.
Whoever will cast his eye over the pages of *Hesperides*
will meet with myriads of original and charming
passages of this kind :

> ' Like to a solemn sober stream
> Bankt all with lilies, and the cream
> Of sweetest cowslips filling them.'

the ' cream of cowslips ' being the rich yellow antlers
of water-lilies.   Or thus, comparing a bride's breath to
the faint, sweet odour of the earth :—

---

[1] I venture to add that Herrick's "Christian Militant" (Vol. II.
p. 40) may take its place beside Wordsworth's "Happy Warrior."

' A savour like unto a blessed field
When the bedabbled morn
Washes the golden ears of corn.'

[I intercalate that in l. 1 the allusion is Biblical, viz.
to Genesis xxvii. 27.]   Or thus, a sketched interior :—

' Yet can thy humble roof maintain a choir
Of singing crickets by the fire,
And the brisk mouse may feed herself with crumbs,
Till that the green-eyed kitling comes.'

"Nor did the homeliest details of the household
escape him.   At Dean Prior his clerical establishment
consisted of Prudence Baldwin, his ancient maid; of
a cock and hen, a goose, a tame lamb, a cat, a spaniel,
and a pet pig, learned enough to drink out of a
tankard; and not only did the genial Vicar divide his
loving attention between the various members of this
happy family, but he was wont, a little wantonly one
fears, to gad about to wakes and wassailings, and to
increase his popular reputation by showing off his
marvellous learning in old rites and ceremonies.   These
he has described with loving minuteness, and not these
only, but even the little acts of cookery do not escape
him.   Of all his household poems not one is more
characteristic and complete than the ' Bride-cake,'

which we remember naving had recited to us years ago
with immense gusto, at the making of a great pound
cake, by a friend now widely enough known as a
charming follower of Herrick's poetic craft :—

' *The Bride-cake.*

This day, my Julia, thou must make
For Mistress Bride, the wedding cake ;
Knead but the dough, and it will be
To paste of almonds turned by thee,
Or kiss it, but once or twice,
And for the bride-cake there'll be spice.' "
(Mr. Gosse, as before, pp. 184-5.)

What a vision of Julia in her radiant beauty all rosy
under such a compliment has the most prosaic reader
in "The Bride-cake." And so it is throughout. Not
one of even the ' household poems ' is without its touch
of imaginative realism.

2. *His realistic imaginativeness.*   I refer here mainly
to his Poems of 'Fairy,' wherein you have not such
thin bodiless Impersonations as in COLLINS' Ode to
the Passions, and even in Gray (if I may dare the
heresy), but substantive and living.   On this Mr. Gosse
(as before) writes finely, though in one place mistakenly, as we shall see :—" Before we turn to more
general matters, there is one section of the *Hesperides*

that demands a moment's attention, that namely, devoted to the description of Fairyland and its inhabi-
tants. ·We have seen that it was, probably, the performance of Ben Jonson's pretty masque of 'Oberon'
that set Herrick dreaming about that misty land where
elves sit eating butterflies' horns round little mushroom
tables, or quaff draughts

> 'Of pure seed-pearl of morning dew,
> Brought and besweetened in a blue,
> And pregnant Violet.'

And with him the poetic literature of Fairyland ended.
He was its last laureate, for the Puritans thought its
rites, though so shadowy, superstitious, and frowned
upon their celebration, while the whole temper of the
Restoration, gross and dandified at the same time, was
foreign to such pure play of the imagination. But
some of the greatest names of the great period had
entered its sacred bounds and sung its praises.
Shakespeare had done it eternal honour in *Midsummer Night's Dream*, and Drayton had written
an elaborate epic (?) *The Court of Faerie*. Jonson's
friend, Bishop Corbet, had composed fairy ballads that
had much of Herrick's lightness about them. It was
these literary traditions that Herrick carried with him

into the West ; it does not seem that he collected any
fresh information about the mushroom world in Devonshire ; we read nothing of river-wraiths or pixies in his
poems. He adds, however, a great deal of ingenious
fancy to the stores he received from his elders, and his
fairy-poems, all written in octo-syllabic verse, as though
forming parts of one projected work, may be read with
great interest as a kind of final compendium of all
that the poets of the 17th century imagined about
fairies " (pp. 186).

Mr. Gosse is again strangely wrong as to the source
of Herrick's ' Fairy ' poems. Misled by the title—and
the mere title or one word ' Oberon ' never could suggest such poems—he assigns to Jonson his inspiration.
But Jonson's ' Oberon ' has nothing whatever on Fairies
or Fairy-land ; nor indeed were such dainty things at all
in his way. One is indeed puzzled at the absence of
the ' Fairies ' in 'Oberon' until it is found that Jonson's
' Oberon ' is a prince of sixteen. Herrick's splendid
praise of ' Rare Ben ' and occasional touches, as in his
" Delight in Disorder " (Vol. I. 46) assure us that he
was his willing subject ; but in not one bit could he
have been indebted to him for his ' Fairy ' creations.
For them it is a pleasure to think of Drayton's *Nymph-
idia* and Shakespeare's *Midsummer's Night Dream* and

Romeo and Juliet. Thither and not at all in Jonson's spectacular ' Oberon' must we look for Herrick's pre-parative reading and impress.[1]

Let the reader turn and return on these 'Fairy' poems. Let him note their quaintness, their apt names, their sly humour, their *fantastique* of exploit, their oddity of invention, their drollery of feasting, their jets of tricksy wit, their quizzical hitting of modern foibles through superstitious rites (the Poet's pen transfixing the vinegar-faced fool as with a needle), their ripple of soft laughter, their swift changefulness (as of peacock's crest, or humming-bird's breast, or dove's neck), their ingenuous credulities. I know not that anywhere we can turn to Poems of Imagination so 'compact,' and at the same time so airy, so real-seeming and yet of subtlest imagination. It is well to read the whole group successively but together, viz. " The Fairie Temple; or Oberon's Chappell " (Vol. I. pp. 156-163), and " Oberon's Feast " (Vol. II. pp. 24-27), and " Oberon's Palace" (Vol. II. pp. 104-9), and " The Beggar" (Vol. II. pp. 202-3), and " The Hagg " (Vol. II. pp. 205-6).[2]

---

[1] See before on Herrick's reading of Marlowe and Greene and Shirley.

[2] Even in Thomas Randolph's *Amyntas* (1638) there are oddi-

His " Epithalamiums " and other marriage and birth-
day poems have the same speciality of realistic imaginativeness.   You have the actual ' fair ladies ' and
' brave men,' but there is a splendour of imagination
prodigally lavished on the use and wont of 'good wishes.'
Of the Epithalamiums Mr. Gosse thus speaks :—" The
epithalamium is a form of verse which had a very bright
period of existence in England, and which has long
been completely extinct.   [Revived gorgeously by
Dante G. Rossetti, as in a quieter way by Coventry
Patmore earlier.]   Its theme and manner gave too
much opportunity to lavish adulation on the one hand,
and unseemly inuendo on the other, to suit the preciser
manners of our more reticent age, but it flourished for
the brief period contained between 1600 and 1650, and
produced some exquisite masterpieces.   The ' Epithalamium' and 'Prothalamion' of Spenser struck the key-
note of a fashion that Drayton, Ben Jonson, [Donne] and

ties of ' Fairy ' possessions that might have been admitted into
" Oberon's Palace," *e.g.* :—
    " *Do.* A curious Parke.
        Pal'd round about with Pick-teeth.
    Io. Besides a house made all of mother of Pearle ;
        An Ivory Tenniscourt.
    Dor. A nut-meg Parlour.
    Io. A Saphyre dary-roome.
    Dor. A Ginger Hall." (1640 ed. p. 34.)

others adorned, and of which Herrick was the last, and far from the least ardent votary. His confidential muse was delighted at being asked in to arrange the ceremonies of a nuptial feast, and described the bride and her surroundings with a world of pretty extravagance. Every admirer of Herrick should read the ' Nuptial Ode on Sir Clipseby Crew and his Lady.' It is admirably fanciful, and put together with consummate skill. It opens with a choral out-burst of greeting to the bride :—

> ' What's that we see from far ? the spring of day
> Bloom'd from the east, or fair enjewelled May
> Blown out of April ? or some new
> Star filled with glory to our view
> Reaching at heaven,
> To add a nobler planet to the seven ? '

Less and less dazzled, he declares her to be some goddess floating out of Elysium in a cloud of tiffany. He leaves the church treading upon scarlet and amber, and spicing the chafed air with fumes of Paradise. Then they watch her coming towards them down the shining street, whose very pavement breathes out spikenard. But who is this that meets her ? Hymen with his fair white feet, and head with marjoram crowned, who lifts his torch, and, behold ! by his side the bridegroom stands, flushed and ardent. Then the maids shower them with shamrock and roses, and so the dreamy verses totter under their load of perfumed words, till they close with a benediction over the new married couple, and a peal of maiden laughter over love and its flower-like mysteries " (p. 186). Fit companion for the Clipseby Crew " Nuptial Ode " is the " Epithalamie to Sir Thomas Southwell and his Ladie" (Vol. I. pp. 90-99) which holds its own even beside Donne's.

Another group of Poems that illustrate his realistic imaginativeness is what may be called his verse-gifts— of which he must have been lavish—to friends and neighbours. These were evidently flung off at the moment; but the most careless (as a rule) reveal the inspired Singer. His celebrations of his own numerous family of brothers and sisters—his guardian-uncle, Sir William Herrick, notably absent, as the old ' curmudgeon ' (*Scotice*) deserved—and his mother's circle of relatives and kinsmen, are charming. Among the former, as though to favour the Poet, was his sweet-named sister ' Mercy.' Among the latter, men of mark in the ' city ' and State, and otherwise—as the Soames and Stones and the like. A careful study of these will reward, for they will be found not exaggerate, but true, imaginative, but realistic. I should scarcely know where to hold my hand if I began quotation from these Poems. I therefore will not begin; but I cannot withhold his own favourite, his " Lilly in a Christal," which in various ways still further exemplifies the present speciality. In this instance the Poet was not as so often wrong in his high and preferring estimate.

" *The Lilly in a Christal.*

You have beheld a smiling *Rose*
   When Virgins hands have drawn
   O'r it a Cobweb-Lawne :
And here, you see, this Lilly shows,
   Tomb'd in a *Christal* stone,
More faire in this transparent case,
   Then when it grew alone ;   [*than*
   And had but single grace.

You see how *Creame* but naked is ;
   Nor daunces in the eye
Without a Strawberrie :
   Or some fine tincture, like to this,
   Which draws the sight thereto,
More by that wantoning with it ;
   Then when the paler hieu   [*than*
   No mixture did admit.

You see how *Amber* through the streams
      More gently stroaks the sight,
    ˙ With some conceal'd delight;
Then when he darts his radiant beams
      Into the boundlesse aire :
Where either too much light, his worth
      Doth all at once impaire,
      Or set it little forth.

Put Purple grapes, or Cherries in-
      To Glasse, and they will send
      More beauty to commend
Them, from that cleane and subtile skin,
      Then if they naked stood,   [*than*
And had no other pride at all,
      But their own flesh and blood,
      And tinctures naturall.

Thus Lillie, Rose, Grape, Cherry, Creame,
      And Straw-berry do stir
      More love, when they transfer
A weak, a soft, a broken beame ;
      Then if they sho'd discover   [*than*
At full their proper excellence ;
      Without some Scean cast over,
To juggle with the sense.

Thus let this *Christal'd Lillie* be
      A Rule, how far to teach,
      Your nakednesse must reach :
And that, no further, then we see

> Those glaring colours laid
> By Arts wise hand, but to this end
> They sho'd obey a shade;
> Lest they too far extend.
>
> So though y'are white as Swan, or Snow,
>   And have the power to move
>   A world of men to love :
> Yet, when your Lawns & Silks shal flow;
>   And that white cloud divide
> Into a doubtful Twi-light; then,
>   Then will your hidden Pride
>   Raise greater fires in men."
>   (Vol. I. p. 129-31.)

I must content myself with two other examples of his
realistic imaginativeness as distinguished from his imaginative realism—a distinction that it may be assumed
will be admitted after our remarks and illustrations—
namely, his " Amber Bead " and " Upon her Feet."
Take them both :—

> " *The Amber Bead.*
>
> I saw a Flie, within a Beade
> Of Amber cleanly burièd :
> The Urne was little, but the room
> More rich then *Cleopatra's* Tombe."   [*than*
>   (Vol. II. p. 280.)

One does not think so much, on reading this little snatch, of . Martial and his epigram (Book IV. 32) which is elsewhere recalled by Herrick himself ("Upon a Flie": Vol. II. p. 140) as of the lines attributed to no less than Milton in our day by Professor Morley. For my part I cannot accept the illustrious authorship ; but it is interesting to find an echo of our Poet in its close, as thus :—

> " For so this little wanton elf
> Most gloriously enshrined itself :—
> A tomb whose beauty might compare
> With Cleopatra's sepulchre."

Perhaps Martial was the source common to each, viz. his 'Viper in Amber' (B. IV. 56); and the point is, that the renowned Queen Cleopatra died by a ' viper ' (Shakespeare's 'worm') and had a tomb (with Anthony) finished by Augustus, that long remained a world's wonder.[1] Now for

---

[1] In respect to the viper, Paley and Stone observe : " This must be taken as a poetic hyperbole for some small creeping thing. The point of the epigram, indeed, turns on its being a real snake ; but this is hardly possible. The ancients were aware of the true nature of amber. See Pliny." These excellent scholars ·are mistaken. A piece of amber has been found in Jutland that weighed twenty-seven pounds ; and in the Royal Mineral Cabinet at Berlin

Upon her feet.

" Her pretty feet
  Like snailes did creep
A little out, and then,
  As if they started at Bo-Beep,
    Did soon draw in agen.''   (Vol. II. p. 153.)

I must pronounce this as truer and finelier wrought than
Sir John Suckling's every-where-known comparison to
mice, thus :—

" Her feet beneath her petticoat,
  Like little mice, stole in and out,
    As if they feared the light :
But oh ! she dances such a way
No sun upon an Easter day
    Is half so fine a sight.''

It was daring in Herrick to write down what he himself
had really seen, the quick movement—as of insects
antennæ—of the snail's ' horns ' if in the slightest
touched, whether by a hindering ' bent ' or falling dew-

---

is another piece weighing 13¼ pounds. It is 13¾ inches long, 8¼
inches broad, 5 inches and five-eighths high on the one side, and
3½ inches on the other. Similar large pieces of gum-copal, with
insects, &c., imbedded, are found in Africa. See Livingstone's
'' Last Journals,'' I. pp. 29, 182.

drop, or sound of human voice—for self-evidently that was what the Poet had in recollection. I feel perfectly satisfied that it originated with our Poet's actual observation, and independent of Suckling's ballad, albeit none would more relish the famous ballad when it reached him, along with his own poems, in "Wit's Recreations" of 1640. The fact of prior publication (not necessarily prior composition) of the "Wedding," and nevertheless "Upon her feet" being given in *Hesperides*, assures us that Herrick knew his own originality. You have only to get over the association with the word and thing 'snail,' and stoop to see the strange beauty of the little creature, ay, even in its track as it innocently 'creeps' along glisteringly, and, above all, its human-eye-like sensitiveness to touch or sound, to clap hands over Herrick's unique comparison of the 'pretty feet' of "Mistresse Susanna Southwell."

3. *His exquisiteness and brightness of fancy.* These are such specialities of Herrick's Poems that no one can miss them—unless, like a blind man trampling over flowers, he is eyeless and earless, and heartless as well. His many Epitaphs and Memorial-verses first of all, strike us for their delicacy and tenderness, in short, for their unsurpassed exquisiteness. As less known than others, I ask the Reader to dwell on this :—

"*An Epitaph upon a Virgin.*

Here a solemne Fast we keepe,
While all beauty lyes asleep
Husht be all things; no noyse here,
But the toning of a teare :
Or a sigh of such as bring
Cowslips for her covering." (Vol. II. p. 113.)

Then how dainty and subtle and original-fancied is his
" Impossibilities to his Friend," as thus :—

" My faithful friend, if you can see
   The Fruit to grow up, or the Tree :
If you can see the colour come
Into the blushing Peare, or Plum :
If you can see the water grow
To cakes of Ice, or flakes of Snow :
If you can see, that drop of raine
Lost in the wild sea, once againe :
If you can see, how Dreams do creep
Into the Brain by easie sleep :
Then there is hope that you may see
Her love me once, who now hates me."
                                   (Vol. I. p. 137.)

The conclusion is somewhat *de trop*, but the imagery
for the 'impossibilities,' of the 'colour' coming into the
plum, of the 'ice,' and of 'dreams,' seems to me super-

latively fine.   Horace has nothing to equal, much less surpass, "His Poetrie his Pillar."   The light-hearted Latin poet knew little of the pathos of this unsurpass- able little Poem, if his shout of 'exegi' tell us he had the Poet's lofty self-estimate.   Let the Reader again 'dwell' on this, and mark the exquisiteness of the opening, and how the softness dilates into strength and gives us a glimpse of Egypt and its thousands- yeared 'pyramids.'

" His Poetrie his Pillar.

Onely a little more
   I have to write,
   Then Ile give o're,
And bid the world Good-night.

'Tis but a flying minute,
   That I must stay,
   Or linger in it ;
And then I must away.

O time that cut'st down all !
   And scarce leav'st here
   Memoriall
Of any men that were.

How many lye forgot
   In Vaults beneath ?
   And piece-meale rot
Without a fame in death ?

Behold this living stone,
 I reare for me,
 Ne'r to be thrown
Downe, envious Time by thee.

Pillars let some set up,
 (If so they please)
 Here is my hope,
And my *Pyramides.*" (Vol. I. p. 146.)

Of the same in *kind* and in elements as exquisitely done
as " His Poetrie His Pillar," and reminding us that he
should scarce have thanked his kinsman for the erection
of the recent great monument, but have preferred a yew
or beech to have flung their greenness and dropped
their cones and nuts in season over his grave, is his

   " *To Laurels.*

  A funerall stone,
  Or Verse I covet none,
 But onely crave
Of you, that I may have
A sacred Laurel springing from my grave :
  Which being seen,
 Blest with perpetuall greene,
  May grow to be
 Not so much call'd a tree,
As the eternall monument of me." (Vol. I. p. 50.)

It were easy to multiply examples and proofs of his exquisiteness of thinking and feeling and workmanship. I can only tarry to illustrate his brightness of fancy as in combination with his exquisiteness. Even when he is pensive and 'melancholy,' there is this colour and brightness. I invite the Student to read and re-read this :—

> " *To Blossoms.*
>
> Faire pledges of a fruitfull Tree,
> Why do yee fall so fast ?" &c.
>
> (Vol. II. p. 124.)

Homelier—as was fitting—but all radiant with the glow of gratitude that burned in his 'thankful heart,' is his "Thanksgiving to God, for his home," wherein too there are touches of exquisite perfectness, and the whole such a poem as inevitably makes us love even to-day the genial old Vicar in his lowly contentment and open-handed bounty. Here it is:—

> " Lord, Thou hast given me a cell
> Wherein to dwell," &c.
>
> (Vol. III. pp. 135-8.)

Next take his peerless "To Daffodils," than which surely there is no flower-poem at once so weighty and

so sweet, so lovely and also impressive, consummate in
its art and enduring in its charm :—

" *To Daffadills.*

1. Faire Daffadills, we weep to see
   You haste away so soone :
   As yet the early-rising Sun
   Has not attain'd his Noone.
   Stay, stay,
   Untill the hasting day
   Has run
   But to the Even-song ;
   And, having pray'd together, we
   Will go with you along.

2. We have short time to stay, as you,
   We have as short a Spring;
   As quick a growth to meet Decay,
   As you, or any thing.
   We die,
   As your hours doe, and drie
   Away,
   Like to the Summers raine ;
   Or as the pearles of Mornings dew
   Ne'r to be found againe."

(Vol. II. p. 35.)

Finally : There is his "To Anthea"—one of various
to this 'fair lady,' which, starting from the mere grass

as starts the lark, lifts us up like the lark into the
blinding summer sky, and fills even that vast cathedral
with melody :—

> " *To* Anthea, *who may command*
> *him any thing.*
>
> Bid me to live, and I will live
>   Thy Protestant to be :
> Or bid me love, and I will give
>   A loving heart to thee.
>
> A heart as soft, a heart as kind,
>   A heart as sound and free,
> As in the whole world thou canst find,
>   That heart Ile give to thee.
>
> Bid that heart stay, and it will stay,
>   To honour thy Decree :
> Or bid it languish quite away,
>   And't shall doe so for thee.
>
> Bid me to weep, and I will weep,
>   While I have eyes to see :
> And having none, yet I will keep
>   A heart to weep for thee.
>
> Bid me despaire, and Ile despaire,
>   Under that *Cypresse* tree :
> Or bid me die, and I will dare
>   E'en Death, to die for thee.

> Thou art my life, my love, my heart,
>   The very eyes of me :
> And hast command of every part,
>   To live and die for thee." (Vol. II. pp. 6-7.)

As distinguished from complete Poems, there are lavishly scattered over *Hesperides* lines and couplets and *bits* that equally show Herrick's exquisiteness and brightness.   Two recur on the instant.   The first is of Tears—" Teares are the noble language of the eye " (Vol. I. p. 100).   The other I will quote because a parallel in a Master of his art, our living Poet-Laureate,—who by the way, in our occasional foot-notes, is seen to have studied Herrick appreciatively— is a typical instance of the ancient Poet's still more ex-quisite instinct in his choice of words.   In his lines " To Dianeme " he thus sang :—

> " If thou compos'd of gentle mould
>   Art so unkind to me ;
> What dismall Stories will be told
>   Of those that cruell be ?" (Vol. II. p. 285.)

Compare Tennyson :—

> " Gently comes the world to those
>   That are cast in gentle mould."

Surely 'cast' here completely spoils the idea? And so everywhere, nearly, you come on unexpected felicities, as Mr. Gosse thus admirably and weightily, and with fine insight sums up:—" We have now rapidly concluded the two volumes on which Herrick claims his place among the best English lyrical poets. Had he written twenty instead of two, he could not have impressed his strong poetic individuality more powerfully on our literature than he has done in the *Hesperides.* It is a storehouse of lovely things, full of tiny beauties of varied kind and workmanship, like a box full of all sorts of jewels, ropes of seed pearl, opals set in old-fashioned shifting settings, antique gilt trifles sadly tarnished by time, here a ruby, here an amethyst, and there a shiny diamond, priceless and luminous, flashing light from all its facets, and dulling the faded jewellery with which it is so promiscuously huddled. What is so very precious about the book is the originality and versatility of the versification. There is nothing too fantastic for the author to attempt, at least; there is one poem written in rhyming triplets, each line having only two syllables [Vol. II. p. 127]. There are clear little trills of sudden song, like the lines to the " Lark"; there are chance melodies that seem like mere wanton-

ings of the air upon a wind-harp; there are such har-
monious endings, as this, ' To Music ':—

> ' Fall on me like a silent dew,
>   Or like those maiden showers
> Which, by the peep of day, do show
>   A baptism o'er the flowers.
>   Melt, melt my pains
>   With thy soft strains,
> That, having ease me given,
>   With full delight
>   I leave this light
>   And take my flight
>   For heaven.'

With such poems as these, and with the delicious songs
of so many of Herrick's predecessors and compeers
before them, it is inexplicable upon what possible
grounds the critics of the eighteenth century can have
founded their astonishing dogma, that the first master
of English versification was Edmund Waller, whose
poems, appearing some fifteen years after the *Hesperides*,
are chiefly remarkable for their stiff and pedantic movement, and the brazen clang, as of stage armour, of the
dreary heroic couplets in which they shut.   Where
Waller is not stilted, he owes his excellence to the
very source from which the earlier lyrists took theirs—a
study of nature and a free but not licentious use of pure

English.   But not one of his poems, except ' Go,
lovely Rose,' is worth the slightest of those delicate
warbles that Herrick piped out when the sun shone on
him, and the flowers were fresh " (p. 189).   *∠*

4. *His allusive reading.*   I prefer ' reading' to 'learning'; for there are proofs that ' learning' was not
Herrick's *forte.*   His career at the University was
probably too much interrupted by ' escapes' to town
and mingling with the gatherings of which Ben Jonson
was sovereign, to admit of steady and full acquirements
such as a College furnishes.   The most that can be
said is that he was fairly well-read in the Greek and
Roman classics, and some of the Fathers—nothing
more.   But his miscellaneous reading must have been
of the type of Robert Burton's or Thomas Fuller's.   In
his "To Live Merrily" (Vol. I. p. 138) we have a vivid
enumeration of the ancient Poets he loved ; and I give
it here in full that there may follow on it Mr. Gosse's
remarks on his obligation to the classics :—

> "*To live merrily, and to trust to
> Good Verses.*
>
> Now is the time for mirth,
>   Nor cheek, or tongue be dumbe :
> For with the flowrie earth,
>   The golden pomp is come.

The golden Pomp is come;
   For now each tree do's weare
(Made of her Pap and Gum)
   Rich beads of *Amber* here.

Now raignes the *Rose,* and now
   Th' *Arabian* Dew besmears
My uncontrollèd brow,
   And my retortèd haires.

Homer, this Health to thee,
   In Sack of such a kind,
That it wo'd make thee see,
   Though thou wert ne'r so blind.

Next, *Virgil,* Ile call forth,
   To pledge this second Health
In Wine, whose each cup's worth
   An Indian Common-wealth.

A Goblet next Ile drink
   To *Ovid;* and suppose,
Made he the pledge, he'd think
   The world had all *one Nose.*

Then this immensive cup
   Of *Aromatike* wine,
Catullus, I quaffe up
   To that Terce Muse of thine.

Wild I am now with heat;
  O *Bacchus !* coole thy Raies !
Or frantick I shall eate
  Thy *Thyrse*, and bite the *Bayes*.

Round, round, the roof do's run;
  And being ravisht thus,
Come, I will drink a Tun
  To my *Propertius*.

Now, to *Tibullus*, next,
  This flood I drink to thee :
But stay; I see a Text,
  That this presents to me.

Behold, *Tibullus* lies
  Here burnt, whose smal return
Of ashes, scarce suffice
  To fill a little Urne.

Trust to good Verses then;
  They onely will aspire,
When Pyramids, as men,
  Are lost, i'th'funerall fire.

And when all Bodies meet
  In *Lethe* to be drown'd;
Then onely Numbers sweet,
  With endless life are crown'd."

                    (Vol. I. pp. 138-41.)

With this in recollection, Mr. Gosse (as before) writes :—" It is an interesting speculation to consider from what antique sources Herrick, athirst for the pure springs of pagan beauty, drank the deep draughts of his inspiration. Ben Jonson it was, beyond doubt, who first introduced him to the classics, but his mode of accepting the ideas he found there, was wholly his own. In the first place, one must contradict a foolish statement that all the editors of Herrick have repeated, sheep-like from one another, namely, that Catullus was his great example and model. In the last edition of the *Hesperides* I find the same old blunder : ' There is no collection of poetry in our language which more nearly resembles the *Carmina* of Catullus.' In reality, it would be difficult to name a lyric poet with whom he has less in common than with the Veronese, whose eagle-flights into the very noonday-depths of passion, swifter than Shelley's, as flaming as Sappho's, have no sort of fellowship with the pipings of our gentle and luxurious babbler by the flowery brooks. In one of his poëms, 'To Live Merrily,' where he addresses the various classical poets, and where, by the way, he tries to work himself into a great exaltation about Catullus, he does not even mention the one that he really took most from of form and colour. No one carefully reading the *Hesperides* can fail to be struck with the extraordinary similarity they bear to the *Epigrams* of Martial, and the parallel will be found to run throughout the writings of the two poets, for good and for bad, the difference being that Herrick is as much a rural as Martial an urban poet. But in the incessant references to himself and his book, the fondness for gums and spices, the delight in the picturesqueness of private life, the art of making a complete and gem-like poem in the fewest possible lines, the curious mixture of sensitiveness and utter want of sensibility, the trick of writing confidential little poems to all sorts of friends, the tastelessness that mixes up obscene couplets with delicate odes 'De Hortis Martialis' or 'To Anthea'; in all those and many more qualities one can hardly tell where to look for a literary parallel more complete. As far as I know, Herrick mentions Martial but once, and then very slightly. He was fond of talking about the old poets in his verse, but never with any critical cleverness. The best thing he says about any of them is said of Ovid in a pretty couplet. In a dream he sees Ovid lying at the feet of Corinna, who presses

> With ivory wrists his laureate head, and steeps
> His eyes in dew of kisses while he sleeps.

q

How much further Herrick's learning proceeded it is difficult to tell. Doubtless he knew some Greek ; he mentions Homer and translates from Anacreon. The English poets of that age, learned as many of them were, do not seem to have gone much further than Rome for their inspiration. Chapman is, of course, a great exception. But none of them, as all the great French poets of the Renaissance, went directly to the Anthology. Perhaps Herrick had read the Planudian Anthology, Theocritus and Anacreon. The little piece called ' Leander's Obsequies ' seems as though it must be a translation of the epigram of Antipater of Thessalonica. Curious to reflect that at the very time that the *Hesperides* was printed, Salmasius, soon to be hunted to death by the implacable hatred of Milton, [?] was carrying about with him in his restless wanderings the MS. of his great discovery, the inestimable Anthology of Constantine Cephalas. One imagines with what sympathetic brotherliness the Vicar of Dean Prior would have gossipped and glowed over the new storehouse of Greek song. That the French poets of the century before were known to Herrick is to me extremely doubtful. One feels how much there was in such a book as *La Bergerie* of Remy Belleau, in which our

poet would have felt the most unfeigned delight, but I
find no distinct traces of their style in his; and unless
the Parisian editions of the classics influenced him, I
cannot think that he brought any honey, poisonous or
other, from France. His inspiration was Latin; that
of Ronsard and Jodelle essentially Greek. It was the
publication of the Anthology in 1531, and of Henry
Estienne's *Anacreon* in 1554, that really set the Pleiad
in movement, and founded *l'école gallo-grecque.* It was
the translation of Ovid, Lucan, Seneca, and Virgil that
gave English Elizabethan poetry the startword."

(pp. 189-91.)

I fear I must repeat the (alleged) "foolish statement" of my editorial predecessors as to Herrick's
indebtedness to Catullus. The foot-notes go to show
frequent reminiscences and adaptations of the poet of
Verona ('adopted' is his own word); and without
traversing the high praise of his "eagle flights" and
"very noonday-depths of passion, swifter than Shelley's,
as flaming as Sappho's," it has been shown earlier that
there was infinitely more of passion in our Poet than is
ordinarily supposed, and than is supposed by Mr.
Gosse, so that it is, I humbly think, a mistake to gen-
eralize on the "pipings of our gentle and luxurious

babbler by the flowery brooks." The *Carmina* of
Catullus, alike in their lyrical fervour and intensity,
find more than "fellowship" in much of the *Hesperides*.
Certes for once that Martial is suggested, Catullus is
three times. More than this—it is in the offensive
Epigrams that had better been spared bodily that
Herrick goes to Martial. Startled by Mr. Gosse's
paradox, I have taken pains to re-read good old
Farnaby's natty edition of the *Epigrammata*, and my
original impression has been confirmed that, except
in instances of all but direct translation, and almost
wholly in the unsavoury Epigrams, Martial exercised but
slight influence, and all of it, unhappily, sinister. On
the other hand, there are in *Hesperides* notable indebtedness to Catullus in what is most imperishable,
e.g. "To Anthea" (in first eight lines : Vol. I. p. 40) :
"Kissing Usurie" (Vol. I. p. 49) : "The Vision"
(*ibid*, p. 86) : "Epithalamie to Sir Thomas Southwell
and his Ladie" (*ibid*, p. 90-9, *et alibi*) : "Corinna
going a Maying" (*ibid*, p. 116) : "An Ode to Master
Endymion Porter upon his Brothers death" (*ibid*, p.
124) : "Lips Tongueless" (*ibid*, pp. 141-2) : "A request to the Graces" (Vol. III. p. 13). Besides these
specific places, the student will again and again catch
the notes of the *Carmina*, often the more assuredly

from the peculiar turn given to the thought or image. Apart from the *Epigrams*, which one must constantly remember are the mere "farcing buckram" of the Book, five or six faint echoes of Martial seem to me to sum up Herrick's obligations to him.[1]

'*Allusive* reading' rather than assimilative is what I discover in Herrick's Poems. Certain of his words and turns of phrase make you think of others, and others keep ringing in your memory as you read; but when you recall them, you begin to suspect coincidence rather than knowledge, and o' times are amused to find that Herrick is the precursor not follower. It

---

[1] Including those in the Index of Names, the following it is believed give references to every Epigram in Martial to which in the slightest way Herrick alludes; most are very slightly indeed remembered: B. I, The Author to his Book (3), To Cæsar (4), To Decianus (8), To Julius (15), To Aelia (19), To Flaccus (57), Of Manneia (83): B. II, To Postumus (10)—perhaps the name of Wickes ('Posthumus') was taken from this and others kindred; To Pannicus (36), To Cæcilianus (37), To Olus (68), To Quintilian (90): B. III, On Sabdidus (17): B. IV, On Cleopatra his wife (22), To Domitian (27), To Hippodamus (31), On a Bee enclosed in Amber (59): B. V, To his Readers (2), To Regulus (10): B. VI, To Marcianus (70): B. VII, To his Book (84), On Papilus (94): B. VIII, To a friend (14): B. XI, To his Readers (16): B. XIII— occasional dishes are recalled. The fingers of a single hand will sum up actual indebtedness to Martial. Catullus and Horace and Anacreon furnish a much more pervading element.

may interest to give a few examples.   In the place I
have quoted Milton in

> "When I thy singing next shall heare
> Ile wish I might turne *all to eare.*" (Vol. I., p. 38.)

Hook's *Amanda*—a sorry affair as a whole, but with
some few glorious things in it—has the same odd
fancy :—

> "Sing on sweet Chauntresse soul of melodie ;
> Closely attentive to thy harmonie :
> The Heavens check't and stop't their rumbling spheres,
> And all the world *turn'd itself into eares.*"   (p. 19.)

Nothing could be more unhappy than 'rumbling'
applied to the great silent 'spheres,' and there is a
dash of the grotesque in the huge impersonation of
'the world '—"turn'd into eares."   Still, the idea is
there, and as Hook's Poems circulated long in Manuscript, it is quite possible it was original to him.
William Cartwright in his " Young Lord to his Mistress who had taught him a Song," has it also :—

> "Whose Sounds do make me wish I were
> Either all Voice, or else all Eare."
>   (Poems 16, p. 208.)

The conceit in "Electra's Tears," that from them sprang sweet flowers, is frequent before and after. None has used it with more graciousness than SIR WILLIAM DAVENANT, as thus :—

"My Grave with Flowers let Virgins strow;
   Which, if thy Teares fall near them,
May so transcend in Scent and Show,
   As thou wilt shortly weare them.

Such Flowers how much will Florists prize,
   Which on a Lover growing,
Are water'd with his Mistress eyes,
   With pity ever flowing.
A Grave so deckt, will, though thou art
   Yet fearful to come nie me.
Provoke thee straite to break thy heart,
   And lie down boldly by me.

Then ev'ry where all Bells shall ring,
   All Light to Darkness turning,
Whilst ev'ry Quire shall sadly sing,
   And Natures self weare mourning.
Yet we hereafter may be found,
   By destinies right placing,
Making, like Flowers, Love under Ground,
   Whose Rootes are still embracing."

               (Works folio p. 318.)

In the lines " To Oenone " we have this appeal :—

> " For shame or pitty now encline,
>   To play a loving part ;
> Either to send me kindly thine,
>   Or give me back my heart."
>
> (Vol. II. p. 111.)

Compare this with SIR JOHN SUCKLING (Remains : 1659, p. 6) :—

> " I prethee send me back my heart,
>   Since I can not have thine :
> For if from yours you will not part,
> . Why then should'st thou have mine ?"

His " Dreame " (Vol. II., p. 84) is of a slighter build than Cartwright's, as thus:—

> " I dream'd I saw my self lye dead,
>   And that my bed my coffin grew :
> Silence and Sleep this strange sight bred,
>   But wak'd I found I liv'd anew.
> Looking next morn on your bright face,
>   Mine Eyes bequeath'd mine Heart fresh pain,
> A Dart rush'd in with every Grace,
>   And so I kill'd my self again :
> . O Eyes, what shall distressèd Lovers do
> If open you can kill, if shut you view."
>
> (Poems, as before, p. 213.)

Again, "Upon Electra":—

> "When out of bed my love doth spring,
>   *'Tis but as day a-kindling :*
>   But when she's up and fully drest,
>   *'Tis then broad Day throughout the East.*"
>
> (Vol. II., p. 86.)

I am willing to believe that Herrick may have thought here of Chaucer :—

> " Up roos the sonne, and up rose Emelye."
> (Knight's Tale : Vol. I., p. 163, Bell.)

Or Davenant again :—

> "Awake, awake, break through your Vailes of Lawne !
> Then draw your Curtains and begin the Dawne."
> (As before, p. 320.)

Daintier than all is Spenser's Una, who "made a sunshine in a shady place" (F.Q. b.I. c. 3). Herrick's, as Sidney's "bean blossoms" and their rich fragrance is one of several like favourites in the *Hesperides*. So too Suckling addressing Herrick's Countess of Carlisle, as did Cartwright and Waller and others, sings :—

> " Didst thou not find the place inspir'd,
>   And flow'rs as if they had desir'd

No other Sun, start from their beds,
And for a sight steal out their heads ?
Heardst thou not musick when she talk't ?
And didst not find that as she walkt
She threw rare perfumes all about
Such as bean-blossoms newly out.
Or chafèd spices give ?————
    " Upon my Lady Carliles walking in Hamp-
        ton Court Garden." (1646, p. 26.)

The " Apron of Flowers " (Vol. II., p. 249) has a fine
parallel in a Poet who is too little known, Thomas
Stanley, as thus :—

" Favonius the milder breath o' th' Spring,
    When proudly bearing on his softer wing
    Rich odours, which from the Panchean groves
    He steals, as by the Phenix pyre he moves,
    Profusely doth his sweeter theft dispence
    To the next Roses blushing innocence,
    But from the grateful Flower, a richer scent
    He back receives then he unto it lent.
    Then laden with his odours richest store,
    He to thy Breath hasts ! to which these are poor ;
    Which whilst the amorous wind to steal essaies,
    He, like a wanton Lover 'bout thee playes, &c."
                        (Poems 1651, p. 6.)

It were easy to add almost *ad infinitum* to such
parallels. They practically leave Herrick's originality

untouched. Of his anticipations of later Poets the most
noteworthy are these two :—

> " *A good death.*
>
> For truth I may this sentence tell
> No man dies ill, that liveth well."
>
> (Vol. III. p. 66.)

and

> " *Sins loath'd, and yet lov'd.*
>
> Shame checks our first attempts ; but then 'tis prov'd,
> Sins first dislik'd, are after that belov'd."
>
> (Vol. III. p. 156.)

The first has been re-written by Pope, thus :—

> " For modes of faith let graceless zealots fight ;
> He can't be wrong whose life is in the right."
>
> (Essay on Man, ep. iii. l. 305.)[1]

The second also by him, thus :—

> " Vice is a monster of so frightful mien,
> As to be hated, needs but to be seen ;
> Yet, seen too oft, familiar with her face,
> We first endure, then pity, then embrace."
>
> (Essay on Man, ep. ii. l. 217.)

---

[1] Better still Cowley on Crashaw :—
" His faith, perhaps, in some nice tenets might
Be wrong; his life, I'm sure was in the right."

Finally here, if the Reader will turn to "The Country Life" (Vol. II. pp. 212-15) and then to "L'Allegro," I shall be indeed mistaken if it be not conceded that Milton remembered it to advantage therein.

5. *His Sacred Verse.* I am aware that it is usual to regard *Noble Numbers* as an infinite falling off from *Hesperides*; nor would I dispute the verdict on his Sacred Verse, taken as a whole. None the less is it true that there are things in *Noble Numbers* that only a man of unique genius could have written. Dr. George Macdonald, in " Antiphon," seems to me to hold the scales evenly, and to bring out specialities worth bringing out. It is a joy to let such a Critic speak for one, as thus (not omitting repetitions of prior given facts) :—" We now come to a new sort, both of man and poet—still a clergyman. It is an especial pleasure to write the name of Robert Herrick among the poets of religion, for the very act records that the jolly careless Anacreon of the church, with his head and heart crowded with pleasures, threw down at length his wine-cup, tore the roses from his head, and knelt in the dust.

"Nothing bears Herrick's name so unrefined as the things Dr. Donne wrote in his youth ; but the impression made by his earlier poems is of a man of far shallower nature, and greatly more absorbed in the delights of the passing hour.   In the year 1648, when he was fifty-seven years of age, being prominent as a Royalist, he was ejected from his living by the dominant Puritans ; and in that same year he published his poems, of which the latter part and later written is his *Noble Numbers*, or religious poems. We may wonder at his publishing the *Hesperides* along with them, but we must not forget that, while the manners of a time are never to be taken as a justification of what is wrong, the judgment of man concerning what is wrong will be greatly influenced by those manners—not necessarily on the side of laxity.   It is but fair to receive his own testimony concerning himself, offered in these two lines printed at the close of his *Hesperides :*

'To his Book's end this last line he'd have plac't,
Jocond his Muse was, but his Life was chast.' [1]

[1] Herrick no doubt was thinking of Ovid (Trist. II. 353-4).
   Crede mihi, mores distant a carmina nostri ;
   Vita veracunda est, Musa jocosa, mihi ;"
and also perhaps of Martial (I. v.) " Lasciva est nobis pagina, vita proba est."   Cartwright was severe on the Poet's apology—for certainly it was intended—when he wrote of Jonson :—" No need to make good count'nance Ill, and use the plea of strict life for a looser muse " (Poems, as before, p. 314).

"We find the same artist in the *Noble Numbers* as in the *Hesperides*, but hardly the same man. However far he may have been from the model of a clergyman in the earlier period of his history, partly, no doubt, from the society to which his power of song made him acceptable, I cannot believe that these later poems are the results of mood, still less the result of mere professional bias, or even sense of professional duty.

"In a good many of his poems he touches the heart of truth ; in others, even those of epigrammatic form, he must be allowed to fail in point as well as in meaning. As to his art-forms, he is guilty of great offences, the result of the same passion for lawless figures and similitudes which Dr. Donne so freely indulged. But his verses are brightened by a certain almost childishly quaint and innocent humour ; while the tenderness of some of them rises on the reader like the aurora of the coming sun of George Herbert. I do not forget that even if some of his poems were printed in 1639 [1635], years before that George Herbert had done his work and gone home : my figure stands in relation to the order I have adopted. Some of his verse is homelier than even George Herbert's homeliest. One of its most remarkable traits is a quaint thanksgiving for the commonest things by name

—not the less real that it is sometimes even queer.
For instance:

' *To God.*

> God gives not onely corne, for need,
> But likewise sup'rabundant seed;
> Bread for our service, bread for shew;
> Meat for our meales, and fragments too:
> He gives not poorly, taking some
> Between the finger, and the thumb;
> But, for our glut, and for our store,
> Fine flowre prest down, and running o're.'

" Here is another, delightful in its oddity.   We can
fancy the merry yet gracious poet chuckling over the
vision of the child and the fancy of his words.

' *A Grace for a Child.*

> Here a little child I stand,
> Heaving up my either hand;
> Cold as Paddocks though they be,
> Here I lift them up to Thee,
> For a Benizon to fall
> On our meat, and on us all. *Amen.*'
>
> (Vol. III. pp. 158-9.)

" I shall now give two or three of his longer poems,
which are not long, and then a few of his short ones.

The best known is the following, but it is not so well known that I must therefore omit it.

' His Letanie, to the Holy Spirit.

1. In the houre of my distresse,
   When temptations me oppresse,' &c.

' The White Island : or place of the Blest.

In this world (the *Isle of Dreames*)
While we sit by sorrowes streames,' &c.

' To Death.

Thou bid'st me come away,
And I'le no longer stay,' &c.

' Eternitie.

1. O Yeares ! and Age ! Farewell :
       Behold I go,
       Where I do know
   Infinitie to dwell.

2. And these mine eyes shall see
       All times, how they
       Are lost i' th' Sea
   Of vast Eternitie.

3. Where never Moone shall sway
      The Starres ; but she
      And Night, shall be
Drown'd in one endlesse Day.

' The goodnesse of his God.

When Winds and Seas do rage
    And threaten to undo me,
Thou dost their wrath asswage,
    If I but call unto Thee.

A mighty storm last night
    Did seek my soule to swallow,
But by the peep of light
    A gentle calm did follow.

What need I then despaire,
    Though ills stand round about me ;
Since mischiefs neither dare
    To bark, or bite without Thee ? '

' To God.

Lord, I am like to *Misletoe*
Which has no root, and cannot grow,
Or prosper, but by that same tree
It clings about ; so I by Thee.
What need I then to feare at all,
So long as I about Thee craule ?
But if that Tree sho'd fall, and die,
Tumble shall heav'n, and down will I.'

r

"Here are now a few chosen from many that—to borrow a term from Crashaw—might be called Divine Epigrams.

' God, when He's angry,' &c.	(Vol. III. p. 121.)
' God can't be wrathful,' &c.	(„ p. 215.)
' 'Tis hard to find God,' &c.	(„ p. 122.)
' God's rod doth watch,' &c.	(„ p. 125.)
' A man's transgression,' &c.	(„ p. 151.)
' God, when He takes,' &c.	(„ p. 156.)
' Humble we must be,' &c.	(„ p. 156.)
' God Who's in Heaven,' &c.	(„ p. 188.)
' The same who crowns,' &c.	(„ p. 189.)
' God is so potent,' &c.	(„ p. 191.)
' Paradise is,' &c.	(„ p. 191.)
' Heaven is not given,' &c.	(„ p. 203.)

One more for the sake of Martha, smiled at by so many because they are incapable either of her blame or her sister's praise.

' The repetition of the name, made known
No other than Christ's full affection.'
(Vol. III. p. 191.)

And so farewell to the very lovable Robert Herrick." (pp. 163-171). Turning back on these " good words," it may be that some, reading his " Letanie" for the first time, or reading it afresh, may be disposed to wonder if not to condemn its levities, and if disposed to be harsh, might even say that the ass's ear persists in peeping out of Herrick's cleanest night-cap.   But in *bits* such as these in his "Letanie"—

> " *When the artlesse doctor sees   =without skill*
> *No one hope, but of his fees,*
> And his skill runs on the lees ;
>   Sweet Spirit, comfort me !
>   . . . .
> When the tapers now burne blew,
> *And the comforters are few,*
> *And that number more then true ;*
>   Sweet Spirit, comfort me !"

there really was no irreverence, nothing save irrepressible humour and sense of the ridiculous side of human nature, and scorn of all unrealities.[1] It is of kin with Sir Thomas More's jest within the gleam of the heads-

[1] 'Art-lesse.'   When I put ' without skill ' in the margin in its place, I thought of the meaning as ▬ skillessness or ignorance, and certainly it might well apply to the then country practitioner in Devonshire.   My good friend Dr. Nicholson suggests that his skillessness *quoad* the patient's state (supposed) is intended, and so ▬ when the doctor's art has become skilless or unable to relieve or save. This seems to be suggested by the 'skill' of third line— which otherwise is contradictory—and yields a finer meaning. There remains the jest on the ' fees,' with its further hint at isolation.

man's axe, and such sallies as have broken from your witty men from stout Gilbert (Raleigh's brother-in-law) to Robert Burns and Sydney Smith. I'd rather have outspoken sincerity than sanctimonious demureness. The incidental mention of George Herbert reminds us that though his contemporary at Cambridge, *Noble Numbers* shews only one distant echo of " The Temple" in "His Saviour's Words, going to the Crosse" (Vol. III. p. 219) and "Good Friday " (Vol. III. 216). It has a touch of " 2. The Sacrifice," just as in " Corinna going a-Maying" there may be heard the sweet urgency of Richard Crashaw in his poem of "The Morning " (Works I. pp. 237-9 in F. W. L.). It is somewhat and inevitably repetitive, but Mr. Gosse's criticism of the sacred Verse must also be given if, in one instance at least, I must again dissent emphatically. Thus he writes :—

" Appended to the *Hesperides*, but bearing date one year earlier, is a little book of poems, similar to these in outward form, but dealing with sacred subjects. Here our pagan priest is seen, despoiled of his vine-wreath and his thyrsus, doing penance in a white sheet, and with a candle in his hand. That rubicund visage, with its sly eye and prodigious jowl, looks ludicrously out of place in the penitential surplice;

but he is evidently sincere, though not very deep, in
his repentance, and sings hymns of faultless orthodoxy,
with a loud and lusty voice, to the old pagan airs. Yet
they are not inspiriting reading, save where they are
least Christian ; there is none of the religious passion
of Crashaw, burning the weak heart away in a flame
of adoration, none of the sweet and sober devotion of
Herbert, nothing, indeed, from an ecclesiastical point
of view, so good as the best of Vaughan the Silurist ;
where the *Noble Numbers* are most readable is where
they are most secular. One sees the same spirit here
as throughout the worldly poems ; in a charming little
Ode to Jesus he wishes the Saviour to be crowned with
roses and daffodils, and laid in a neat white osier
cradle ; in *The Present*, he will take a rose to Christ,
and sticking it in His stomacher, beg for one 'melli-
fluous kiss.' The epigrams of the earlier volume are
replaced in the *Noble Numbers* by a series of couplets,
attempting to define the nature of God, of which none
equals in neatness this, which is the last :—

> 'Of all the good things whatsoe'er we do
> God is the 'Αρχὴ and the Τέλος too.'

As might be expected, his religion is as grossly
anthropomorphic as it is possible to be. He almost

surpasses those mediæval priests of Picardy who
brought such waxen images to the Madonna's shrine
as no altar had seen since the cult of the Lampsacene,
in certain verses on the Circumcision, verses that are
more revolting in their grossness than any of those
erotic poems—

> 'unbaptised rhymes
> Writ in my wild unhallowed times '—

for which he so ostentatiously demands absolution.   It
is pleasant to turn from these to the three or four
pieces that are in every way worthy of his genius.   Of
these the tenderest is the *Thanksgiving*, where he is
delightfully confidential about his food, thus :—

> ' Lord, I confess, too, when I dine
>   The pulse is Thine,
> And all those other bits, that be
>   Placed there by Thee ;
> The worts, the purslain, and the mess
>   Of water-cress.
>
> .   .   .   .   .   .
>
> 'Tis thou that crown'st my glittering hearth
>   With guiltless mirth,
> And giv'st me wassail-bowls to drink,
>   Spiced to the brink.'

And about his house :—

'Like as my parlour, so my hall
.   And kitchen's small,
A little buttery, and therein
    A little bin.'

" The wild and spirited *Letanie* is too well known to
be quoted here, but there are two very fine odes in the
Noble Numbers that are hardly so familiar.   One is the
'Dirge of Jepthah's Daughter,' written in a wonder-
fully musical and pathetic measure, and full of fine
passages, of which this is a fair sample :—

'May no wolf howl, or screech-owl stir
A wing about thy sepulchre !
No boisterous winds or storms come hither
    To starve or wither
Thy soft sweet earth, but, like a spring,
Love keep it ever flourishing.'

" But beyond question the cleverest and at the same
time the most odd poem in the *Noble Numbers* is
'The Widow's Tears ; or, Dirge of Dorcas,' a lyrical
chorus supposed to be wailed out by the widows over
the death-bed of Tabitha.   The bereaved ladies dis-
grace themselves, unfortunately, by the greediness of
their regrets, dwelling on the loss to them of the bread
—'ay ! and the flesh, for and the fish'—that Dorcas

was wont to give them; but the poem has stanzas of marvellous grace and delicacy, and the metre in which it is written is peculiarly sweet. But truly Herrick's forte did not lie in hymn-writing, nor was he able to refrain from egregious errors of taste, whenever he attempted to reduce his laughing features to a proper clerical gravity. Of all his solecisms, however, none is so monstrous as one almost incredible poem 'To God,' in which he gravely encourages the Divine Being to read his secular poems, assuring Him that

> 'Thou, my God, may'st on this impure look,
> Yet take no tincture from my sinful book.'

For unconscious impiety this rivals the famous passage in which Robert Montgomery exhorted God to 'pause and think.'" (pp. 187-8). The supposed 'solecism' is surely a misapprehension. It is the utterance of penitent humility which discerns imperfection and stain on its best, and rejoices to think of Him who is the Light condescending to look on his Poems forgivingly; and the 'take no tincture' is not a bathetic but a pathetic version of Isaiah's cry: "Wo is me! for I am undone; because I am a man of unclean lips, and I dwell in the midst of a people of unclean lips: for mine eyes have seen the King, the Lord of Hosts" (VI. 5).

Accordingly I have enforced it *(in loco)* with a line from Cowper. ⌐

V. *His assurance of fame.* This is too large an ele- . ment in the Poetry of Herrick to be left un-noted. Any / one who studies the early literature of England must have been struck with the grotesquely impossible expec- tations of immortality cherished and published by mere ˙ Versifiers. You have the most serene self-laudation and accusing committal of their Poems to the next cen- tury as distinguished from an ignorant and unsympa- thetic present time. The contrast between the Hope and its failure has no doubt its ludicrous side, but it has also something of pathos. But when you find not merely aspiration but achievement, not only prediction but the very ' stuff' of the imperishable, you do well to pause and meditate ; for no man who could write the " Mad Maid's Song," or " The Prim- roses fill'd with dew," or other of Herrick's pieces already marked and examined, is to be regarded as an Egotist in joyously and in perfect words singing his assurance of fame, especially when, as in his case, the immortality counted on is unexaggerate and modest, and symbolized by the dew from the sky, not the great dome of the sky itself, or as least and lowliest wild- flowers live securely from age to age, carrying ˙ in their bosom the tiny *bit* of colour, or the censer of fragrance given them by Him who is The Gardener. The pretender's assurance of 'fame' is a tribute as it is a foil to the true man's. It is to be questioned if there can be actuality of possession of capacity above the ordinary and yet unconsciousness of it; and if consciously held, it is simple trueness to the fact to utter it out. Herrick's possession will not be gainsayed; nor his positive guerdons; nor the certainty of an undying memory within his own self-chosen realm of bright and dainty, rural-breathed and divinely simple Poetry, with o' times celestial tones as of the Lark "soaring and singing, singing and soaring," right up to "Heaven's gate." Quotations already made might suffice to confirm his assurance of fame. But the "thirst for fame," as Mr. Gosse shews, "is unsatiable, and his hope of gaining it intense"; his poetry is "his life and his pyramides," a living pillar, never "to be thrown down by envious Time," and it shall be the "honour of great musicians to set his pieces to music when he is dead" (as before, p. 180). Hence it demands more specific exemplification. His anticipation as to 'good musicians' deeming it an 'honour' to 'set' his poems to music, was abundantly fulfilled. Laniere and Wilson, the Lawes and the most famous of the next generation did so; and 'tis pity that to-day the *Hesperides* is not more searched for worthier words than are furnished for contemporary music. 'At Court' both his sacred and secular pieces were " set to music," and sung at Whitehall and elsewhere. But this was a mere accident of that 'fame' concerning which he cherished an assurance. He 'sang' perfectly, certain that his notes were true. He 'described,' and he was equally certain that he gave back in his poems what *he* saw. He 'painted' and there could be no question of the genuineness of his colours (as his epithets). He gave 'praise' to another and another who sought a place in his 'Book of the Just,' and he had the seer's burdened eye to discern that it would endure, whatever might become of the personality celebrated. And so throughout.

The most absolute expression of his assurance of fame as a Poet is " His Poetrie his Pillar " (Vol. I., p. 146) ; but others strike the same key, e.g.

" *On himselfe.*

Live by thy Muse thou shalt; when others die,
Leaving no Fame to long Posterity :
When Monarchies trans-shifted are, and gone;
Here shall endure thy vast Dominion."

(Vol. II. p. 182.)

"*To his Booke.*

Thou art a plant sprung up to wither never,
But like a Laurell, to grow green for ever."

(Vol. I. p. 171.)

Nor must his before-mentioned hope through musicians be omitted:—

"*Upon himself.*

Thou shalt not All die; for while Love's fire
    shines
Upon his Altar, men shall read thy lines;
And learn'd Musicians shall to honour *Herricks*
Fame, and his Name, both set, and sing his Lyricks."

(Vol. II. p. 66.)

Still more characteristic is his

"*Poetry perpetuates the Poet.*

Here I my selfe might likewise die,
And utterly forgotten lye,
But that eternall Poetrie
Repullulation gives me here
Unto the thirtieth thousand yeere,
When all now dead shall re-appeare."

(Vol. II. p. 273.)

Finer and deeper still is his "To live merrily, and to trust to good verses":—

" Trust to good Verses then ;
They onely will aspire,
When Pyramids, as men,
Are lost, i'th'funerall fire.

And when all Bodies meet
In *Lethe* to be drown'd ;
Then onely Numbers sweet,
With endless life are crown'd."
(Vol. I. p. 140.)

These must suffice. The assurance is positive, but, I
repeat, is modest. It is as the Poet of Love's altar-fire
and as 'sweet' he grounds his Hope. There are
behind this—like the horizon stretching away beyond
the barest patch of moorland—gnome-words declarative of a 'vast dominion' and of 'eternall' renown ;
yet is his self-estimate humble and nicely true to his
self-knowledge. I think our dwelling upon it ought to
guide to more proportionate recognition of his genius,
that is, to the full extent he asserts.

VI. *His Portrait.* It will be noticed that Mr.
Gosse speaks of the "prodigious jowl" of Herrick.
This suffices to convince me that he has been taking
either the preposterous enlargement by Schiavonetti
(in Nott's Selections, 1810), or the equally untrue
lesser enlargement of Worthington (Pickering, 1846),

or the still more monstrous lithograph in Walford's
edition (1869)—coarse and vulgar—as the real like-
ness of our Poet.   None of these has any truth in it,
contrariwise, are lying in feature and expression and
everything.   Lord Dundrennan's woodcut (1823) is
an outrage.   That in the Library of Old Authors
(nominally Mr. Hazlitt's) which reproduces the whole
of the original engraving of *Hesperides* (1648) is a
great advance on all the others, or, rather, while it
shows conscientious work, the others are not for a moment to be regarded.   I was extremely anxious to give
one truer still ; and, unless I very much mistake, ours
will be accepted as closer to the original than anything
hitherto.   The engraver (Mr. W. J. Alais) has made it
a task of love ; and the admirer of Herrick has now a
genuine replica (enlarged) of that Portrait which he
himself gave to the world, and which in its most
commanding aquiline nose, and twinkling eye under its
arched and shaggy pent-house, and slight moustache,
and short upper lip, and massive under-jaw, and
' juicy' neck, with much of the voluptuous force of the
best type among the Roman emperors, and affluent
curls, interprets to us his Book, and unmistakably gives
us assurance of a Man, every inch of him.   It speaks
much for his independence that at a time when pre-

fatory verse-eulogies were the rule, and their absence
almost the exception, his Book came out with his own
self in it alone, save in the engraved Latin lines under-
neath his bust-portrait. The I. H. C. of these Lines I
take to have been young John Hall, of Cambridge—to
whom in turn Herrick addressed a panegyric (Vol. III.,
pp. 27-8). Curiously enough, even Lord Dundrennan
and other after-critics have left uncorrected such plain
errors as ' minor es ' for ' minores,' and ' major es ' for
' majores,' which, as Marshall was the engraver, recalls
Milton's Greek, that he caused his unfortunate engraver
innocently to place under his portrait. It may fitly
close these specialities to give the Verses and our verse-
translation :—

"Tempora cinxisset Foliorum densior umbra :
    Debetur Genio Laurea Sylva tuo.
Tempora et Illa Tibi mollis redimîsset Oliva ;
    Scilicet excludis Versibus Arma tuis.
Admisces Antiqua Novis, Jocunda Severis :
    Hinc Juvenis discat, Fœmina, Virgo, Senex
Vt solo minores Phœbo, sic majores Unus
    Omnibus Ingenio, Mente Lepore, Stylo.
            Scripsit I. H. C."

In English take this :—

A denser shade of leaves thy brows should bind ;
A laurel grove is due to such a mind.

The peaceful olive should those brows entwine,
For arms are banished from such verse as thine.
Old things with new thou blendest, grave with gay :
Hence young and old, mother and maid may say,
Phœbus except, all else thou dost outvie
In style, and beauty, and capacity.

Let Charles Short (" Selections " 1839) and the
Retrospective Review, now close these 'critical' observations.   The former thus speaks :—" Forgetting his
blemishes, and only estimating the character and effusions of his felicitous genius, Herrick may safely be
pronounced one of the greatest of the English lyric
poets ; alternately gay and serious, lively and tender,
descriptive and didactic, his pages also record many
curious national customs and traditions ; and if this
had been his only merit, he might have deserved
thanks at least, and not severe censure.   Then again,
he makes incursions into fairy-land with infinite success,
and these may be truly said to rival even Shakespeare
himself " (p. 34).   Next, the *Retrospective Review*
(Vol. V. 1822) :—" Herrick is the most joyous and
gladsome of the bards, singing like the grasshopper, as
if he never would grow old ; he is as fresh as the
Spring, as blithe as Summer, and as ripe as Autumn.
We know of no English poet who is so abandonné, as

the French term it, who so wholly gives himself up to
his present feelings, who is so much heart and soul in
what he writes, and this not on one subject only, but
on all subjects alike. The spirit of song dances in his
veins, and flutters around his lips—now bursting into
the joyful and hearty voice of the Epicurean, sometimes breathing forth strains soft as the sigh of ' buried
love '; and sometimes uttering feelings of the most
delicate pensiveness. His poems resemble a luxuriant
meadow, full of king-cups and wild flowers, or a July
firmament sparkling with a myriad of stars. His fancy
fed upon all the fair and sweet things of nature; it is
redolent of roses and geraniums; it is as bright and
airy as the thistle-down, or the bubbles which laughing
boys blow into the air, where they float in a waving line
of beauty. Like the sun, it communicates a delight
and gladness to everything it shines upon, and is as
bright and radiant as his beams ; and yet many of his
pieces conclude with the softest touches of sensibility
and feeling. Indeed, it is that delicate pathos which
is, at the same time, natural and almost playful, which
most charms us in the writings of Herrick. And as for
his versification, it presents one of the most varied
specimens of the rhythmical harmony in the language,

flowing with an almost wonderful grace and flexibility"
(pp. 157-8). Again: "And now farewell, young
Herrick! for young is thy poetry as thy wisdom is old:
and mayest thou flourish in immortal youth, thou boon
companion and most jocund songster! May thy purest
poems be piped from hill to hill, throughout England;
and thy spirit, tinged with superstitious lore, be glad-
dened by the music! May the flowers breath incense
to thy fame, for thou hast not left one of them unsung!
May the solitary springs and circumambient air murmur
thy praises as thou hast warbled theirs! And may
those who love well sing, and those who love well, sigh
sweet panegyrics to thy memory! Ours shall not be
wanting, for we have read thee much, and would fain
hope that this our paper, being nearly all made of thy
thoughts and language, may be liked as well as one like
thee is" (pp. 179-180).

A "sweet singer" of Devonshire (Mortimer Collins)
has paid recent tribute to our Poet; and if it be somewhat thin, and if it be an anachronism at this time o'
day to connect 'hypocrite' with Oliver Cromwell, and
an impertinence to characterize the heroic and most
real Christianity of the Puritans and Nonconformists
as 'cant,' it were pity to lose the little lilt. So "an'
it please thee," Reader, you have it:—

Herrick.

1.

Strangely quiet are Devon's green glades
    Under Apollo's noontide anger;
And the madid eyes of Devonshire maids [moist (*ma-*
    Are full of a sweet and dreamy languor,   *didus*)
Terribly twaddles the dreary " Times,"—
    Little is good that's neoteric;
So I'll lie on the turf beneath the limes
    With a bottle of claret and rare old Herrick.

2.

Rare old Herrick, the Cavalier Vicar
    Of pleasant Dean Prior by Totnes Town,—
Rather too wont in foaming liquor
    The cares of those troublous times to drown,—
Of wicked wit by no means chary,—
    Of ruddy lips not at all afraid;
If you gave him milk in a Devonshire Dairy
    He'd probably kiss the Dairymaid.

3.

But loyal and true to Charles the Martyr,
    To his high profession not untrue,
A poet who strained the poet's charter
    Beyond its limits a point or two;
Lover of ruby and amber wine,
    Of joyous humour and charming girls,
Hater of cant about things divine,
    Of hypocrite Cromwell and all his churls.

4.

None ever touched with so fine a finger
   The delicate lyre of English rhyme;
He loved amid fresh flowers to linger
   And he made their fragrance last through time ;
And the daffodil growing in Spring's soft track
   Has a beauty mystic and esoteric,
Since its brief bright life, two centuries back,
   Was made into verse by our Devonshire Herrick.

5.

Well the poet liked fair London city ;
   He polished some of its choicest gems,
And wrote full many a lyric ditty,
   In taverns over the sparkling Thames :
For those were the days when the Thames ran clear
   Palace and shadowy lawn between,
And bays glittered with stately cheer,
   And light feet danced upon Charing green.

6.

London town is another affair
   Since Herrick wrote his perfect rhymes ;
But Devon has the same Elysian air
   It had in the fine old Cavalier times ;
And he who cares little for all the hysteric
   Trash which the " well-informed " reader sees,
Can't do better than study Herrick
   With a flask of claret under the trees."
   (Summer Songs by Mortimer Collins (1860) p. 114.)

ALEXANDER B. GROSART.

APPENDIX

TO

MEMORIAL-INTRODUCTION.

APPENDIX.

A.

THE HERRICKS OF BEAUMANOR.

From the relationship to the Poet, it is thought well to give here the pedigree of Herrick of Beaumanor from Nichols' Leicestershire (Vol. III. p. 148), with a few corrections from the Beaumanor copy as in Mr. Hazlitt's edn. of *Hesperides.* (Vol. II. pp. 502-3.) It is to be regretted that this pedigree did not come within the scope of Mr. Hill's "Market Harborough," etc., as before.

Sir William Herrick, knt. fifth son of John and Mary Eyrick of Leicester;══Joan, dau. of Richard May, esq. of London born 1557; mar. 1596; knighted 1605; M.P. for the borough of Lei-│ and sister to Sir Humphry May, chancellor cester, 1601, 1605, 1629; died March 2, 1652-3, in his 96th year. │ of the dutchy of Lancaster.

1. William Herrick,══Elizabeth, dau.
   esq. born 1597; │ of Humphry
   married 1623; d. │ Fox, esq. d.
   1671; æt. 74. │ 1683, æt. 84.

2. Robert, born 1598;
   died s.p. 1639.

3. Richard, born 1600;
   d. Warden of Man-
   chester in 1667.

4. Thomas, b. 1602.

5. Elizabeth, b. 1603.

6. Henry, 1604.

7. Roger, fellow of All
   Souls 1628-9.

8. John, 1612.

9. Mary, d. ætat. 20.

10. Martha, married in 1634 to
    John Holmstead, esq. of Lynn
    Norfolk.

11. Dorothy, married in 1628
    the Rev. James Lancashire.

12. Elizabeth, mar. in 1633 Beau-
    mont Pight, esq. of Beaumanor

Anne, dau. of William Bainbrigge, esq.══William Herrick, esq. born 1624;══Frances, dau. of Will. Milward, esq. of Chil-
of Lockington, first wife; d. 1655. │ marr. 1649; died 1693, æt. 69.│ cot, co. Derb. second wife; d. before 1681.

1. William══Dorothy, dau.
   Heyrick │ of Ja. Woot-
   b. 1650; │ ton, of Wes-
   d. 1705; │ ton, co.
   æt. 55. │ Derby, esq.
   │ died 1749,
   │ æt. 100.

2. John, of the══Mary, dau. of
   Outwoods in │ Beaumont
   the parish of │ Pight, esq,
   Loughboro'; │ of Denton,
   d. 1724. │ co. Lincoln;
   │ d. 1727.

3. Benjamin
   Herrick,
   M.D. æt.
   circa 26,
   1681; d.
   1720.

4. Elizabeth,
   married to
   John
   Levesley,
   esq. of
   Belton.

1. Thomas, d. 1682,
   aged 20.

2. Frances, d. young,
   1664.

3. Mary, b. 1665; m.
   Will. Lucas, esq.

4. Christiana, born
   1666; m. Clifton

P

Q

1. Elizabeth, bo. 1684; marr. Robert Bunny, gent. died 1745.
2. William, born 1685; died 1686.
3. Anne, born 1687; died 1759 unmarried.

4. William Herrick, esq. born 1689; married 1740; died 1773, æt. 84. = Lucy, dau. of John Gage, esq. of Bentley Park, Sussex, d. 1778, aged 64.

5. John Herrick, born 1691, married 1715; died 1760; æt. 68. = Elizabeth, dau. of Samuel Marshall, of Burton-on-the-Woulds, gent. d.1757, æt. 75.

6. Thomas Herrick, esq. of Leicester.

1. William Bainbrigge, Herrick, d. 1733.
2. A dau.

1. Lucy, born 1741. = Richard Gildart, esq. of Norton Hall, co. Stafford; high sheriff of that county, 1784.
2. Dorothy, b. 1743; d. 1745.
3. Dorothy, d. 1747.

4. William Herrick, esq. b. 1745. = Sarah Stokes, of Woodhouse.

5. John Herrick, esq. b. 1749.

6. Thomas Bainbrigge Herrick, esq. b. 1754. = Mary, only dau. of Jas. Perry, esq. of Eardsley Park, co. Hereford.

Richard, born 1772; a gentleman commoner of University College, Oxford. Died 1802 unmarried.

1. William, born June 29, 1794.

1. William, born = Sophia, daughter of Jonathan Henry Christie, esq. of London, barrister-at-law.
2. Mary-Anne, born June 9, 1796.
3. Lucy, born March 21, 1798, died 1832 unmarried.

Two sons and two dau. all dead.

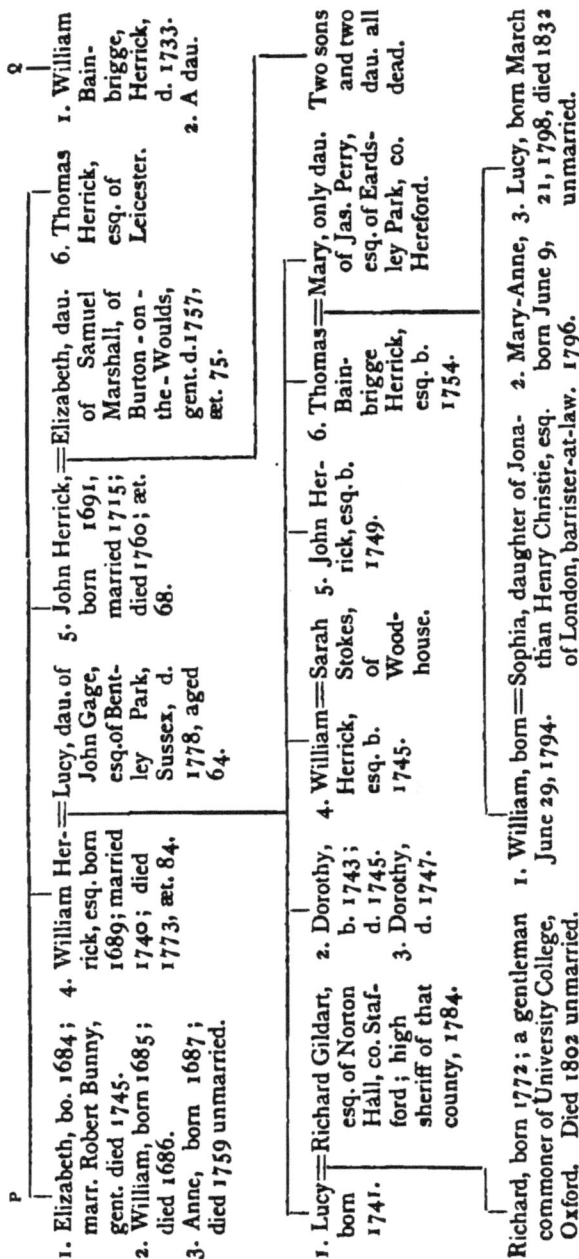

With reference to the 'knighthood' of Sir William Herrick, the following quotation from Winwood's Memorials of Affairs of State, 1725 (Vol. II. p. 57) is curious. Samuel Calvert writes to Ralph Winwood on 6th April, 1605: "On Easter Tuesday, one Mr. William Herrick, a goldsmith in Cheapside, was Knighted for making a Hole in the great Diamond the King doth wear. The party little expected the honour, but he did his work so well as won the King to an extraordinary liking of it." The King was James I. G.

B.

RICHARD HEYRICK, OR HERRICK.

Richard Heyrick (or Herrick) is by far the most notable of the Herricks (the Poet excepted), and as a striking contrast with his cousin, and as, moreover, hitherto overlooked very much, it is most satisfactory to be able to add here the following notices of him, for which I am indebted to my excellent friend W. A. Abram, Esq., of Blackburn, the Historian of Blackburn.

"Richard Heyrick, third son of Sir William Heyrick, of Beaumanor Park, co. Leicester, was born in London the 9th Sept., 1600. After receiving the elements of learning at Merchant Taylor's school, he entered at All Saints' College, Oxford; took the degree of M. A. at the age of 20, and four years later, in 1624, was elected a fellow of his College. On the petition of his father, to whom the Royal house was under obligation for pecuniary assistance, Richard Heyrick obtained from Charles the First, in the year 1626, the promise of the reversion of the Wardenship of Manchester

College after the decease of Richard Murray, Knt. By
the King's Charter to Christ's College, Manchester,
dated 30th Sept., 1635, Richard Heyrick was consti-
tuted 'first warder of the said perpetual College.' He
came into possession of this appointment, then worth
about £700 per annum, at the age of 36. In his
ecclesiastical views, Warden Heyrick was a puritan of
Presbyterian tendencies in church government, and a
vehement hater of Popery and all its works. He
preached several set discourses in the Manchester
Collegiate Church, during the years 1638-40, against
Popery, which exhibit the intensity of his antagonism
to the Roman system and its adherents in England.
In 1641, he published in duodecimo 'Three Sermons
preached at the Collegiate Church, Manchester,' dedicated to the House of Commons; one of the three
sermons was preached on the public Fast Day, 8th
July, 1640. Warden Heyrick drafted the address of
the Puritans of Lancashire to the King, at the outset of
the Civil War in 1644, which was subscribed by sixty-
four Knights and esquires, fifty-five divines, 740 gentle-
men, and 7,000 freeholders and others. The same
year, somewhat later on, he was the first in Manchester
to subscribe the Solemn League and Covenant. During
the war, the Warden stoutly upheld the cause of Par-

liament, and is said to have given the larger proportion of his official income to provide pay for the forces garrisoning Manchester. In 1646, the sequestration by Parliament included the revenues of the College and Church of Manchester; but Warden Heyrick took the opportunity of an invitation to preach before the House of Commons to urge an appeal, which was successful, for the restoration of the estate of his College. He was a chief agent in the establishment of the Lancashire Presbytery, Oct., 1646; and made a journey to London in that year. In 1649, the Republican soldiers under Col. Thomas Birch broke into the Chapter House of Manchester Collegiate Church, and seized the charters of its endowment, which the Warden vainly essayed to protect. These deeds were sent to London, and were never recovered thereafter. The Commissioners of sequestration granted to Herrick a small stipend of £100 per annum; but he regarded the College as dissolved, and ceased to use the title of Warden. In 1651, Richard Heyrick was so imprudent as to proceed to London for the purpose of joining with some Presbyterians there in an attempt to excite a revolt against the Republican party then in the ascendant; the consequence being that after the battle of Worcester Heyrick was arrested in Manchester, taken to London,

and imprisoned, along with his son-in-law, Mr. Johnson.
Some of his confederates in the scheme of disaffection
were sentenced to death ; but friends at court protected
Heyrick, and obtained his liberation. Mr. Heyrick is
found presiding as Moderator at the synod of the
Lancashire Presbytery in October, 1657 ; and in May,
1658, he made a journey to London on church business. On the Restoration in 1660, the College of
Manchester was re-instated, and its endowments restored ; but Heyrick was temporarily in danger of being
supplanted in the office of Warden by one Dr. Woolley,
a royalist partizan. Henry Newcome in his journal
writes :—' July 2, 1660. I heard of Mr. Heyrick's
going to London ; the cause was his wardenship was
claimed by Dr. Wolley, to whom King Charles I. in
the beginning of the war had granted it, for Mr. H.'s
delinquency; and so he was forced to go up to look after
it.' Eventually, the old Warden was restored to his
function. Heyrick preached the sermon at the Collegiate Church, Manchester, on the Coronation Day
of Charles II., Tuesday, April 23, 1661. This dis-
course was printed by the Manchester Royalists, with
an epistle to the preacher prefixed, who was not con-
sulted in the publication. Warden Heyrick conformed,
but with some show of reluctance and humiliation,

under the Act of Uniformity in 1662. He survived this change in his profession five years, and died, aged 67, Aug. 6th, 1667. Mr. Newcome, his associate, records the event:—'I heard of the sudden and dangerous sickness of poor Mr. Heyrick; insomuch that August 1st [1667], I went on purpose to see him. I found him very ill. We returned to town on the Saturday, August 3rd. August 5th was kept in private on his behalf. I went every day to see him; and on Tuesday in the evening we had a report that he was better, and went up to see him towards evening, and he was declining fast, insomuch that Mrs. Heyrick desired us not to leave her; and we did stay, and was at prayer for him just as he died, about nine at night, on August 6th (Tuesday)... August 9th (Friday) we buried my old friend and colleague." By his first wife, Hellen, daughter of Thomas Corbit, of Spranston, co. Norfolk, Richard Heyrick had issue a son, Thomas, born Sept. 9th, 1632; and daughters, Mary, married Mr. John Johnson, of Manchester; and Elizabeth, married, April 17th, 1661, Rev. Richard Holbrook, of Salford. His second wife was Anna Maria, daughter of Mr. Erasmus Britton, merchant, of Hamburg; by her he had a son John, born in 1652, and died young; and a daughter Hellen, married Thomas Radcliffe, Esq.

Warden Heyrick's will bears date May 6th, 1661. His memorial in Manchester Collegiate Church is a plate of copper, within an oaken frame, and is fixed over the entrance to the Chapter House.

HESPERIDES.

2

HESPERIDES:
OR,
THE WORKS
BOTH
HUMANE & DIVINE
OF
ROBERT HERRICK *Esq.*

OVID.

Effugient avidos Carmina noftra Rogos.

LONDON,
Printed for *John Williams*, and *Francis Eglesfield*,
and are to be fold at the Crown and Marygold
in Saint *Pauls* Church-yard. 1 6 4 8 .

TO THE MOST

ILLVSTRIOVS,

AND

Moft Hopefull P R I N C E,

C H A R L E S,

Prince of *Wales*.[1]

Ell may my Book come forth like
Publique Day,
When fuch a *Light* as *You* are leads
the way:
Who are my Works *Creator*, and alone
The *Flame* of it, and the *Expanfion*.
And look how all thofe heavenly Lamps acquire
Light from the Sun, that *inexhaufted*[2] *Fire:*
So all my *Morne*, and *Evening Stars* from You
Have their *Exiftence*, and their *Influence* too.
Full is my Book of Glories; but all Thefe
By You become *Immortall Subftances*.

[1] Afterwards Charles II.   [2] = inexhaustible.

F Or *thefe Tranfgrefsions which thou here doft fee,*
Condemne the Printer, Reader, and not me ;
Who gave them forth good Grain, though he miftook
The Seed ; fo fow'd thefe Tares throughout my Book.

E R R A T A.

P Age 33. line 10. read *Rods* [for 'rod']. p. 41. l. 19. r.
Gotiere [for 'Goteire']. p. 65 l. 12. r. *only one* [for
'our']. p. 83. l. 28. r. *soft* [for 'foft']. p. 88. l. 26. r. *the
flowrie* [for 'flowrie' without 'the'] p. 91. l. 29. r. *such fears*
[for 'Flesh-quakes']. p. 136. l. 9. r. *to thee the* [for 'the'
dropped]. p. 155. l. 10. r. *washt or's to tell* [for 'Washt o're'].
p. 166. l. 10. r. *his Lachrimæ* [for 'Lacrime']. p. 181. l. 10. r.
Ah woe is me, woe, woe is me [for 'Ah! woe woe woe woe
woe is me']. p. 183. l. 9. r. *and thy brest* [for 'bed'] p. 201. l.
22. r. *let chast* [for 'yet']. p. 230. l. 21. r. *and hauing drunk* [for
'havink']. p. 260. l. 26. r. *to rise* [for 'to kisse'] p. 335. l. 17. r.
a wife as [for 'or a wife'].

In the Divine.
Pag. 22. line 14. read *where so ere he sees* [for 'when he sees'].

Hitherto omitted e.g. by Dundrennan, Singer, Walford,
Hazlitt. Dr. Nott adopts and adapts the verses to the errata of his
" Selections," (1810). The whole of these errata have been silently
corrected in our text.

HESPERIDES.

The Argument of his Book.

SING of *Brooks*, of *Blossomes*, Birds,
and *Bowers :*
Of *April*, *May*, of *June*, and *July*-
Flowers.
I sing of *May-poles, Hock-carts,*[4] *Wassails,*[5] *Wakes,*[6]
Of *Bride-grooms, Brides*, and of their *Bridall-cakes.*
I write of *Youth*, of *Love*, and have Accesse
By these, to sing of cleanly-*Wantonnesse.*

[4] Harvest-home cart: the last loaded in the harvest. So Hock-tide or festival. It is curiously mixed up with the history of the Danes in England. See Bailey, *s. v.* "The Hock-cart, Vol. I. pp. 172-.8

[5] Wassail or wassel (waes hael A. S. 'be in health')—a liquor made of apples, sugar and ale, which being freely partaken of at Christmas or Twelfth-tide, led to the word meaning ▬ hilarious, if not drunken, bouts. So Shakespeare, "at wakes and wassails" (Love's Labour Lost, v. 2).

[6] A watch or vigil, ordinarily with a corpse at night.

I sing of *Dewes*, of *Raines*, and piece by piece
Of *Balme*, of *Oyle*, of *Spice*, and *Amber-Greece.*[7]
I sing of *Times trans-shifting;* and I write
How *Roses* first came *Red*, and *Lillies White.*
I write of *Groves*, of *Twilights*, and I sing
The Court of *Mab*, and of the *Fairie-King.*
I write of *Hell;* I sing (and ever shall)
Of *Heaven*, and hope to have it after all.

To his Muse.

WHITHER, *Mad maiden*, wilt thou roame?
    Farre safer 'twere to stay at home:
Where thou mayst sit, and piping please
The poore and private *Cottages.*
Since *Coats*,[8] and *Hamlets*, best agree
With this thy meaner Minstralsie.

[7] = Sea-born amber, *i.e.* amber gris (French)—one of the varieties of amber. See Cotgrave and notes in Marvell and Herbert, s. v. (Fuller Worthies' Library and Aldine Poets).

[8] = cots, cottages, named in preceding line. Barnfield so spells (Roxburghe Club edn). On the ' lore' of the word ' cote,' see H. Leo in his treatise on Saxon Names of Places (Rectitudines Singularum Personarum), translated by B. Williams: London, 1852, p. 55. Dr. Nott, in his "Selections" (1810), on ll. 19-20 onward, annotates: Thus, too, Petrarch addresses and concludes his 26th *Canzone*:

    O poverella mia, come se' rozza;
    Credo che tel corioschi;
    Rimanti in questi hoschi.

There with the Reed, thou mayst expresse
The Shepherds Fleecie happinesse :
And with thy *Eclogues* intermixe
Some smooth, and harmlesse *Beucolicks.*[9]
There on a Hillock thou mayst sing
Unto a handsome Shephardling ; [1]
Or to a Girle (that keeps the Neat) [2]
With breath more sweet then Violet.
There, there, (perhaps) such Lines as These
May take the simple *Villages.*
But for the Court, the Country wit
Is despicable unto it.
Stay then at home, and doe not goe
Or flie abroad to seeke for woe.
Contempts in Courts and Cities dwell ;
No *Critick* haunts the Poore mans Cell :
Where thou mayst hear thine own Lines read
By no one tongue, there, censurèd.
That man's unwise will search for Ill,
And may prevent it, sitting still.

---

[9] = pastoral songs or poems (bucolics).
[1] Herrick affects such diminutives : see Glossarial Index, s. v.
[2] = oxen or cows.

To his Booke.

WHILE thou didst keep thy *Candor* [3] undefil'd,
  Deerely I lov'd thee ; as my first-borne child :
But when I saw thee wantonly to roame
From house to house, and never stay at home ;
I brake my bonds of Love, and bad thee goe,
Regardlesse whether well thou sped'st, or no.
On with thy fortunes then, what e're they be ;
If good I'le smile, if bad I'le sigh for Thee.

Another.

TO read my Booke the Virgin shie
  May blush, (while *Brutus* [4] standeth by ;)
But when He's gone, read through what's writ,
And never staine a cheeke for it.

Another.

WHO with thy leaves shall wipe (at need)
  The place, where swelling *Piles* do breed :
May every Ill, that bites, or smarts,
Perplexe him in his hinder-parts.

---

[3] = sincerity or integrity : metaphorically whiteness, as being unpublished and so unhandled and unsoiled. See Glossarial-Index,
s. v.

[4] Brutus and Cato are common-places of examples of severe virtue, as in " When he would have his verses read," (l. 10) p. 6.

1234567890

To the soure Reader.

IF thou dislik'st the Piece thou light'st on first ;
  Thinke that of All, that I have writ, the worst :
But if thou read'st my Booke unto the end,
And still do'st this, and that verse, reprehend :
O Perverse man ! If All disgustfull be,
The Extreame Scabbe take thee, and thine, for me.

To his Booke.

COME thou not neere those men, who are like *Bread*
  O're-leven'd ; or like *Cheese* o're-renetted.[5]

When he would have his verses read.

IN sober mornings, doe not thou reherse
  The holy incantation of a verse ;
But when that men have both well drunke,[6] and fed,
Let my Enchantments then be sung, or read.
When Laurell spirts 'ith' fire,[7] and when the Hearth
Smiles to it selfe, and guilds the roofe with mirth ;

[5] From rennet, the maw of a calf, used for making curds in curds and cream and cheese.
[6] St. John, ii., 10. [7] Folk-lore.

When up the *Thyrse*[8] is rais'd, and when the sound
Of sacred *Orgies*[9] flyes, A round, A round;[1]
When the *Rose* raignes, and locks with ointments shine,
Let rigid *Cato* read these Lines of mine.

Upon Julias *Recovery.*

DROOP, droop no more, or hang the head,
　　Ye *Roses* almost witherèd ;
Now strength, and newer Purple get,
Each here declining *Violet.*
O *Primroses /* let this day be
A Resurrection unto ye ;
And to all flowers ally'd in blood,
Or sworn to that sweet Sister-hood :
For Health on *Julia's* cheek hath shed
Clarret, and Creame comminglèd.
And those her lips doe now appeare
As beames[2] of *Corrall*, but more cleare.

---

[8] A *Javelin* twind with *Ivy.* H. [And headed with pine-cones—
used in the rites and orgies of Bacchus.]

[9] Songs to *Bacchus.* H.　　[1] =a call to dance ' a round,' not
' around, around.'　　　　　　[2] =branches or twigs.

To Silvia *to wed.*

LET us (though late) at last (my *Silvia*) wed ;
   And loving lie in one devoted bed.
Thy Watch may stand, my minutes fly poste haste ;
No sound calls back the yeere that once is past.
Then sweetest *Silvia*, let's no longer stay ;
True love, we know, precipitates delay.
Away with doubts, all scruples hence remove ;
No man at one time, can be wise, and love.

The Parliament of Roses to Julia.

I DREAMT the Roses one time went
   To meet and sit in Parliament :
The place for these, and for the rest
Of flowers, was thy spotlesse breast :
Over the which a State[3] was drawne
Of Tiffanie,[4] or Cob-web Lawne ;[5]
Then in that *Parly,*[6] all those powers
Voted the Rose, the Queen of flowers.
But so, as that her self should be
The maide of Honour unto thee.

---

[3] =canopy.   [4] =thin silk or fine gauze.   [5] =lawn as delicately wrought as a spider's web.

[6] Diminutive of Parliament (cf. L 2): Parley=conference and discussion between enemies, while war is suspended.

No Bashfulnesse in begging.

TO get thine ends, lay bashfulnesse aside ;
　Who feares to aske, doth teach to be deny'd.

The Frozen Heart.

I FREEZE, I freeze, and nothing dwels
　In me but Snow, and *ysicles.*
For pitties sake, give your advice,
To melt this snow, and thaw this ice ;
I'le drink down Flames, but if so be
Nothing but love can supple me ;
I'le rather keepe this frost, and snow,
Then to be thaw'd, or heated so.

To Perilla.

AH, my *Perilla !* do'st thou grieve to see
　Me, day by day, to steale away from thee ?
Age cals me hence, and my gray haires bid come,
And haste away to mine eternal home ;
'Twill. not be long *(Perilla)* after this,
That I must give thee the *supremest* kisse :
Dead when I am, first cast in salt, and bring
Part of the creame from that *Religious Spring;*[7]

---

[7] = sacred fountain : 'creame.' Qu : foam or froth ?　See Brand
under "Wells and Fountains."

With which *(Perilla)* wash my hands and feet ;
That done, then wind me in that very sheet
Which wrapt thy smooth limbs (when thou didst
    implore
The Gods protection, but the night before)
Follow me weeping to my Turfe, and there
Let fall a *Primrose*, and with it a teare :
Then lastly, let some weekly-strewings [8] be
Devoted to the memory of me :
Then shall my *Ghost* not walk about, but keep
Still in the coole, and silent shades of sleep.

A Song to the Maskers.

1 COME down, and dance ye in the toyle
    Of pleasures, to a Heate ;
    But if to moisture, Let the oyle
    Of Roses be your sweat.

2 Not only to your selves assume
    These sweets, but let them fly ;
    From this, to that, and so Perfume
    E'ne all the standers by.

[8] = of flowers on the grave. See Brand *s. v.* for a full account.

3 As Goddesse *Isis* [9] (when she went,
　　Or glided through the street)
　Made all that touch't her, with her scent,
　　And whom she touch't, turne sweet.

To *Perenna.*

WHEN I thy Parts runne o're, I can't espie
　　In any one, the least indecencie : [1]
But every Line and Limb diffusèd thence,
A faire, and unfamiliar excellence :
So, that the more I look, the more I prove,　　　＇
Ther's still more cause, why I the more should love.

Treason.

THE seeds of *Treason* choake up as they spring,
　He Acts the Crime, that gives it Cherishing.

Two Things Odious.

TWO of a thousand things, are disallow'd,
　A lying *Rich* man, and a *Poore* man proud.

---

[9] Cf. " Love perfumes all paths " onward : l. 7, mythical.
[1] = inelegance or disorder.　So Milton, "Over thy *decent* shoulders drawn " (Il Penseroso, l. 36).

To his Mistresses.

H ELPE me ! helpe me ! now I call
  To my pretty *Witchcrafts* all ;
Old I am, and cannot do
That, I was accustom'd to.
Bring your *Magicks, Spels, and Charmes,*
To enflesh my thighs, and armes :
Is there no way to beget
In my limbs their former heat ?
Æson had (as *Poets* faine) [2]
Baths that made him young againe :
Find that *Medicine* (if you can)
For your drie-decrepid man :
Who would faine his strength renew,
Were it but to pleasure you.

The Wounded Heart.

C OME bring your *sampler,*[3] and with Art,
  Draw in't a wounded Heart :
  And dropping here, and there :
Not that I thinke, that any Dart,

---

[2] Ovid. *Met.* vii. 163, 250, &c.
[3] Fine canvas on which ornamental wool-work, and sometimes in silk, was wrought with the needle.

Can make your's bleed a teare :
Or peirce it any where ;
Yet doe it to this end : that I,
May by
This secret see,
Though you can make
That *Heart* to bleed, your's ne'r will ake
For me.

No Loathsomnesse in love.

WHAT I fancy, I approve,
No Dislike there is in love :
Be my Mistresse short or tall,
And distorted there-withall :
Be she likewise one of those,
That an *Acre* hath of Nose :
Be her forehead, and her eyes
Full of incongruities :
Be her cheeks so shallow too,
As to shew her *Tongue* wag through :
Be her lips ill hung, or set,
And her grinders black as jet ;
Ha's she thinne haire, hath she none,
She's to me a *Paragon.*[4]

---

[4] = equal, or compeer, *i. e.,* the peerless or pattern one. See
Glossarial Index s. v.

To Anthea.

I F, deare *Anthea*, my hard fate it be
 To live some few-sad-howers after thee :
Thy *sacred Corse* with *Odours* I will burne ;
And with my *Lawrell* crown thy *Golden Vrne.*
Then holding up (there) such religious Things,
As were (time past) thy holy *Filitings* : [5]
Nere to thy *Reverend Pitcher* [6] I will fall
Down dead for grief, and end my woes withall :
So three in one small plat [7] of ground shall ly,
Anthea, *Herrick*, and his *Poetry.*

The Weeping Cherry.

I SAW a Cherry weep, and why ?
 Why wept it ? but for shame,
Because my *Julia's* lip was by,
 And did out-red the same.
But, pretty Fondling, [8] let not fall
 A teare at all for that :
Which *Rubies*, *Corralls*, *Scarlets*, all
 For tincture, [9] wonder at.

---

[5] = binding with fillets or bandages, and in the fillets themselves
as bindings, there were bands.
 [6] = that from which she made libations and sacrificed.
 [7] = small piece of ground : sometimes ' plot.'
 [8] = foolish little thing.   [9] = colour or hue.

Soft Musick.

THE mellow touch of musick most doth wound
  The soule, when it doth rather sigh, then sound.

The Difference betwixt
Kings and Subiects.

TWIXT Kings and Subjects ther's this mighty
    odds,
Subjects are taught by *Men ;* Kings by the *Gods.*

His Answer to a Question.

SOME would know
      Why I so
  Long still doe tarry,
      And ask why
      Here that I
  Live, and not marry ?
      Thus I those
      Doe oppose ;
  What man would be here,
      Slave to Thrall,
      If at all
  He could live free here ?

Upon *Julia's Fall.*

JVLIA was carelesse, and withall,
   She rather took,[1] then [2] got a fall:
The wanton *Ambler* chanc'd to see
Part of her leggs sinceritie:[3]
And ravish'd thus, It came to passe,
The Nagge (like to the *Prophets Asse,*)
Began to speak, and would have been
A telling what rare sights h'ad seen:
Añd had told all; but did refraine,
Because his Tongue was ty'd againe.

Expences Exhaust.

LIVE with a thrifty, not a needy Fate;
   Small shots [4] *paid often, waste a vast estate.*

Love what it is.

LOVE is a circle that doth restlesse move
   In the same sweet eternity of love.

---

[1] *i. e.* she might be said to have merited it.
[2] = than—and so throughout as placed in the margin.
[3] = pureness.   [4] = debts.

Presence and Absence.

WHEN what is lov'd is Present, love doth spring ;
But being absent, Love lies languishing.[5]

No Spouse but a Sister.

A BACHELOUR I will
   Live as I have liv'd still,
And never take a wife
To crucifie my life :
But this I'le tell ye too,
What now I meane to doe ;
A Sister (in the stead
Of Wife) about I'le lead ; [6]
Which I will keep embrac'd,
And kisse, but yet be chaste.

The Pomander[7] Bracelet.

TO me my *Julia* lately sent
   A Bracelet richly Redolent :
The Beads I kist, but most lov'd her
That did perfume the Pomander.

---

[5] Allusion to the flower Love-Lies-Bleeding.

[6] 1 Corinthians, ix. 5.

[7] = Pomme d'ambre (French), *i. e.* an amber apple (and sometimes a pear) having been the form of a silver case within which the

The shooe tying.

A *NTHEA* bade me tye her shooe;
   I did; and kist the Instep too:
And would have kist unto her knee,
Had not her Blush rebukèd me.

The Carkanet.[8]

I NSTEAD of Orient Pearls, of Jet,
   I sent my Love a Karkanet:
About her spotlesse neck she knit
The lace,[9] to honour me, or it:
Then think how wrapt[1] was I to see
My Jet t'enthrall such Ivorie.

ball of various scents, mainly *ambergris,* was enclosed, having holes
pierced throughout, for escape of the perfume. A pomander bracelet
was made of these balls, &c. Such balls were supposed to be use-
ful against infection so late as 1610. The Plague that year being
in Oxford, George Radcliffe (afterwards Sir George) wrote that his
tutor " had sent him out of town, if he had desired it, and made him
a *Pomander* " (Churton's Life of Dean Nowell, pp. 21-2). Becon
named a rare little book of his " The Pomander of Prayers," (1578).
   [8] The carcanet was a gold or other ornamental chain, or necklace, worn round the neck. *Carcan* originally signified an iron
collar to confine malefactors to a post. Nicot, in his *Grand Dic-
tionaire,* defines it, *ornement d'or qu'on imst au col des demoiselles. N.*
   [9] = the string of the carkanet or necklace.
   [1] = rapt, enraptured.

C

His sailing from Julia.

WHEN that day comes, whose evening sayes I'm
　　　gone
Unto that watrie Desolation :
Devoutly to thy *Closet-gods*[2] then pray,
That my wing'd Ship may meet no *Remora.*[3]
Those Deities which circum-walk the Seas,
And look upon our dreadfull passages,
Will from all dangers, re-deliver me,
For one *drink offering*, pourèd out by thee.
Mercie and *Truth* live with thee ! and forbeare
(In my short absence) to unsluce[4] a teare :
But yet for Loves-sake, let thy lips doe this,
Give my dead picture one engendring kisse :
Work that to life, and let me ever dwell
In thy remembrance (*Julia*).　So farewell.

How the Wall-flower came first, and why so called.

WHY this Flower is now call'd so,
　　　List' sweet maids, and you shal know.

---

[2] = lares, of whom Herrick is so fond.
[3] = hindrance : from the small fish or worm called a sea-lamprey or suckstone, of which it was long a Vulgar Error that by attaching itself to a ship's bottom it arrested its motion.　See Bailey, s. v.
[4] = lift the sluice to make way for a tear.

Understand, this First-ling⁵ was
Once a brisk and bonny Lasse,
Kept as close as *Danae* was :
Who a sprightly *Springall*⁶ lov'd,
And to have it fully prov'd,
Up she got upon a wall,
Tempting down to slide withall :
But the silken twist unty'd,
So she fell, and bruis'd, she dy'd.
Love, in pitty of the deed,
And her loving-lucklesse speed,
Turn'd her to this Plant, we call
Now, *The Flower of the Wall.*

Why Flowers change colour.

THESE fresh beauties (we can prove)
    Once were Virgins sick of love,
Turn'd to Flowers. Still in some
Colours goe, and colours come.

To his Mistresse objecting to him neither Toying or Talking.

YOU say I love not, 'cause I doe not play
    Still with your curles, and kisse the time away.

---

⁵ = first produce or offspring. G. ⁶ = a youth or stripling.

You blame me too, because I cann't devise
Some sport, to please those Babies [7] in your eyes :
By *Loves Religion,* I must here confesse it,
The most I love, when I the least expresse it.
Small griefs find tongues: [8] Full Casques [9] are ever found
To give, (if any, yet) but little sound.
Deep waters noyse-lesse are; And this we know,
That chiding streams betray small depth below. [1]
So when Love speechlesse is, she doth expresse
A depth in love, and that depth, bottomlesse.
Now since my love is tongue-lesse, know me such,
Who speak but little, 'cause I love so much.

[7] = the tiny face-reflection in the pupil of the eyes.   This sportive
conceit, says Dr. Nott, was imagined perhaps before, and certainly
since Herrick wrote.

>   See where little Cupid lies
>   Looking babies in the eyes.
> Thus in our looks some propagation lies,
>   For we make babies in each others eyes.
>   LITTLE, alias MOORE.

[8] A common-place from classical times.   The greatest of all is in
Shakespeare : " The grief that does not speak, whispers the o'er-
fraught heart, and bids it break " (Macbeth iv. 3).

[9] = casks or barrels.   [1] A classical common-place from
Ovid onward, and frequent in the Elizabethan poets.

Upon the losse of his Mistresses.

I HAVE lost, and lately, these
   Many dainty Mistresses :
Stately *Julia*, prime of all ;
Sapho next, a principall :
Smooth *Anthea*, for a skin
White, and Heaven-like Chrystalline :
Sweet *Electra*, and the choice
Myrha, for the Lute, and Voice.
Next, *Corinna*, for her wit,
And the graceful use of it :
With *Perilla :* All are gone ;
Onely *Herrick's* left alone,
For to number sorrow by
Their departures hence, and die.

The Dream.

ME thought (last night) Love in an anger came,
   And brought a rod, so whipt me with the same :
Mirtle the twigs were, meerly to imply,
Love strikes, but 'tis with gentle crueltie.
Patient I was : Love pitifull grew then,
And stroak'd the stripes, and I was whole agen.
Thus like a Bee, *Love-gentle* stil doth bring
Hony to salve, where he before did sting.

The Vine.

I DREAM'D this mortal part of mine
   Was Metamorphoz'd to a Vine ;
Which crawling one and every way,
Enthrall'd my dainty *Lucia.*
Me thought, her long small legs & thighs .
I with my *Tendrils* did surprize ;
Her Belly, Buttocks, and her Waste
By my soft *Nerv'lits*[2] were embrac'd :
About her head I writhing[3] hung,
And with rich clusters (hid among
The leaves) her temples I behung :
So that my *Lucia* seem'd to me
Young *Bacchus* ravisht by his tree.[4]
My curles about her neck did craule,
And armes and hands they did enthrall :
So that she could not freely stir,
(All parts there made one prisoner).
But when I crept with leaves to hide
Those parts, which maids keep unespy'd,
Such fleeting pleasures there I took,
That with the fancie I awook ;
And found (Ah me !) this flesh of mine
More like a *Stock*, then like a *Vine.*

---

² = diminutive of nerves.   ³ = entwining.
⁴ Ivy, the vine—one of many myths concerning Dionysius.

To Love.

I'M free from thee ; aud thou no more shalt heare
　My puling Pipe to beat against thine eare :
Farewell my shackles, (though of pearle they be)
Such precious thraldome ne'r shall fetter me.
He loves his bonds, who when the first are broke,
Submits his neck unto a second yoke.

On himselfe.

YOUNG I was, but now am old,
　　But I am not yet grown cold ;
I can play, and I can' twine
'Bout a Virgin like a Vine :
In her lap too I can lye
Melting, and in fancie die:
And return to life, if she
Claps my cheek, or kisseth me ;
Thus, and thus it now appears
That our love out-lasts our yeeres.

Love's play at Push-pin. [5]

LOVE and my selfe (beleeve me) on a day
　At childish Push-pin (for our sport) did play :
I put, he pusht,[6] and heedless of my skin,
Love prickt my finger with a golden pin :

---

[5] A child-game, with pins 'pushed' alternately. [6] I placed, he pushed.

Since which, it festers so, that I can prove
'Twas but a trick to poyson me with love :
Little the wound was ; greater was the smart ;
The finger bled, but burnt was all my heart.

The Rosarie.

ONE ask'd me where the roses grew ?
    I bade him not goe seek ;
But forthwith bade my *Julia* shew
    A bud in either cheek.[7]

Upon Cupid.

OLD wives have often told, how they
    Saw *Cupid* bitten by a flea :
And thereupon, in tears half drown'd,
He cry'd aloud, Help, help the wound :
He wept, he sobb'd, he call'd to some
To bring him *Lint*, and *Balsamum*,
To make a *Tent*,[8] and put it in,
Where the *Steletto*[9] pierc'd the skin:
Which being done, the fretfull paine
Asswag'd, and he was well again.

---

[7] Cf. 'The Rock of Rubies' onward.
[8] = plug for a wound.   [9] = stilletto or dagger.

The Parcæ, or, *Three dainty Destinies.*

The Armilet.[1]

THREE lovely Sisters working were
  (As they were closely set)
Of soft and dainty Maiden-haire,[2]
  A curious *Armelet.*
I smiling, ask'd them what they did ?
  (Faire *Destinies* all three)
Who told me, they had drawn a thred
  Of Life, and 'twas for me.
They shew'd me then, how fine 'twas spun :
  And I reply'd thereto,
I care not now how soone 'tis done,
  Or cut, if cut by you. .

Sorrowes succeed.

WHEN one is past, another care we have,
  Thus woe succeeds a woe ; as wave a wave.

[1] ▬armlet : armilla, a bracelet worn on the wrist or arm.
[2] ▬A fern so called, found on walls and ruins, with an inner play
on the hair of a maiden.

Cherry-pit.

JULIA and I did lately sit
    Playing for sport, at Cherry-pit : [3]
She threw ; I cast ; and having thrown,
I got the Pit, and she the Stone.

To Robin Red-brest.

LAID out for dead, let thy last kindnesse be
    With leaves and mosse-work for to cover me :
And while the Wood-nimphs my cold corps inter,
Sing thou my Dirge, sweet-warbling Chorister !
For Epitaph, in Foliage, next write this,
    Here, here the Tomb of Robin Herrick is.

Discontents in Devon.

MORE discontents I never had
    Since I was born, then here ;
Where I have bee'n, and still am sad,
    In this dull *Devon-shire :*
Yet justly too I must confesse ;
    I ne'r invented such
Ennobled numbers for the Presse,
    Then where I loath'd so much.

---

[3] A child-game, in which they threw cherry-stones into a small hole: "play at cherry-pit" (Twelfth Night, iii. 4).

To his Paternall Countrey.

O EARTH ! Earth ! Earth ! heare thou my voice,
    and be
Loving, and gentle for to cover me :
Banish'd from thee I live ; ne'r to return,
Unlesse thou giv'st my small Remains an Urne.

Cherrie-ripe.

CHERRIE-ripe, Ripe, Ripe, I cry,
    Full and faire ones ; come and buy :
If so be, you ask me where
They doe grow ? I answer, There,
Where my *Julia's* lips doe smile ;
There's the Land, or Cherry-Ile :
Whose Plantations fully show
All the yeere, where Cherries grow.

To his Mistresses.

PUT on your silks ; and piece by piece
    Give them the scent of Amber-Greece :[4]
And for your breaths too, let them smell
Ambrosia-like, or *Nectarell ;*[5]
While other Gums their sweets perspire,
By your owne jewels set on fire.

---

[4] See Glossarial Index, 2 v.   [5] Probably a new-coined adjective
from nectar — nectar-like.

To Anthea.

NOw is the time, when all the lights wax dim ;
    And thou (*Anthea*) must withdraw from him
Who was thy servant.   Dearest, bury me
Under that *Holy-oke*, or *Gospel-tree :*[6]
Where (though thou see'st not) thou may'st think upon
Me, when thou yeerly go'st Procession :
Or for mine honour, lay me in that Tombe
In which thy sacred Reliques shall have roome.
For my Embalming (Sweetest) there will be
No Spices wanting, when I'm laid by thee.

The Vision to Electra.

I DREAM'D we both were in a bed
    Of Roses, almost smother'd :
The warmth and sweetnes had me there
Made lovingly familiar ;
But that I heard thy sweet breath say,
Faults done by night, will blush by day :
I kist thee (panting), and I call
Night to the Record ! that was all.
But ah ! if empty dreames so please,
Love, give me more such nights as these.

---

[6] At the processions or perambulations of the parish, the Gospel
was read at certain trees, thence called ‘ Gospel trees.’ See Brand
(ed. Hazlitt) i. 112.

Dreames.

H ERE we are all, by day : By night w'are hurl'd
By dreames, each one, into a sev'rall world.

Ambition.

I N man, Ambition is the common'st thing ;
Each one, by nature, loves to be a king.

His request to Julia.

J *ULIA,* if I chance to die
Ere I print my Poetry ;
I most humbly thee desire
To commit it to the fire :
Better 'twere my Book were dead,
Then to live not perfected.

Money gets the masterie.

F IGHT thou with shafts of silver, and o'rcome,
When no force else can get the masterdome.

The Scar-fire.[7]

W ATER, water I desire,
Here's a house of flesh on fire :

[7] ■ a fright by fire : query—a beacon of alarm (as of invasion).

Ope' the fountains and the springs,
And come all to Buckittings :[8]
What ye cannot quench, pull downe ;
Spoile a house, to save a towne :
Better 'tis that one shu'd fall,
Then by one to hazard all.

Upon Silvia, *a Mistresse.*

WHEN some shall say, Faire once my *Silvia* was ;
    Thou wilt complaine, False now's thy Looking-
        glasse :
Which renders that quite tarnisht, which was green ;
And Priceless[9] now, what Peerless once had been :
Upon thy Forme more wrinkles yet will fall,
And comming downe, shall make no noise at all.

Cheerfulnesse in Charitie : or,
The sweet Sacrifice.

TIS not a thousand Bullocks thies
    Can please those Heav'nly Deities,
If the Vower don't express
In his Offering, Cheerfulness.

---

[8] = filling of buckets.   [9] = valueless.

Once poore, still penurious.

GOES the world now, it will with thee goe hard :
    The fattest Hogs we grease the more with Lard.
To him that has, there shall be added more ;
Who is penurious, he shall still be poore.

Sweetnesse in Sacrifice.

'TIS not greatness they require,
    To be offer'd up by fire :
But 'tis sweetness that doth please
Those Eternall Essences.

Steame in Sacrifice.

IF meat the Gods give, I the steame
    High-towring wil devote to them :
Whose easie natures like it well,
If we the roste have, they the smell.

Upon Julia's *Voice.*

SO smooth, so sweet, so silv'ry is thy voice,
    As, could they hear, the Damn'd would make no
        noise ;
But listen to thee, (walking in thy chamber)
Melting melodious words to Lutes of Amber.[1]

---

[1] Amber was used to adorn musical instruments : here used by
stress of rhyme.

Againe.

WHEN I thy singing next shall heare,
 Ile wish I might turne all to eare,[2]
To drink in Notes, and Numbers ; such
As blessed soules cann't heare too much :
Then melted down, there let me lye
 Entranc'd, and lost confusedly ;
And by thy Musique strucken mute,
Die and be turn'd into a Lute.

All things decay and die.

ALL *things decay with Time :* The Forrest sees
 The growth, and down-fall of her aged trees ;
That Timber tall, which three-score *lusters* stood
The proud *Dictator* of the State-like wood :[3]
I meane (the Soveraigne of all Plants) the Oke
Droops, dies, and falls without the cleavers stroke.

The succession of the foure sweet months.

FIRST, *April,* she with mellow showrs
 Opens the way for early flowers ;
Then after her comes smiling *May,*
In a more rich and sweet aray ;

---

[2] Cf. Milton "all ear to hear" (P. L. IV. l. 410).
[3] Cf. Keats, " those green-robed senators of mighty woods."

Next enters *June*, and brings us more
Jems, then those two, that went before :
Then (lastly) *July* comes, and she
More wealth brings in, then all those three.

No Shipwrack of Vertue.   To a friend.

THOU sail'st with others in this *Argus* here ;
    Nor wrack or *Bulging*[4] thou hast cause to feare :
But trust to this, my noble passenger ;
Who swims with Vertue, he shall still be sure
(*Ulysses*-like) all tempests to endure ;
And 'midst a thousand gulfs to be secure.

Upon his Sister-in-Law, Mistresse
Elizab : Herrick.

FIRST, for Effusions [5] due unto the dead,
    My solemne Vowes have here accomplishèd :
Next, how I love thee, that my griefe must tell,
Wherein thou liv'st for ever.   Deare farewell.

Of Love.   A Sonet.

HOW Love came in, I do not know,
    Whether by th' eye, or eare, or no ;

---

[4] Originally bilging, from bilge or the lower part of a ship, where
it swells out.   [5] =outpourings.

D

Or whether with the soule it came
(At first) infusèd with the same ;
Whether in part 'tis here or there,
Or, like the soule, whole every where :
This troubles me : but I as well
As any other, this can tell ;
That when from hence she does depart,
The out-let then is from the heart.

To Anthea.[6]

AH my *Anthea !* Must my heart still break ?
    (Love makes me write, what shame forbids to
        speak.)
Give me a kisse, and to that kisse a score ;
Then to that twenty, adde an hundred more :
A thousand to that hundred : so kisse on,
To make that thousand up a million.
Treble that million, and when that is done,
Let's kisse afresh, as when we first begun.
But yet, though Love likes well such Scenes as these,
There is an Act that will more fully please :
Kissing and glancing, soothing, all make way
But to the acting of this private Play :
Name it I would ; but being blushing red,
The rest Ile speak, when we meet both in bed.

     [6] Imitation of Catullus in the first eight lines.

The Rock of Rubies : and
The quarrie of Pearls.[7]

SOME ask'd me where the *Rubies* grew?
   And nothing I did say :
But with my finger pointed to
   The lips of *Julia.*
Some ask'd how *Pearls* did grow, and where?
   Then spoke I to my Girle,
To part her lips, and shew'd them there
   The Quarelets[8] of Pearl.

Conformitie.

CONFORMITY was ever knowne
   A foe to Dissolution :
Nor can we that a ruine call,
   Whose crack gives crushing unto all.

TO THE KING, Upon his comming with his
   Army into the West.[9]

WELCOME, most welcome to our Vowes and us,
   Most great, and universall *Genius !*

---

[7] Cf. ' The Rosarie ' before.

[8] A 'quarrel' is anything squared, glass, stone, tile, &c. (Fr : Quarreau, verb quarrer, to square). A stone-quarry in various English counties is called a ' quarrel.'

[9] The King pursued Essex into Cornwall in August, 1644, where he forced him to capitulate—a brief success in abounding disaster.

The Drooping West, which hitherto has stood
As one, in long-lamented-widow-hood,
Looks like a Bride now, or a bed of flowers,
Newly refresh't, both by the Sun, and showers.
War, which before was horrid, now appears
Lovely in you, brave Prince of Cavaliers !
A deale of courage [1] in each bosome springs
By your accesse ; *(O you the best of Kings !)*
Ride on with all white [2] *Omens ;* so that where,
Your Standard's up, we fix a Conquest there.

Upon Roses.

U NDER a Lawne, then skyes more cleare,
       Some ruffled Roses nestling were :
And snugging [3] there, they seem'd to lye
As in a flowrie Nunnery :
They blush'd, and look'd more fresh then flowers [*than*
Quickned of late by Pearly showers ;
And all, because they were possest
But of the heat of *Julia's* breast :
Which as a warme, and moistned spring,
Gave them their ever flourishing.

[1] See Glossarial Index, s. v.
[2] = auspicious. See Glossarial Index, s. v.
[3] Snug—to lie close, to snudge.

HESPERIDES.

To the King and Queene, upon their
unhappy distances.[4]

WOE, woe to them, who (by a ball of strife)
    Doe, and have parted here a Man and Wife :
CHARLS the best Husband, while MARIA strives
To be, and is, the very best of Wives :
Like Streams, you are divorc'd ; but 't will come, when
These eyes of mine shall see you mix agen.
Thus speaks the *Oke*,[5] here ; C. and M. shall meet,
Treading on *Amber*, with their silver-feet :
Nor wil't be long, ere this accomplish'd be ;
The words found true, C. M. remember me.

Dangers wait on Kings.

AS oft as Night is banish'd by the Morne,
    So oft, we'll think, we see a King new born.

The Cheat of Cupid : or,
The ungentle guest.[6]

ONE silent night of late,
    When every creature rested,

---

[4] The Queen's absence from England is doubtless merely intended, but there were rumours of domestic strife and consequent coldness, or 'distances.'   [5] = the oracular tree, as the oaks of Dodona.
[6] Anacreon : Ode 3 imitated.

Came one unto my gate,
　　And knocking, me molested.

Who's that (said I) beats there,
　　And troubles thus the Sleepie?
Cast off (said he) all feare,
　　And let not Locks thus keep ye.

For I a Boy am, who
　　By Moonlesse nights[7] have swerved ;[8]
And all with showrs wet through,
　　And e'en with cold half starved.

I pittifull arose,
　　And soon a Taper lighted ;
And did my selfe disclose
　　Unto the lad benighted.

I saw he had a Bow,
　　And Wings too, which did shiver ;
And looking down below,
　　I spy'd he had a Quiver.

I to my Chimney's shine
　　Brought him (as Love professes)

---

[7] " In the hush of moonless nights," Tennyson.
[8] = strayed or roved.

And chaf'd his hands with mine,
　And dry'd his dropping Tresses :

But when he felt him warm'd,
　Let's try this bow of ours,
And string, if they be harm'd,
　Said he, with these late showrs.

Forthwith his bow he bent,
　And wedded string and arrow,
And struck me, that it went
　Quite through my heart and marrow.

Then laughing loud, he flew
　Away, and thus said flying,
Adieu, mine Host, Adieu,
　Ile leave thy heart a dying.

*To the reverend shade of his religious
Father.*

THAT for seven *Lusters* I did never come
　To doe the *Rites* to thy Religious Tombe ;
That neither haire was cut, or true teares shed
By me, o'r thee, *(as justments[9] to the dead)*

---

[9] From the Latin *justa*, funeral obsequies : query—a coinage of
Herrick ?

Forgive, forgive me; since I did not know
Whether thy bones had here their Rest, or no.[1]
But now 'tis known, Behold; behold, I bring
Unto thy Ghost th' Effusèd Offering:
And look, what Smallage,[2] Night-shade, Cypresse, Yew,
Unto the shades have been, or now are due,
Here I devote;[3] And something more then so;
I come to pay a Debt of Birth I owe.
Thou gav'st me life (but Mortall); For that one
Favour, Ile make full satisfaction;
For my life mortall, Rise from out thy Herse,
And take a life immortall from my Verse.

Delight in Disorder.

A SWEET disorder in the dresse
    Kindles in cloathes a wantonnesse:
A Lawne about the shoulders thrown
Into a fine distraction:
An erring[4] Lace, which here and there
Enthralls the Crimson Stomacher:

---

[1] Herrick was a baby of a year old only when his father died; but on this somewhat enigmatical celebration of him see our Memorial-Introduction. Line 2nd 'seven Lusters' is = 35 years, *i. e.* 1626 for date of composition.

[2] Herb. See Glossarial Index, s. v.   [3] = dedicate or consecrate.

[4] = wandering.

A Cuffe neglectfull, and thereby
Ribbands to flow confusedly :
A winning wave (deserving Note)
In the tempestuous petticote :
A carelesse shooe-string, in whose tye
I see a wilde civility :[5]
Doe more bewitch me, then when Art   [*than*
Is too precise in every part.

To his Muse.

WERE I to give thee *Baptime*,[6] I wo'd chuse
    To *Christen* thee, the *Bride*, the *Bashfull*
    Muse,
Or *Muse* of *Roses :* since that name does fit
Best with those *Virgin-verses* thou hast writ :
Which are so cleane, so chast, as none may feare
Cato the *Censor*, sho'd he scan each here.

Upon Love.

LOVE scorch'd my finger, but did spare
    The burning of my heart ;

---

[5] = good manners, easiness. Milton has " civil-suited morn."
(Il Penseroso, l. 122): later Dryden, "the sweet civilities of life."
See Memorial-Introduction for Ben Jonson's song in The Silent
Woman, " Still to be neat, still to be drest," &c.
   [6] = baptism. Query : from the French Baptême ?

To signifie, in Love my share
    Sho'd be a little part.

Little I love ; but if that he
    Wo'd but that heat recall :
That joynt to ashes sho'd be burnt,
    Ere I wo'd love at all.

To Dean-bourn, *a rude River in* Devon : *by
    which sometimes he lived.*

DEAN-BOURN, farewell ; I never look to see
    Deane, or thy watry incivility.
Thy rockie bottome, that doth teare thy streams,
And makes them frantick, ev'n to all extreames ;
To my content, I never sho'd behold,
Were thy streames silver, or thy rocks all gold.
Rockie thou art ; and rockie we discover
Thy men ; and rockie are thy wayes all over.
O men, O manners ; There and ever knowne
To be *A Rockie Generation !*
A people currish ; churlish as the seas ;
And rude (almost) as rudest Salvages :[7]
With whom I did, and may re-sojourne when
Rockes turn to Rivers, Rivers turn to Men.

[7] =savages or uncivilized.

Kissing Usurie.

B*IANCHA*, Let
    Me pay the debt
I owe thee for a kisse
    Thou lend'st to me ;
    And I to thee
Will render ten for this :

    If thou wilt say,
    Ten will not pay
For that so rich a one ;
    Ile cleare the summe,
    If it will come
Unto a Million.

    He must of right,
    To th'utmost mite,
Make payment for his pleasure ;[8]
    By this, I guesse,
    Of happinesse
Who has a little measure.

[8] By Hazlitt and others the commencement is put first in this stanza. Dr. Nott annotates—These lines breathe of Catullus and Secundus. See of the former Carmen 5 ; and of the latter Basiam 6.

To Julia.

HOW rich and pleasing thou, my *Julia* art,
    In each thy dainty, and peculiar part !
First, for thy *Queen-ship* on thy head is set
Of flowers a sweet commingled Coronet :
About thy neck a Carkanet [9] is bound,
Made of the *Rubie, Pearle, and Diamond :*
A golden ring, that shines upon thy thumb : [1]
About thy wrist, the rich *Dardanium.* [2]
Between thy Breasts (then Doune of Swans more white)
There playes the *Saphire* with the *Chrysolite.*
No part besides must of thy selfe be known,
But by the *Topaze, Opal, Calcedon.*

To Laurels.

A FUNERALL stone,
    Or Verse I covet none,
      But onely crave
    Of you, that I may have
A sacred Laurel springing from my grave :
    Which being seen,
      Blest with perpetuall greene,

---

[9] = chain for the neck, as before.
[1] Rings used to be, oddly enough, worn on the thumb.
[2] *A Bracelet, from Dardanus so call'd.* H.

May grow to be
Not so much call'd a tree,
As the eternall monument of me.

His Cavalier.

GIVE me that man, that dares bestride
The active sea-horse, & with pride,
Through that huge field of waters ride :[3]

Who, with his looks too, can appease
The ruffling winds and raging Seas,
In mid'st of all their outrages.

This, this a virtuous man can doe,
Saile against Rocks, and split them too ;
I ! and a world of Pikes passe through.

Zeal required in Love.

I'LE doe my best to win, when'ere I wooe :
That man loves not, who is not zealous too.

The Bag of the Bee.

ABOUT the sweet bag of a Bee,
Two *Cupids* fell at odds ;

---

[3] Cf. Byron of the Sea in close of Childe Harrold :—
　　　"I was as it were a child of thee,
　　　And trusted to thy billows far and near,
　　　And laid my hands upon thy mane."

And whose the pretty prize shu'd be,
   They vow'd to ask the Gods.

Which *Venus* hearing, thither came,
   And for their boldness stript them :
And taking thence from each his flame ;
   With rods of *Mirtle* whipt them.

Which done, to still their wanton cries,
   When quiet grown sh'ad seen them,
She kist, and wip'd thir dove-like eyes ;
   And gave the Bag between them.[4]

Love kill'd by Lack.

LET me be warme ; let me be fully fed :
   Luxurious Love by Wealth is nourishèd.
Let me be leane, and cold, and once grown poore,
I shall dislike, what once I lov'd before.

To his Mistresse.

CHOOSE me your Valentine :[5]
   Next, let us marry :

---

[4] This little elegant composition is likewise found in a collection
of poetry entitled, *Wit a sporting in a Pleasant Grove of new Fancies,*
by H. B. 1657. N.

[5] No chronicle affords us any satisfactory information respecting
the rites of Saint Valentine, a Roman bishop beheaded under the

Love to the death will pine,
  If we long tarry.

Promise, and keep your vowes,
  Or vow ye never :
Loves doctrine disallowes
  Troth-breakers ever.

You have broke promise twice
  (Deare) to undoe me ;
If you'prove faithlesse thrice,
  None then will wooe you.

To the generous Reader.

S EE, and not see ; and if thou chance t'espie
  Some Aberrations in my Poetry ;
Wink at small faults, the greater, ne'rthelesse
Hide, and with them, their Father's nakedness.
Let's doe our best, our Watch and Ward to keep :
Homer himself, in a long work, may sleep.[6]

---

emperor Claudius, whose festival is observed on the 14th of February.
There is a rural tradition, that about this period birds chuse their
mates ; and it is a very ancient custom, on the day of the festival,
for young people, particularly among the lower orders, to select Val-
entines, or sweethearts, by drawing of lots. N. See Brand s. n.
Chaucer and Lydgate celebrate the festival.

  ⁶ Quandoque bonus dormitat Homerus.   Horace : Art. Poet.,
l. 359.

To Criticks.

ILE write, because Ile give
　　You Criticks means to live :
For sho'd I not supply
The Cause, th'effect wo'd die.

Duty to Tyrants.

GOOD princes must be pray'd for : for the bad
　　They must be borne with, and in rev'rence had.
Doe they first pill⁷ thee, next, pluck off thy skin ?
Good children kisse the rods, that punish sin.
Touch not the Tyrant ; Let the Gods alone
To strike him dead, that but usurps a Throne.

Being once blind, his request to Biancha.

WHEN age or Chance has made me blind,
　　So that the path I cannot find :
And when my falls and stumblings are
More then the stones i'th' street by farre :
Goe thou afore ; and I shall well
Follow thy Perfumes by the smell :
Or be my guide ; and I shall be
Led by some light that flows from thee.
Thus held, or led by thee, I shall
In wayes confus'd, nor slip or fall.

---

⁷ = strip or peel : hence to spoil, to take away.

Upon Blanch.

BLANCH swears her Husband's lovely; when a
 scald
Has blear'd his eyes : Besides, his head is bald.
Next, his wilde eares, like Lethern wings full spread,
Flutter to flie, and beare away his head.

No want where there's little.

TO Bread and Water none is poore ;
 And having these, what need of more ?
Though much from out the Cess[8] be spent,
Nature with little is content.

Barly-Break : or, Last in Hell.[9]

WE two are last in Hell : what may we feare
 To be tormented, or kept Pris'ners here ?
Alas ! If kissing be of plagues the worst,
We'll wish, in Hell we had been Last and First.

The Definition of Beauty.

BEAUTY, no other thing is, then a Beame
 Flasht out between the Middle and Extreame.

---

[8] = the count or accompt, *i. e.* the (total of the) income.
[9] A country game, celebrated finely by Sidney : Poems in Fuller
Worthies' Library, ii. 36 et seq.

To Dianeme.

DEARE, though to part it be a Hell,
    Yet *Dianemè*, now farewell :
Thy frown (last night) did bid me goe ;
But whither, onely Grief do's know.
I doe beseech thee, ere we part,
(If mercifull, as faire thou art ;
Or else desir'st that Maids sho'd tell
Thy pitty by Loves-Chronicle)
O *Dianemè*, rather kill
Me, then to make me languish stil !
'Tis cruelty in thee to'th'height,
Thus, thus to wound, not kill out-right :
Yet there's a way found (if thou please)
By sudden death to give me ease :
And thus devis'd, doe thou but this,
Bequeath to me one parting kisse :
So sup'rabundant joy shall be
The Executioner of me.

To Anthea *lying in bed.*

SO looks *Anthea*, when in bed she lyes,
    Orecome, or halfe betray'd by Tiffanies : [1]

---

[1] = fine silk or gauze, as before.

Like to a Twi-light, or that simpring[2] Dawn,

That Roses shew, when misted o're with Lawn.

Twilight is yet, till that her Lawnes give way;

Which done, that Dawne, turnes then to perfect day.

To Electra.

MORE white then whitest Lillies far,

    Or Snow, or whitest Swans you are :

More white then are the whitest Creames,   [*than*

Or Moone-light tinselling the streames :

More white then Pearls, or *Juno's* thigh ;

Or *Pelops* Arme of *Yvorie.*

True, I confesse ; such Whites as these

May me delight, not fully please :

Till, like *Ixion's* cloud[3] you be

White, warme, and soft to lye with me.

A Country-life : to his Brother,
M. Tho : Herrick.[4]

THRICE, and above, blest (my soules halfe) art

    thou,

    In thy both **Last,** and **Better Vow :**

---

[2] ⸺pleasant—as a smile : deteriorated since.
[3] ⸺the cloud in which Juno lay with him.
[4] See Memorial-Introduction on this brother.

Could'st leave the City, for exchange, to see
 The Countries sweet simplicity :
And it to know, and practice ; with intent
 To grow the sooner innocent :
By studying to know vertue ; and to aime
 More at her nature, then her name : [*than*
The last is but the least ; the first doth tell
 Wayes lesse to live, then to live well :
And both are knowne to thee, who now can'st live
 Led by thy conscience ; to give
Justice to soone-pleas'd nature ; and to show,
 Wisdome and she together goe,
And keep one Centre : This with that conspires,
 To teach Man to confine desires ;
And know, that Riches have their proper stint,[5]
 In the contented mind, not mint.
And can'st instruct, that those who have the itch
 Of craving more, are never rich.
These things thou know'st to'th'height, and dost
  prevent
 That plague ; because thou art content
With that Heav'n gave thee with a warie hand,
 (More blessed in thy Brasse,[6] then Land)

---

[5] = quantity.   [6] = cash : a vulgarism since.

To keep cheap Nature even, and upright ;
  To coole, not cocker [7] Appetite.
Thus thou canst tearcely [8] live to satisfie
  The belly chiefly ; not the eye :
Keeping the barking stomach wisely quiet,
  Lesse with a neat,[9] then needfull diet.   [*than*
But that which most makes sweet thy country life,
  Is, the fruition of a wife :
Whom (stars consenting with thy Fate) thou hast
  Got, not so beautifull, as chast :
By whose warme side thou dost securely sleep
  (While Love the Centinell doth keep)
With those deeds done by day, which n'er affright
  Thy silken slumbers in the night.
Nor has the darknesse power to usher in
  Feare to those sheets, that know no sin.
But still thy wife, by chast intentions led,
  Gives thee each night a Maidenhead.
The Damaskt medowes, and the peebly streames
  Sweeten, and make soft your dreames : [1]
The Purling springs, groves, birds, and well-weav'd
  Bowrs,
  With fields enameled with flowers,

---

[7] = pamper.   [8] = cleanly.   [9] = elegant.
[1] Intentionally a syllable short, as in others following.

Present their shapes ; while fantasie discloses
  Millions of *Lillies* mixt with *Roses.*
Then dream, ye heare the Lamb by many a bleat
  Woo'd to come suck the milkie Teat :
While *Faunus* in the Vision comes to keep,
  From rav'ning wolves, the fleecie sheep.
With thousand such enchanting dreams, that meet
  To make sleep not so sound, as sweet :
Nor can these figures so thy rest endeare,
  As not to rise when *Chanticlere*
Warnes the last Watch ; but with the Dawne dost rise
  To work, but first to sacrifice ;
Making thy peace with heav'n, for some late fault,
  With Holy-meale, and spirting-salt.[2]
Which done, thy painfull Thumb[3] this sentence tells us
  Jove for our labour all things sells us.
Nor are thy daily and devout affaires
  Attended with those desp'rate cares,
Th' industrious Merchant has ; who for to find
  Gold, runneth to the Western Inde,
And back again, (tortur'd with fears) doth fly,
  Untaught to suffer Poverty.
But thou at home, blest with securest ease,
  Sitt'st, and beleev'st that there be seas,

---

[2] Folk-lore. But cf. Leviticus c. ii.   [3] *Ibid*, but cf. S. Mark
ix. 49.

And watrie dangers ; while thy whiter hap,
    But sees these things within thy Map.
And viewing them with a more safe survey,
    Mak'st easie Feare unto thee say,
A heart thrice wall'd with Oke, and brasse, that man
    Had, first, durst plow the Ocean.[4]
But thou at home without or tyde or gale,
    Canst in thy Map securely saile :
Seeing those painted Countries ; and so guesse
    By those fine Shades, their Substances :
And from thy Compasse taking small advice,
    Buy'st Travell at the lowest price.
Nor are thine eares so deafe, but thou canst heare,
    (Far more with wonder, then with feare) [*than*
Fame tell of States, of Countries, Courts, and Kings ;
    And beleeve there be such things :[5]
When of these truths, thy happyer knowledge lyes,
    More in thine eares, then in thine eyes.
And when thou hear'st by that too-true-Report,
    Vice rules the Most, or All at Court :
Thy pious wishes are, (though thou not there)
    Vertue had, and mov'd her Sphere.
But thou liv'st fearlesse ; and thy face ne'r shewes
    Fortune when she comes, or goes.

[4] Horace : Illi robur, &c., Odes i. 3.
[5] See previous note on a lacking syllable.

But with thy equall thoughts, prepar'd dost stand,
   To take her by the either hand :
Nor car'st which comes the first, the foule or faire ;
   A wise man ev'ry way lies square.[6]
And like a surly *Oke* with storms perplext ;
   Growes still the stronger, strongly vext.
Be so, bold spirit ; Stand Center-like, unmov'd ;
   And be not onely thought, but prov'd
To be what I report thee ; and inure
   Thy selfe, if want comes to endure :
And so thou dost : for thy desires are
   Confin'd to live with private *Larr :* [7]
Not curious whether Appetite be fed,
   Or with the first, or second bread.
Who keep'st no proud mouth for delicious cates :
   Hunger makes coorse meats, delicates.
Can'st, and unurg'd, forsake that Larded fare,
   Which Art, not Nature, makes so rare ;
To taste boyl'd Nettles, Colworts, Beets, and eate
   These, and sowre herbs, as dainty meat ?

---

[6] Tennyson : " four-square to all the winds that blow." Originally quoted by Aristotle (Ethics i. 11, and Rhetoric iii. 11, 2) from
Simonides : traced back to Pythagoras.

[7] = Household god or house itself. ' Lara ' was a later mythical
coinage to acconnt for the existence of the Lar. See Glossarial Index
s. v.

While soft Opinion makes thy _Genius_ say,
    Content makes all Ambrosia.
Nor is it, that thou keep'st this stricter size [8]
    So much for want, as exercise :
To numb the sence of Dearth, which sho'd sinne
        haste it,
    Thou might'st but onely see't, not taste it.
Yet can thy humble roofe maintaine a Quire
    Of singing Crickits by thy fire :
And the brisk Mouse may feast her selfe with crums,
    Till that the green-ey'd Kitling comes.
Then to her Cabbin, blest she can escape
    The sudden danger of a Rape.
And thus thy little-well-kept stock doth prove,
    Wealth cannot make a life, but Love.
Nor art thou so close-handed, but can'st spend
    (Counsell concurring with the end)
As well as spare : still conning o'r this Theame,
    To shun the first, and last extreame.
Ordaining that thy small stock find no breach,
    Or to exceed thy Tether's reach :
But to live round, and close, and wisely true
    To thine owne selfe ; [9] and knowne to few.

---

[8] =assize.   [9] " To thine own self be true " (Hamlet i. 3).

Thus let thy Rurall Sanctuary be
    Elizium to thy wife and thee;
There to disport your selves with golden measure :
    For seldome [1] *use commends the pleasure.*
Live, and live blest; thrice happy Paire ; Let Breath,
    But lost to one, be th' others death.
And as there is one Love, one Faith, one Troth,
    Be so one Death, one Grave to both. [2]
Till when, in such assurance live, ye may
    Nor feare, or wish your dying day.

Divination by a Daffadill.

WHEN a Daffadill I see,
    Hanging down his head t'wards me ;
Guesse I may, what I must be :
First, I shall decline my head ;
Secondly, I shall be dead ;
Lastly, safely buryèd.

[1] = unfrequent.
[2] " We two will die the self-same day." Tennyson.

To the Painter, to draw him a Picture.

COME, skilfull *Lupo*[3], now, and take
　　Thy Bice,[4] thy *Vmber*,[5] *Pink*, and *Lake ;*[6]
And let it be thy Pensils strife,
To paint a Bridgeman[7] to the life :
Draw him as like too, as you can,
An old, poore, lying, flatt'ring man :
His cheeks be-pimpled, red and blue ;
His nose and lips of mulbrie hiew.
Then for an easie fansie ; place
A Burling[8] iron for his face :
Next, make his cheeks with breath to swell,
And for to speak, if possible :
But do not so ; for feare, lest he
Sho'd by his breathing, poyson thee.

---

[3] Martial ?　[4] A painting colour, either green or blue. Bailey s. v.

[5] A dark and yellowish colour, so called from *umbra*, a shadow.

[6] A darker colour and not so rich as carmine—further removed from vermilion than carmine.

[7] Query—a real name of some (now forgotten) parishioner ?　It is a Devonshire name, usually misprinted here ' bridgeman.'

[8] = pincers or nippers.

Upon Cuffe. *Epig.*

CUFFE comes to church much ; but he keeps
    his bed
Those Sundayes onely, whenas Briefs [9] are read.
This makes *Cuffe* dull ; and troubles him the most,
Because he cannot sleep i'th' Church, free-cost.

Upon Fone *a School-master.* Epig.

FONE sayes, those mighty whiskers he do's weare
    Are twigs of Birch, and willow, growing there :
If so, we'll think too (when he do's condemne
Boyes to the lash) that he do's whip with them.

A Lyrick to Mirth.

WHILE the milder Fates consent,
    Let's enjoy our merryment :
    Drink, and dance, and pipe, and play ;
    Kisse our *Dollies* [1] night and day :
    Crown'd with clusters of the Vine ;
    Let us sit, and quaffe our wine.

---

[9] = letters-patent or licence for a collection for some charitable object.

[1] = sweet-hearts : deteriorated to prostitutes provincially, albeit a 'dolly-mop' is still distinct from the open prostitute. Burns uses it in his " Jolly Beggars," under the form of 'doxy,'
    " His doxy lay within his arm " (l. 18).

Call on *Bacchus ;* chaunt his praise ;
Shake the *Thyrse,* and bite the *Bayes :*
Rouze *Anacreon* from the dead ;
And return him drunk to bed :
Sing o're *Horace ;* for ere long
Death will come and mar the song :
Then shall *Wilson* [2] and *Gotiere* [3]
Never sing, or play more here.

To the Earle of Westmerland. [4]

WHEN my date's done, and my gray age
    must die ;
Nurse up, great Lord, this my posterity :
Weak though it be ; long may it grow, and stand,
Shor'd [5] up by you, *(Brave Earle of Westmerland.)*

---

[2] A celebrated composer and musician. See Memorial-Introduction.

[3] In the errata this is corrected from ' Goteire ' to Gotiere ' : query —guitar? (See Glossarial Index, s. v.) Certainly no composer of the name is known, albeit spelling his name Goutire, Dr. Nott describes him as "a celebrated musical composer and lutanist, much in favour with Charles the First." Probably in its variants it is the French form of Walter. A friend informs me ' Cutierrer ' is a common Spanish name.

[4] This was Mildmay Fane, second Earl of Westmoreland. He succeeded to the title on the death of his father, on 23rd March, 1628-9 ; was twice married : died 12th Feb., 1665-6, and was buried at Apthorpe co., Northampton. He was a Poet—as noticed onward.

[5] = propped.

Against Love.

WHEN ere my heart, Love's warmth, but enter-
    taines,
O Frost ! O Snow ! O Haile ! forbid the Banes.[6]
One drop now deads a spark ; but if the same
Once gets a force, Floods cannot quench the flame
Rather then love, let me be ever lost ;   [*than*
Or let me 'gender with eternall frost.

Upon Julia's *Riband.*

AS shews the Aire, when with a Rain-bow grac'd ;
    So smiles that Riband 'bout my *Julia's* waste : [7]
Or like——Nay 'tis that *Zonulet* [8] of love,
Wherein all pleasures of the world are wove.

The frozen Zone : or, Julia *disdainfull.*

WHITHER ? Say, whither shall I fly,
    To slack these flames wherein I frie ? [9]
To the Treasures, shall I goe,
Of the Raine, Frost, Haile, and Snow ?

---

[6] = bans.
[7] = waist. See Glossarial Index s. v.   [8] Diminutive of zone.
[9] Often used as Herrick does by Crashaw : deteriorated since.

Shall I search the under-ground,
Where all Damps and Mists are found?
Shall I seek (for speedy ease)
All the floods, and frozen seas?
Or descend into the deep,
Where eternall cold does keep?
These may coole; but there's a Zone
Colder yet then any one:
That's my *Julia's* breast: where dwels
Such destructive Ysicles;
As that the Congelation will
Me sooner starve, then those can kill.

An Epitaph upon a sober Matron.

WITH blamelesse carriage, I liv'd here,
    To' th' (almost) sev'n and fortieth yeare.
Stout sons I had, and those twice three;
One onely daughter lent to me:
The which was made a happy Bride,
But thrice three Moones before she dy'd.
My modest wedlock, that was known
Contented with the bed of one.

To the Patron of Poets, M. End : Porter.[1]

LET there be Patrons; Patrons like to thee,
    Brave *Porter !* Poets ne'r will wanting be :
Fabius, and *Cotta, Lentulus*, all live
In thee, thou Man of Men ! who here do'st give
Not onely subject-matter for our wit,
But likewise Oyle of Maintenance to it :
For which, before thy Threshold, we'll lay downe
Our Thyrse, for Scepter ; and our Baies for Crown.
For to say truth, all Garlands are thy due ;
The *Laurell, Mirtle, Oke*, and *Ivie* too.

The sadnesse of things for Sapho's *sicknesse.*

LILLIES will languish ; Violets look ill ;
    Sickly the Prim-rose ; Pale the Daffadill :
That gallant Tulip will hang down his head,
Like to a Virgin newly ravishèd.
Pansies will weep ; and Marygolds will wither ;
And keep a Fast, and Funerall together,
If *Sapho* droop ; Daisies will open never,
But bid Good-night, and close their lids for ever.

---

[1] One of the Wits of the period, but more famous for the many verse and prose tributes paid him by contemporaries. He seems to have been a kind of more prudent Benlowes, though not like him, a poet. See Memorial-Introduction.

Leanders *Obsequies.*

WHEN as *Leander* young was drown'd,
  No heart by love receiv'd a wound ;
But on a Rock himselfe sate by,
There weeping sup'rabundantly.
Sighs numberlesse he cast about,
And all his Tapers thus put out :
His head upon his hand he laid ;
And sobbing deeply, thus he said,
Ah, cruell Sea ! and looking on't,
Wept as he'd drowne the Hellespont.
And sure his tongue had more exprest,
But that his teares forbad the rest.

Hope heartens.

NONE goes to warfare, but with this intent ;
  The gaines must dead the feare of detriment.

Foure things make us happy here.

HEALTH is the first good lent to men ;
  A gentle disposition then :
Next, to be rich by no by-wayes ;
Lastly, with friends t'enjoy our dayes.[2]

---

[2] From a Greek Scolion, doubtfully ascribed to Simonides : cf.
Fragments, &c.

His parting from Mrs. Dorothy Keneday.[3]

WHEN I did goe from thee, I felt that smart,
    Which Bodies do, when Souls from them depart.
Thou did'st not mind it ; though thou then might'st see
Me turn'd to tears ; yet did'st not weep for me.
'Tis true, I kist thee ; but I co'd not heare
Thee spend a sigh, t'accompany my teare.
Me thought 'twas strange, that thou so hard sho'dst
        prove,
Whose heart, whose hand, whose ev'ry part spake love.
Prethee (lest Maids sho'd censure thee) but say
Thou shed'st one teare, whenas I went away ;
And that will please me somewhat : though I know,
And Love will swear't, my Dearest did not so.

The Teare sent to her from Stanes.[4]

1. GLIDE, gentle streams, and beare
        Along with you my teare
            To that coy Girle ;
            Who smiles, yet slayes
            Me with delayes ;
        And strings my tears as Pearle.

---

[3] See Memorial-Introduction on this friend.
[4] See Memorial-Introduction : = Stains, the royal residence.

2. See ! see, she's yonder set,
 Making a Carkanet
  Of Maiden-flowers !
  There, there present
  This Orient,
 And Pendant Pearle of ours.

3. Then say, I've sent one more
 Jem to enrich her store ;
  And that is all
  Which I can send,
  Or vainly spend,
 For tears no more will fall.

4. Nor will I seek supply
 Of them, the spring's once drie ;
  But Ile devise,
  (Among the rest)
  A way that's best
 How I may save mine eyes.

5. Yet say ; sho'd she condemne
 Me to surrender them ;
  Then say ; my part
  Must be to weep
  Out them, to keep
 A poore, yet loving heart.

6. Say too, She wo'd have this ;
　　She shall : Then my hope is,
　　　　That when I'm poore,
　　　　And nothing have ·
　　　　To send, or save ;
　　I'm sure she'll ask no more.

Upon one Lillie, *who marryed with a maid*
call'd Rose.

WHAT times of sweetnesse this faire day fore-
　　shows,
Whenas the Lilly marries with the Rose !
What next is lookt for? but we all sho'd see
To spring from these a sweet Posterity.

An Epitaph upon a child.

VIRGINS promis'd when I dy'd,
　　That they wo'd each Primrose-tide,
Duely, Morne and Ev'ning, come,
And with flowers dresse my Tomb.
Having promis'd, pay your debts,
Maids, and here strew Violets.

Upon Scobble. *Epig.*

S COBBLE⁵ for Whoredome whips his wife ; and
    cryes,
He'll slit her nose ; But blubb'ring, she replyes,
Good Sir, make no more cuts i'th' outward skin,
One slit's enough to let Adultry in.

The Houre-glasse.

T HAT Houre-glasse, which there ye see
    With Water fill'd, (Sirs, credit me)
The humour was, (as I have read)
But Lovers tears inchristallèd.
Which, as they drop by drop doe passe
From th' upper to the under-glasse,
Do in a trickling manner tell,
(By many a watrie syllable)
That Lovers tears in life-time shed,
Do restless run when they are dead.

⁵ This is a Devonshire name—Scobell. In the Dean Priory Register we read : Jeffery Scobble th' elder buried the fifth day of February, 1654: he had a son named Ellis baptized in 1632.   See
Memorial-Introduction on Devonshire names introduced by Herrick
in his Epigrams.

His Fare-well to Sack.

FAREWELL thou Thing, time-past so knowne, so
　　deare
To me, as blood to life and spirit : Neare,
Nay, thou more neare then kindred, friend, man, wife,
Male to the female, soule to body : Life　　　　[*than*
To quick [our] action,[6] or the warme soft side
Of the resigning, yet resisting Bride.
The kisse of Virgins ; First-fruits of the bed ;
Soft speech, smooth touch, the lips, the Maiden-head :
These, and a thousand sweets, co'd never be
So neare, or deare, as thou wast once to me.
O thou the drink of Gods, and Angels ! Wine
That scatter'st Spirit and Lust ; whose purest shine,
More radiant then the Summers Sun-beams shows ;
Each way illustrious, brave ; and like to those
Comets we see by night ; whose shagg'd [7] portents
Fore-tell the comming of some dire events :
Or some full flame, which with a pride aspires,
Throwing about his wild, and active fires.

---

　[6] The meaning is that sack is to the male life to quick, *i. e.* make
lively his action—to the bride it is life to make quick or give life to
' her soft side.'　Hence a distinctive pronoun is required, and I venture to fill in ' our.'　These early Poets allowed themselves licence of
speech on things about which silence had been golden.

　[7] =shaggy, hairy.

'Tis thou, 'bove [8] Nectar, O Divinest soule !
(Eternall in thy self) that canst controule
That, which subverts whole nature, grief and care ;
Vexation of the mind, and damn'd Despaire.
'Tis thou, alone, who with thy Mistick Fan, [9]
Work'st more then Wisdome, Art, or Nature can, [*than*
To rouze the sacred madnesse ; and awake
The frost-bound-blood, and spirits ; and to make
Them frantick with thy raptures, flashing through
The soule, like lightning, and as active too.
'Tis not *Apollo* can, or those thrice three
Castalian sisters, sing, if wanting thee.
Horace, Anacreon both had lost their fame,
Hadst thou not fill'd them with thy fire and flame.
Phœbean splendour ! and thou *Thespian* spring !
Of which, sweet Swans must drink, before they sing
Their true-pac'd Numbers, and their Holy-Layes,
Which makes them worthy *Cedar*,[1] and the *bayes*.
But why ? why longer doe I gaze upon
Thee with the eye of admiration ?

[8] I print 'bove for ' above.'
[9] = the *mystica vannus Iacchi* of the 1st Georgic.
[1] Used for caskets ; or the oil used to preserve MSS. See Glossarial Index.

Since I must leave thee ; and enforc'd, must say
To all thy witching beauties, Goe, Away.
But if thy whimpring looks doe ask me why ?
✗ Then know, that Nature bids thee goe, not I.
'Tis her erroneous self has made a braine
Uncapable of such a Soveraigne,
As is thy powerfull selfe.   Prethee not smile ;
Or smile more inly ; lest thy looks beguile
My vowes denounc'd in zeale, which thus much show
      thee,
That I have sworn, but by thy looks to know thee.
Let others drink thee freely ; and desire
Thee and their lips espous'd ; while I admire,
And love thee ; but not taste thee.   Let my Muse
Faile of thy former helps ; and onely use
Her inadult'rate strength : what's done by me
Hereafter, shall smell of the Lamp,[2] not thee.

Upon Glasco. *Epig.*

GLASCO had none, but now some teeth has got ;
    Which though they furre,[3] will neither ake, or
      rot.

---

[2] The classical common-place.
[3] = grow foul. Cf. Martiall *frequenter.*

Six teeth he has, whereof twice two are known
Made of a Haft, that was a Mutton-bone.
Which not for use, but meerly for the sight,
He weares all day, and drawes those teeth at night.

Upon Mrs. Eliz : Wheeler, *under the name of* Amarillis.[4]

SWEET *Amarillis*, by a Spring's
    Soft and soule-melting murmurings,
Slept ; and thus sleeping, thither flew
A *Robin-red-brest ;* who at view,
Not seeing her at all to stir,
Brought leaves and mosse to cover her :
But while he, perking,[5] there did prie
About the Arch of either eye ;
The lid began to let out day ;
At which poore *Robin* flew away :
And seeing her not dead, but all disleav'd ;
He chirpt for joy, to see himself disceav'd.

[4] The lady complimented in this poem was probably a relation by marriage. Herrick's first cousin, Martha, the seventh daughter of his uncle Robert, married Mr. John Wheeler. N. See Memorial-Introduction and onward. [5] ═ to hold, or toss up the head, pertly.

The Custard.

FOR second course, last night, a Custard came
    To th'board, so hot, as none co'd touch the same :
Furze, three or foure times with his cheeks did blow
Upon the Custard, and thus coolèd so ;
It seem'd by this time to admit the touch :
But none co'd eate it, 'cause it stunk so much.

To Myrrha hard-hearted.

FOLD now thine armes; and hang the head,
    Like to a Lillie witherèd :
Next, look thou like a sickly Moone ;
Or like *Jocasta* in a swoone.[6]
Then weep, and sigh, and softly goe,
Like to a widdow drown'd in woe :
Or like a Virgin full of ruth,
For the lost sweet-heart of her youth :
And all because, Faire Maid, thou art
Insensible of all my smart ;
And of those evill dayes that be
Now posting on to punish thee.
The Gods are easie, and condemne
All such as are not soft like them.

---

[6] Probably some (forgotten) Play is referred to.

The Eye.

MAKE me a heaven ; and make me there
    Many a lesse and greater spheare.
Make me the straight, and oblique lines ;
The Motions, Lations,[7] and the Signes.
Make me a Chariot, and a Sun ;
And let them through a Zodiac run :
Next, place me Zones, and Tropicks there ;
With all the Seasons of the Yeare.
Make me a Sun-set ; and a Night :
And then present the Mornings-light
Cloath'd in her Chamlets[8] of Delight.
To these, make Clouds to poure downe raine ;
With weather foule, then faire againe.
And when, wise Artist, that thou hast,
With all that can be, this heaven grac't ;
Ah ! what is then this curious skie,
But onely my *Corinna's* eye ?

Upon the much lamented, Mr. J. Warr.[9]

WHAT Wisdome, Learning, Wit, or Worth,
    Youth, or sweet Nature, co'd bring forth,

---

[7] In full—translations, or local motions.
[8] =camlet : originally made of camel's hair and silk : camelot.
[9] Not known.

Rests here with him ; who was the Fame,
The Volumne of himselfe, and Name.
If, Reader, then thou wilt draw neere,
And doe an honour to thy teare ;
Weep then for him, for whom laments
Not one, but many Monuments.

Upon Gryll.

G*RYLL* eates, but ne're sayes Grace ; To speak the
        troth,
Gryll either keeps his breath to coole his broth ;
Or else because *Grill's* roste do's burn his Spit,
Gryll will not therefore say a Grace for it.

The suspition upon his over-much familiarity with a Gentlewoman.

A ND must we part, because some say,
        Loud is our love, and loose our play,
And more then well becomes the day ?   [*than*
Alas for pitty ! and for us
Most innocent, and injur'd thus
Had we kept close, or play'd within,
Suspition now had been the sinne,
And shame had follow'd long ere this,
T'ave plagu'd, what now unpunisht is.
But we as fearlesse of the Sunne,
As faultlesse ; will not wish undone,

What now is done : since *where no sin*
Unbolts the doore, no shame comes in.
Then, comely and most fragrant Maid,
Be you more warie, then afraid   [*than*
Of these Reports ; because you see
The fairest most suspected be.
The common formes have no one eye,
Or eare of burning jealousie
To follow them : but chiefly, where
Love makes the cheek, and chin a sphere
To dance and play in : (Trust me) there
Suspicion questions every haire.
Come, you are faire ; and sho'd be seen
While you are in your sprightfull green :
And what though you had been embrac't
By me,—were you for that unchast ?
No, no, no more then is yond' Moone,
Which shining in her perfect Noone ;
In all that great and glorious light,
Continues cold, as is the night.
Then, beauteous Maid, you may retire ;
And as for me, my chast desire
Shall move t'wards you ; although I see
Your face no more : So live you free
From Fames black lips, as you from me.

Single life most secure.

SUSPICION, Discontent, and Strife,
Come in for Dowrie with a Wife.

The Curse. A Song.

GOE, perjur'd man ; and if thou ere return
    To see the small remainders in mine Urne :
When thou shalt laugh at my Religious dust ;
And ask, Where's now the colour, forme and trust
Of Womans beauty ? and with hand more rude
Rifle the Flowers which the Virgins strew'd :
Know, I have pray'd to Furie, that some wind
May blow my ashes up, and strike thee blind.

The wounded Cupid. *Song.*[1]

CUPID as he lay among
    Roses, by a Bee was stung.
Whereupon in anger flying
To his Mother, said thus crying ;
Help ! O help ! your Boy's a dying.
And why, my pretty Lad, said she ?
Then blubbering, replyèd he,

---

[1] Imitation of Anacreon : Od. 40.

A wingèd Snake has bitten me,
Which Country people call a Bee.
At which she smil'd ; then with her hairs
And kisses drying up his tears :
Alas ! said she, my Wag ! if this
Such a pernicious torment is :
Come tel me then, how great's the smart
Of those, thou woundest with thy Dart !

To Dewes.   A Song.

I BURN, I burn ; and beg of you
    To quench, or coole me with your Dew.
I frie [2] in fire, and so consume,
Although the Bile be all perfume.
Alas ! the heat and death's the same ;
Whether by choice, or common flame :
To be in Oyle of *Roses* drown'd,
Or water ; where's the comfort found ?
Both bring one death ; and I die here,
Unlesse you coole me with a Teare :
Alas ! I call ; but ah ! I see
Ye coole, and comfort all, but me.

[2] See Glossarial Index s. v.

Some comfort in calamity.

TO conquer'd men, some comfort 'tis to fall
By th'hand of him who is the Generall.

The Vision.

SITTING alone (as one forsook)
   Close by a Silver-shedding Brook ;
With hands held up to Love, I wept ;
And after sorrowes spent, I slept :
Then in a Vision I did see
A glorious forme appeare to me :
A Virgins face she had ; her dresse
Was like a sprightly *Spartanesse.*
A silver bow with green silk strung,
Down from her comely shoulders hung :
And as she stood, the wanton Aire
Dangled the ringlets of her haire.
Her legs were such *Diana* shows,
When tuckt up [3] she a-hunting goes ;
With Buskins shortned to descrie
The happy dawning of her thigh :
Which when I saw, I made accesse
To kisse that tempting nakednesse :

---

[3] Cf. Hymn to Ceres (erroneously) ascribed to Homer, 176, and
Catullus Nupt. Pel. et Thet., 128.

But she forbad me, with a wand
Of Mirtle she had in her hand :
And chiding me, said, Hence, Remove,
Herrick, thou art too coorse to love.

Love me little, love me long.

YOU say, to me-wards your affection's strong ;
    Pray love me little, so you love me long.
Slowly goes farre : the meane is best : Desire
Grown violent, do's either die, or tire.

Upon a Virgin kissing a Rose.

'TWAS but a single *Rose*,
    Till you on it did breathe ;
But since (me thinks) it shows
    Not so much *Rose*, as Wreathe.

Upon a Wife that dyed mad with Jealousie.

IN this little Vault she lyes,
    Here, with all her jealousies :
Quiet yet ; but if ye make
Any noise, they both will wake,
And such spirits raise, 'twill then
Trouble Death to lay agen.

Upon the Bishop of Lincolne's *Imprisonment.*[4]

NEVER was Day so over-sick with showres,
 But that it had some intermitting houres.
Never was night so tedious, but it knew
The Last Watch out, and saw the Dawning too.
Never was Dungeon so obscurely deep,
Wherein or Light, or Day, did never peep.
Never did Moone so ebbe, or seas so wane,
But they left Hope-seed to fill up againe.
So you, my Lord, though you have now your stay,
Your Night, your Prison, and your Ebbe ; you may
Spring up afresh ; when all these mists are spent,
And Star-like, once more, guild [5] our Firmament.
Let but That Mighty *Cesar* speak, and then,
All bolts, all barres, all gates shall cleave ; as when
That Earth-quake shook the house, and gave the stout
Apostles, way (unshackled) to goe out.[6]
This, as I wish for, so I hope to see ;
Though you (my Lord) have been unkind to me : [7]

---

[4] This 'imprisoned' Bishop was the Statesman-Bishop Williams.
He was elected Bishop of Lincoln 3rd Aug., 1621, and consecrated
11th Nov: translated to York in 1641.
 [5] = gild.   [6] Acts of the Apostles, c. xvi.
 [7] See Memorial-Introduction.

To wound my heart, and never to apply,
(When you had power) the meanest remedy :
Well ; though my griefe by you was gall'd,[8] the more ;
Yet I bring Balme and Oile to heal your sore.

Disswasions from Idlenesse.

CYNTHIUS pluck ye by the eare,
    That ye may good doctrine heare.
Play not with the maiden-haire ; [9]
For each Ringlet there's a snare.
Cheek, and eye, and lip, and chin ;
These are traps to take fooles in.
Armes, and hands, and all parts else,
Are but Toiles, or Manicles
Set on purpose to enthrall
Men, but Slothfulls most of all.
Live employ'd, and so live free
From these fetters ; like to me
Who have found, and still can prove,
The lazie man the most doth love.[1]

[8] = to fret or rub.   [9] See Glossarial Index s. v.
[1] Thus the great master of Love's art : Cedit amor rebus ; res age, tutus eris. Ovid. Remed. Amor. v. 151. N.

Upon Strut.

STRUT, once a Fore-man of a Shop we knew;
  But turn'd a Ladies Usher now, ('tis true :)
Tell me, has *Strut* got ere a title more?
No; he's but Fore-man, as he was before.

An Epithalamie to Sir Thomas Southwell
and his Ladie.[2]

I.

NOW, now's the time; so oft by truth
  Promis'd sho'd come to crown your youth.
  Then Faire ones, doe not wrong
  Your joyes, by staying long :
  Or let Love's fire goe out,
  By lingring thus in doubt :
  But learn, that Time once lost,
  Is ne'r redeem'd by cost.
Then away; come, *Hymen* guide
To the bed, the bashfull Bride.

[2] There appears to have been two Sir Thomas Southwells: one
settled in Ireland, and too early for this ' Epithalamie,' The other
was knighted 21st July, 1615, and died in 1642. His relict, Mary,
administered to his estate 16th December, 1642, when he was described as of Angleton, in Sussex (=Hangleton, near Brighton).
She died almost immediately after, as on 30th January following,

II.

Is it (sweet maid) your fault, these holy
Bridall-Rites goe on so slowly?
    Deare, is it this you dread,
    The losse of Maiden-head?
    Beleeve me; you will most
    Esteeme it when 'tis lost :
    Then it no longer keep,
    Lest Issue lye asleep.
Then away; come, *Hymen* guide
To the bed, the bashfull Bride.

III.

These Precious-Pearly-Purling [3] teares,
But spring from ceremonious feares.
    And 'tis but Native shame,
    That hides the loving flame :
    And may a while controule
    The soft and am'rous soule;
    But yet, Loves fire will wast
    Such bashfulnesse at last.
Then away; come, *Hymen* guide
To the bed, the bashfull Bride.

Sir Matthew Menes, K. B., administered to his estate, the relict Mary
being dead. This ' Epithalamie' must have been written early.
   [3] See Glossarial Index s. v.

IV.

Night now hath watch'd her self half blind ;
Yet not a Maiden-head resign'd !
  'Tis strange, ye will not flie
  To Love's sweet mysterie.
  Might yon Full-Moon the sweets
  Have, promis'd to your sheets ;
  She soon wo'd leave her spheare,
  To be admitted there.
Then away; come, *Hymen* guide
To the bed, the bashfull Bride.

V.

On, on devoutly, make no stay ;
While *Domiduca* [4] leads the way :
  And *Genius* who attends
  The bed for luckie ends : [5]
  With *Juno* goes the houres,
  And Graces strewing flowers.
  And the boyes with sweet tune sing,
  Hymen, O *Hymen* bring

---

[4] A coined word, I presume, for the *paranympha pronuba*, or bride-maid attending the bride. N.   Dr. Nott is mistaken: it is one of the eight nymphal names of Juno. Cf. Ben Jonson's Masque of Hymen, and his notes thereon.

[5] =the power that begets, the lingam deity.

Home the Turtles; *Hymen* guide
To the bed, the bashfull Bride.

VI.

Behold! how *Hymens* Taper-light
Shews you how much is spent of night.
   See, see the Bride-grooms Torch
   Halfe wasted in the porch.
   And now those Tapers five,
   That shew the womb shall thrive:
   Their silv'rie flames advance,
   To tell all prosp'rous chance
Still shall crown the happy life
Of the good man and the wife.[6]

VII.

Move forward then your Rosie feet,
And make, what ere they touch, turn sweet.[7]

[6] Borne by the Quinque Cerei in Roman marriages, and supposed
by some to represent the highest number of births at one time.
Throughout Herrick combines classical customs with English, even
when speaking of home festivities and evening merriments and
drinking.

[7] "The meadows your walks have left so sweet,"—Tennyson: and
again, "Her feet have touched the meadows and left the daisies
rosy" (Maud). Earlier in Herrick's great friend:
   "Where she went the flowers took thickest root,
    As she had sow'd them with her odorous foot."
           (Sad Shepherd i. 1).

May all, like flowrie Meads
Smell, where your soft foot treads;
And every thing assume
To it, the like perfume :
As *Zephirus* when he 'spires
Through *Woodbine*, and *Sweet-bryers.*
Then away; come *Hymen*, guide
To the bed, the bashfull Bride.

VIII.

And now the yellow Vaile,[8] at last,
Over her fragrant cheek is cast.
Now seems she to expresse
A bashfull willingnesse :[9]
Shewing a heart consenting;
As with a will repenting.
Then gently lead her on
With wise suspicion :
For that, Matrons say, a measure
Of that Passion sweetens Pleasure.

[8] Saffron, the colour appropriated to marriage, and in which
Hymen is always supposed to be dressed.

[9] Tardet ingenuus pudor : Catullus. Epithal. Julie et Manlii.

Transfer omine cum bono
Limen aureolos pedes. Idem. N.

IX.

You, you that be of her neerest kin,
Now o're the threshold force her in.[1]
    But to avert the worst ;
    Let her, her fillets first
    Knit to the posts[2]: this point
    Remembring, to anoint
    The sides : for 'tis a charme
    Strong against future harme :
And the evil deads, the which
There was hidden by the Witch.

X.

O *Venus !* thou, to whom is known
The best way how to loose the Zone
    Of Virgins ! Tell the Maid,
    She need not be afraid :
    And bid the Youth apply
    Close kisses, if she cry :
    And charge, he not forbears
    Her, though she wooe with teares.

---

[1] The wife in Roman marriages was lifted over the threshold, for which various differing reasons were alleged.

[2] A custom in Roman marriages, as is the anointing with its supposed averting power.

Tel them, now they must adventer,
Since that Love and Night bid enter.

XI.

No Fatal Owle the Bedsted keeps,
With direful notes to fright your sleeps :
  No Furies, here about,
  To put the Tapers out,
  Watch, or did make the bed :
  'Tis *Omen* full of dread :
  But all faire signs appeare
  Within the Chamber here.
Juno here, far off, doth stand
Cooling sleep with charming wand.

XII.

Virgins, weep not ; 'twill come, when,
As she, so you'l be ripe for men.
  Then grieve her not, with saying
  She must no more a Maying :
  Or by Rose-buds devine,
  Who'l be her Valentine.[3]
  Nor name those wanton reaks[4]
  Y'ave had at Barly-breaks.

---

[3] St. Valentine's day, Feb. 14th—the name drawn by lot thereon.
See Glossarial Index s. v.   [4] =pranks.

But now kisse her, and thus say,
Take time Lady while ye may.

XIII.

Now barre the doors, the Bride-groom puts
The eager Boyes to gather Nuts.[5]
   And now, both Love and Time
   To their full height doe clime :
   O ! give them active heat
   And moisture, both compleat :
   Fit Organs for encrease,
   To keep, and to release
That, which may the honour'd Stem
Circle with a Diadem.[6]

XIV.

And now, Behold ! the Bed or Couch
That ne'r knew Brides, or Bride-grooms touch,
   Feels in it selfe a fire ;
   And tickled with Desire,

[5] The ceremony of throwing nuts at a wedding, which boys scrambled for, was of Athenian origin. Besides Catullus, Virgil and many other classic writers mention the custom ; hence *nucibus relictis* became proverbial, for the renouncing of childhood. See Persius, Sat. i., ver. 10. N. On line preceding : Claudite ostia virgines : Catullus, as before.

[6] Proverbs xvii. 6.

Pants with a Downie brest,
As with a heart possest :
    Shrugging as it did move,
    Ev'n with the soule of love.
And (oh !) had it but a tongue,
Doves, 'two'd say, yee bill too long.

XV.

O enter then ! but see ye shun
A sleep, untill the act be done.
    Let kisses, in their close,
    Breathe as the Damask Rose :
    Or sweet, as is that gumme
    Doth from *Panchaia* [7] come.
    Teach Nature now to know,
    Lips can make Cherries grow
Sooner, then she, ever yet,
In her wisdome co'd beget.

XVI.

On your minutes, hours, dayes, months, years,
Drop the fat blessing of the sphears.
    That good, which Heav'n can give
    To make you bravely live ;

[7] See Glossarial Index s. v.

Fall, like a spangling dew,[8]
By day, and night on you.
May Fortunes Lilly-hand
Open at your command ;
With all luckie Birds to side
With the Bride-groom, and the Bride.

XVII.

Let bounteous Fate your spindles full
Fill, and winde up with whitest wooll.[9]
Let them not cut the thred
Of life, untill ye bid.
May Death yet come at last ;
And not with desp'rate hast :
But when ye both can say,
Come, Let us now away.
Be ye to the Barn then born,
Two, like two ripe shocks of corn.

[8] Cf. " The benediction of these covering heavens
       Fall on your heads like dew,"
            (Cymb., v. 5, ll. 350-1 : cf. Henry VIII., iv. 2, l. 133.
[9] Cf. Ben Jonson's Hue and Cry after Cupid :—
    [James coming]
        " That was reserved until the Parcae spun
          Their whitest wool ; and then his thread begun."

Teares are Tongues.

WHEN *Julia* chid, I stood as mute the while,
    As is the fish, or tonguelesse Crocodile.[1]
Aire coyn'd to words, my *Julia* co'd not heare ;
But she co'd see each eye to stamp [2] a teare :
By which, mine angry Mistresse might descry,
Teares are the noble language of the eye.
And when true love of words is destitute,
The Eyes by tears speak, while the Tongue is mute.[3]

[Epitaph] *Upon a young mother of many children.*

LET all chaste Matrons, when they chance to see
    My num'rous issue: Praise, and pitty me.
Praise me, for having such a fruitfull wombe :
Pity me too, who found so soone a Tomb.

To Electra.

I LE come to thee in all those shapes
    As *Jove* did, when he made his rapes :
    Onely, Ile not appeare to thee,
    As he did once to *Semele.*

---

[1] Long a vulgar error.

[2] = Coin—there being a parallelism with former line.

[3] Cf. Sidney 'dumb eloquence,' and Daniel 'silent rhetoric' in Memorial-Introduction.

Thunder and Lightning Ile lay by,
To talk with thee familiarly.
Which done, then quickly we'll undresse
To one and th'others nakednesse.
And ravisht, plunge into the bed,
(Bodies and souls comminglèd)
And kissing, so as none may heare,
We'll weary [4] all the Fables [5] there.

His wish.

IT is sufficient if we pray
    To *Jove*, who gives, and takes away :
Let him the Land and Living finde ;
Let me alone to fit the mind.

His *Protestation to* Perilla.

NOONE-DAY and Midnight shall at once be
    seene:
Trees, at one time, shall be both sere and greene:
Fire and water shall together lye
In one-self-sweet-conspiring sympathie :
Summer and Winter shall at one time show
Ripe eares of corne, and up to th'eares in snow :

---

[4] = wear out or exhaust.   [5] *i. e.* told of Jove's amours.

Seas shall be sandlesse ; Fields devoid of grasse ;
Shapelesse the world (as when all *Chaos* was)
Before, my deare *Perilla*, I will be
False to my vow, or fall away from thee.

Love perfumes all parts.

IF I kisse *Anthea's* brest,
   There I smell the Phenix nest :
If her lip, the most sincere [6]
Altar of Incense, I smell there.
Hands, and thighs, and legs, are all
Richly Aromaticall.
Goddesse *Isis* cann't transfer
Musks and Ambers more from her : [7]
Nor can *Juno* sweeter be,
When she lyes with *Jove*, then she.   [*than*

To Julia.

PERMIT me, *Julia,* now to goe away ;
   Or by thy love, decree me here to stay.
If thou wilt say, that I shall live with thee :
Here shall my endless Tabernacle be :
If not, (as banisht) I will live alone
There, where no language ever yet was known.

[6] = pure.   [7] See Glossarial Index s. v.

On himselfe.

LOVE-SICK I am, and must endure
  A desp'rate grief, that finds no cure.
Ah me.! I try ; and trying, prove,
No Herbs have power to cure Love.
Only one Soveraign salve, I know,
And that is Death, the end of Woe.

Vertue is sensible of suffering.

THOUGH a wise man all pressures can sustaine ;
  His vertue still is sensible of paine :
Large shoulders though he has, and well can beare,
He feeles when Packs[8] do pinch him ; and the where.

The cruell Maid.

AND,[9] Cruell Maid, because I see
  You scornfull of my love, and me :
Ile trouble you no more ; but goe
My way, where you shall never know
What is become of me : there I
Will find me out a path to die ;
Or learne some way how to forget
You, and your name, for ever yet

[8] = loads. [9] Unusual to begin with 'And.' In our own generation Dibdin starts off with " And have you not heard of a jolly
young waterman," &c. See Glossarial Index s. v.

H

Ere I go hence; know this from me,
What will, in time, your Fortune be :
This to your coynesse I will tell ;
And having spoke it once, Farewell.
The Lillie will not long endure ;
Nor the Snow continue pure :
The Rose, the Violet, one day
See, both these Lady-flowers decay :
And you must fade, as well as they.
And it may chance that Love may turn,
And (like to mine) make your heart burn
And weep to see't ; yet this thing doe,
That my last Vow commends to you :
When you shall see that I am dead,
For pitty let a teare be shed ;
And (with your Mantle o're me cast)
Give my cold lips a kisse at last :
If twice you kisse, you need not feare,
That I shall stir, or live more here.
Next, hollow out a Tombe to cover
Me ; me, the most despisèd Lover :
And write thereon, *This, Reader, know,*
Love kill'd this man.[1]   No more but so.

---

[1] Huic misero fatum dura puella fuit.   Propertius : Eleg. I. Lib.
2, ver. ult. N.

To Dianeme.

SWEET, be not proud of those two eyes,
　　Which Star-like sparkle in their skies :
Nor be you proud, that you can see
All hearts your captives; yours, yet free :
Be you not proud of that rich haire,
Which wantons with the Love-sick aire :
Whenas that *Rubie,* which you weare,
Sunk from the tip of your soft eare,
Will last to be a precious Stone,
When all your world of Beautie's gone.

TO THE KING,
To cure the Evill.[2]

TO find that Tree of Life, whose Fruits did feed,
　　And Leaves did heale, all sicke of humane seed :
To finde *Bethesda,* and an Angel there,
Stirring the waters,[3] I am come ; and here,
At last, I find, (after my much to doe)
The Tree, Bethesda, and the Angel too :

---

[2] Scrofula being ' the King's evil' the reference is to scrofulous disease of the joints and limbs. See line 8. It is astonishing and humiliating how long this superstitious belief in the royal touch lingered. Originally it held a noble tradition. 　[3] St. John, c. v.

And all in Your Blest Hand, which has the powers
Of all those suppling-healing herbs and flowers.
To that soft *Charm*, that *Spell*, that *Magick Bough*,
That high Enchantment I betake me now :
And to that Hand, (the Branch of Heavens faire Tree)
I kneele for help ; O ! lay that hand on me,
Adorèd *Cesar !* and my Faith is such,
I shall be heal'd, if that my *KING* but touch.
The Evill is not Yours : my sorrow sings,
Mine is the Evill, but the Cure, the *KINGS.*

His misery in a Mistresse.

WATER, Water I espie :
    Come, and coole ye ; all who frie [4]
In your loves ; but none as I.

Though a thousand showres be
Still a falling, yet I see
Not one drop to light on me.

Happy you, who can have seas
For to quench ye, or some ease
From your kinder Mistresses.

I have one, and she alone,
Of a thousand thousand known,
Dead to all compassion.

[4] See Glossarial Index s. v.

Such an one, as will repeat
Both the cause, and make the heat
More by Provocation great.

Gentle friends, though I despaire
Of my cure, doe you beware
Of those Girles, which cruell are.

Upon Jollies *wife.*

FIRST, *Jollies* wife is lame ; then next, loose-hipt :
Squint ey'd, hook-nos'd ; and lastly, Kidney-lipt.

To a Gentlewoman objecting to him his gray haires.

AM I despis'd, because you say,
And I dare sweare, that I am gray ?
Know, Lady, you have but your day :
And time will come when you shall weare
Such frost and snow upon your haire ;
And when (though long, it comes to passe)
You question with your Looking-glasse ;
And in that sincere[5] *Christall* seek,
But find no Rose-bud in your cheek :
Nor any bed to give the shew
Where such a rare Carnation grew.

[5] —truth-telling.

Ah ! then too late, close in your chamber keeping,
   It will be told
   That you are old ;
By those true teares y'are weeping.

To Cedars.

IF 'mongst my many Poems, I can see
  One, onely, worthy to be washt by thee :[6]
I live for ever ; let the rest all lye
In dennes of Darkness, or condemn'd to die.

Upon Cupid.

LOVE, like a Gypsie, lately came ;
  And did me much importune
To see my hand ; that by the same
  He might fore-tell my Fortune.

He saw my Palme ; and then, said he,
  I tell thee, by this score here ;
That thou, within few months, shalt be
  The youthfull Prince *D'Amour* here.

---

[6] From Horace
  . . . . " carmina fingi
   Posse linenda cedro. . . ." (Epist. ad Pis. 332: vi. ll. 331-2).
Cf. "A Dirge . . . . . Bernard Stuart," and Glossarial Index s. v.
But could the Bible-use of 'cedar' be intended ? See Leviticus xiv.
4: Num. xix. 6.

I smil'd ; and bade him once more prove,[7]
And by some crosse-line show it ;
That I co'd ne'r be Prince of Love,
Though here the Princely Poet.[8]

How Primroses came green.

VIRGINS, time-past, known were these,
 Troubled with Green-sicknesses,
Turn'd to flowers : Stil the hieu,
Sickly Girles, they beare of you.

To Jos : Lo : Bishop of Exeter.[9]

WHOM sho'd I feare to write to, if I can
 Stand before you, my learn'd *Diocesan?*
And never shew blood-guiltinesse, or feare
To see my Lines *Excathedrated* here.
Since none so good are, but you may condemne ;
Or here so bad, but you may pardon them.
If then, (my Lord) to sanctifie my Muse
One onely Poem out of all you'l chuse ;
And mark it for a Rapture nobly writ,
'Tis Good Confirm'd ; for you have Bishop't it.

---

[7] =try.   [8] See Memorial-Introduction.
 [9] The illustrious and venerable Joseph Hall : born 1574 : died 1656. His "Satires" are still quick as well as his "Meditations" &c. &c.

Upon a black Twist, rounding the Arme of the Countesse of Carlile.[1]

I SAW about her spotlesse wrist,
  Of blackest silk, a curious twist;
Which, circumvolving gently, there
Enthrall'd her Arme, as Prisoner.
Dark was the Jayle; but as if light
Had met t'engender with the night;
Or so, as Darknesse made a stay
To shew at once, both night and day.

[1] This was most probably Margaret 3rd. d. of Francis Earl of Bedford and lady of James Hay, the 2nd. of that name Earl of Carlisle; who succeeded his father James 1636; she being the then Countess at the time Herrick published his *Hesperides.* Yet might the poet have written his Lines on the Lady Lucy, 2nd wife of James, 1st earl of Carlisle, who was celebrated for her wit and beauty, and at the time Herrick's book came out must have been about the age of fifty; she was d. of Henry Percy, 9th earl of Northumberland: her character is found drawn up at the head of A Collection of Letters made by Sir Tobie Mathews, Knight, and dedicated to her ladyship: it is a curious and now rare little book, printed 1660. Waller wrote many elegant verses on this " Bright Carlisle of the court of heaven." N. The latter was all but certainly Herrick's Countess. Davies of Hereford places her among his " Worthy Persons."

One[2] fancie more ! but if there be
Such Freedome in Captivity ;
I beg of Love, that ever I
May in like Chains of Darknesse lie.

On himselfe.

I FEARE no Earthly Powers ;
But care for crowns of flowers :
And love to have my Beard
With Wine and Oile besmear'd.
This day Ile drowne all sorrow ;
Who knowes to live to morrow ?[3]

Upon Pagget.

PAGGET, a School-boy, got a Sword, and then
He vow'd Destruction both to Birch, and Men :
Who wo'd not think this Yonker[4] fierce to fight ?
Yet comming home, but somewhat late, (last night)
Untrusse, his Master bade him ; and that word
Made him take up his shirt, lay down his sword.

---

[2] Misprinted " I " self-evidently an error for " one " which was probably written as I ▬ one fancy more.

[3] So Mickle in the well-known Scottish song :
"The present moment is our ain
The neist we never saw."

[4] ▬ Youngster, youth.

A Ring presented to Julia.

JULIA, I bring
    To thee this Ring,[5]
Made for thy finger fit ;
    To shew by this,
    That our love is
(Or sho'd be) like to it.

    Close though it be,
    The joynt is free : ·
So when Love's yoke is on,
    It must not gall,
    Or fret at all
With hard oppression.

    But it must play
    Still either way ;
And be, too, such a yoke,
    As not too wide,
    To over-slide ;
Or be so strait to choak.

    So we, who beare,
    This beame, must reare
Our selves to such a height :

[5] Probably a gemmal ring.

As that the stay
Of either may
Create the burden light.

And as this round
Is no where found
To flaw, or else to sever :
So let our love
As endless prove ;
And pure as Gold for ever.

To the Detracter.

WHERE others love, and praise my Verses ; still
   Thy long-black-Thumb-nail marks 'em out
      for ill :
A fellon take it, or some Whit-flaw[6] come
For to unslate, or to untile that thumb !
But cry thee Mercy : Exercise thy nailes
To scratch or claw, so that thy tongue not railes :
Some numbers prurient are, and some of these
Are wanton with their itch ; scratch, and 'twill please.

---

[6] = Whit-low : a swelling at end of finger next the nail : vulgarly whit-flow or flaw.

Upon the same.

I ASK'T thee oft, what Poets thou hast read,
  And lik'st the best?   Still thou reply'st, The dead.
I shall, ere long, with green turfs cover'd be;
Then sure thou't like, or thou wilt envie me.

Julia's *Petticoat.*

THY Azure Robe, I did behold,
  As ayrie as the leaves of gold :
Which erring[7] here, and wandring there,
Pleas'd with transgression ev'ry where : ___
Sometimes 'two'd pant, and sigh, and heave,
As if to stir it scarce had leave :
But having got it ; thereupon,
'Two'd make a brave expansion.
And pounc't[8] with Stars, it shew'd to me
Like a *Celestiall Canopie.*
Sometimes 'two'd blaze, and then abate,
Like to a flame growne moderate :
Sometimes away 'two'd wildly fling ;
Then to thy thighs so closely cling,

---

[7] = blowing aside or deviating.
   = sprinkled as was dust, before blotting-paper, over writing.

That some conceit did melt me downe,
As Lovers fall into a swoone :
And all confus'd, I there did lie
Drown'd in Delights ; but co'd not die.
That Leading Cloud, I follow'd still,
Hoping t'ave seene of it my fill ;
But ah ! I co'd not : sho'd it move
To Life Eternal, I co'd love.

To Musick.

BEGIN to charme, and as thou stroak'st mine eares
With thy enchantment, melt me into tears.
Then let thy active hand scu'd o're thy Lyre :
And make my spirits frantick with the fire.
That done, sink down into a silv'rie straine ;
And make me smooth as Balme, and Oile againe.

Distrust.

TO safe-guard Man from wrongs, there nothing
must
Be truer to him, then a wise Distrust. [than
And to thy selfe be best this sentence knowne,
Heare all men speak; but credit few or none.

Corinna's *going a Maying.*[9]

G ET up, get up for shame, the Blooming Morne
    Upon her wings presents the god unshorne.[1]
    See how *Aurora* throwes her faire
    Fresh-quilted colours[2] through the aire :
    Get up, sweet Slug-a-bed, and see
    The Dew bespangling Herbe and Tree.
Each Flower has wept, and bow'd toward the East,
Above an houre since ; yet you not drest,
        Nay ! not so much as out of bed ?
        When all the Birds have Mattens seyd,
        And sung their thankfull Hymnes : 'tis sin,
        Nay, profanation to keep in,
Whenas a thousand Virgins on this day,
Spring, sooner then the Lark, to fetch in May.   [*than*

Rise ; and put on your Foliage, and be seene
To come forth, like the Spring-time, fresh and greene ;

[9] See Memorial-Introduction for parallels.   Dr. Nott annotates
here : The ceremony of *going a Maying*, and the *May Festivities*, were
once of great notoriety : though now almost in disuse, or but faintly
shadowed in the lower orders of people : they were observed by
royalty even.   Stowe, quoting Hall, gives an account of Henry VIII's
riding a Maying, with his queen, Catharine, to the high ground on
Shooter's Hill, accompanied by a train of the nobility.
  [1] = Apollo.   [2] Cf. Milton's ' Nativity,' l. 146, ' tissued clouds.'

And sweet as *Flora.* Take no care
For Jewels for your Gowne, or Haire :
Feare not ; the leaves will strew
Gemms in abundance upon you :
Besides, the childhood of the Day has kept,
Against you come, some *Orient Pearls* unwept :
Come, and receive them while the light
Hangs on the Dew-locks of the night :
And *Titan* on the Eastern hill
Retires himselfe, or else stands still
Till you come forth. Wash, dresse, be briefe in
praying :
Few Beads[3] are best, when once we goe a Maying.

Come, my *Corinna*, come ; and comming, marke
How each field turns a street ; each street a Parke
Made green, and trimm'd with trees : see how
Devotion gives each House a Bough,
Or Branch : Each Porch, each doore, ere this,
An Arke a Tabernacle is
Made up of white-thorn neatly enterwove ;
As if here were those cooler shades of love.[4]

[3] = prayers.
[4] It is an ancient custom in Devon and Cornwall to deck the porches of houses with boughs of sycamore and hawthorn on May-day.

Can such delights be in the street,

And open fields, and we not see't?

Come, we'll abroad; and let's obay

The Proclamation made for May:

And sin no more, as we have done, by staying;

But my *Corinna*, come, let's goe a Maying.

There's not a budding Boy, or Girle, this day,

But is got up, and gone to bring in May.

A deale of Youth,[5] ere this, is come

Back, and with *White-thorn* laden home.

Some have dispatcht their Cakes and Creame,

Before that we have left to dreame:

And some have wept, and woo'd, and plighted Troth,

And chose their Priest, ere we can cast off sloth:

Many a green-gown[6] has been given;

Many a kisse, both odde and even:

Many a glance too has been sent

From out the eye, Love's Firmament:

Many a jest told of the Keyes betraying

This night, and Locks pickt,[7] yet w'are not a Maying.

---

[5] See Glossarial Index s. v.

[6] Giving a maid a green gown was, in its purer sense, throwing her on the grass sportively.

[7] The usual rural tricks of sweathearts, with (unhappily) a double meaning.

Come, let us goe, while we are in our prime ;
And take the harmlesse follie of the time.
    We shall grow old apace, and die
    Before we know our liberty.
    Our life is short ; and our dayes run
    As fast away as do's the Sunne :
And as a vapour, or a drop of raine
Once lost, can ne'r be found againe :
    So when or you or I are made
    A fable, song, or fleeting shade ;
    All love, all liking, all delight
    Lies drown'd with us in endlesse night.[8]
Then while time serves, and we are but decaying ;
Come, my *Corinna*, come, let's goe a Maying.

On Julia's *breath*.

BREATHE, *Julia*, breathe, and I'le protest,
    Nay more, I'le deeply sweare,
That all the Spices of the East
    Are circumfusèd[9] there.

---

[8] This concluding stanza is in the same spirit with Catullus's fifth *Carmen*. N.   [9] = shed round about.

I

Upon a Child.   An Epitaph.

BUT borne, and like a short Delight,
    I glided by my Parents sight.
That done, the harder Fates deny'd
My longer stay, and so I dy'd.
If pittying my sad Parents Teares,
You'l spil a tear or two, with theirs :
And with some flowrs my grave bestrew,
Love and they'l thank you for't.   Adieu.

A Dialogue betwixt Horace *and* Lydia, *Translated*[1] Anno 1627, *and set by Mr.* Ro : Ramsey.[2]

Hor. WHILE, *Lydia,* I was lov'd of thee,
        Nor any was preferr'd 'fore me
    To hug thy whitest neck : Then I,   [*than*
    The Persian King liv'd not more happily.

Lyd. While thou no other didst affect,
    Nor *Cloe* was of more respect ;
    Then *Lydia,* far-fam'd *Lydia,*
    I flourish't more then Roman *Ilia.*

---

[1] Horace : Carm. III. 9.

[2] The name of this Composer is not found in any of the musical authorities.

Hor. Now *Thracian Cloe* governs me,
　　　 Skilfull i' th' Harpe, and Melodie :
　　　 For whose affection, *Lydia*, I
　　　 (So Fate spares her) am well content to die.

Lyd. My heart now set on fire is
　　　 By *Ornithes* sonne,[3] young *Calais ;*
　　　 For whose commutuall flames here I
　　　 (To save his life) twice am content to die.

Hor. Say our first loves we sho'd revoke,
　　　 And sever'd, joyne in brazen yoke :
　　　 Admit I *Cloe* put away,
　　　 And love again love-cast-off *Lydia ?*

Lyd. Though mine be brighter then the Star ;
　　　 Thou lighter then the Cork by far ;　　　 [*than*
　　　 Rough as th' *Adratick sea*, yet I
　　　 Will live with thee, or else for thee will die.

The captiv'd Bee: or, The Little Filcher.

A S *Julia* once a-slumb'ring lay,
　　 It chanc't a Bee did flie that way,

---

[3] Me torret face mutua
　　　 Thurini Calais filius Ornyti (ll. 14-15.)

(After a dew, or dew-like shower)
To tipple freely in a flower.
For some rich flower, he took the lip
Of *Julia*, and began to sip;
But when he felt he suckt from thence
Hony, and in the quintessence:
He drank so much he scarce co'd stir;
So *Julia* took the pilferer.
And thus surpriz'd (as Filchers use)
He thus began himselfe t'excuse:
Sweet *Lady-Flower*, I never brought
Hither the least one theeving thought:
But taking those rare lips of yours
For some fresh, fragrant, luscious flowers:
I thought I might there take a taste,
Where so much sirrop ran at waste.
Besides, know this, I never sting[4]
The flower that gives me nourishing:

[4] One would almost imagine that Herrick here had in view the caution which Secundus gives the bee, in his *Basia :* and that the little insect attended to it.

> Heu ! non est stimulis compungite molle labellum ;
> 　　Ex oculis stimulos vibrat et illa pareis.
> Credite non ullum patietur vulnus inultum :
> 　　Leniter innocuæ mella legatis apes.
> 　　　　　　　　Joan. Sec. Basium, 19. N.

But with a kisse, or thanks, doe pay
For Honie, that I beare away.
This said, he laid his little *scrip*
Of hony, 'fore her Ladiship :
And told her, (as some tears did fall)
That that, he took, and that was all.
At which she smil'd ; and bade him goe
And take his bag ; but thus much know,
When next he came a-pilfring so,
He sho'd from her full lips derive,
Hony enough to fill his hive.

Upon Prig.

Prig now drinks Water, who before drank Beere :
    What's now the cause? we know the case is cleere :
Look in *Prig's* purse, the chev'rell[5] there tells you
Prig mony wants, either to buy, or brew.

Upon Batt.

Batt he gets children, not for love to reare 'em ;
    But out of hope his wife might die to beare 'em.

---

[5] =cheveril leather (purse) made of wild goats' skin : kid.

An Ode to Master Endymion Porter,
upon his Brothers death.[6]

NOT all thy flushing Sunnes are set,
             Herrick, as yet :
Nor doth this far-drawn Hemisphere
Frown, and look sullen ev'ry where.
Daies may conclude in nights ; and Suns may rest,[7]
             As dead, within the West ;
Yet the next Morne, re-guild the fragrant East.[8]

        Alas for me ! that I have lost
                    E'en all almost :
        Sunk is my sight ; set is my Sun ;
        And all the loome of life undone :
The staffe,[9] the Elme, the prop, the shelt'ring wall
             Whereon my Vine did crawle,
Now, now, blowne downe ; needs must the old stock fall.

[6] See Memorial-Introduction, as before.
[7] Here we have a beautiful amplification of the three following lines from Catullus :—

        Soles occidere, et redire possunt ;
        Nobis, cum semel occidit brevis lux,
        Nox est perpetua una dormenda.
                    Carm. 5. N.

[8] The first stanza is to be supposed as spoken by Porter.
[9] = support or frame-work.

Yet, *Porter*, while thou keep'st alive,
        In death I thrive :
And like a *Phenix* re-aspire
From out my Narde,[1] and Fun'rall fire :
And as I prune my feather'd youth, so I
        Doe mar'l how I co'd die,
When I had Thee, my chiefe Preserver, by.

I'm up, I'm up, and blesse that hand,
        Which makes me stand
Now as I doe ; and but for thee,
I must confesse, I co'd not be.
The debt is paid : for he who doth resigne[2]
        Thanks to the gen'rous Vine ;
Invites fresh Grapes to fill his Presse with Wine.

To his dying Brother, Master William Herrick.[3]

LIFE of my life, take not so soone Thy flight,
   But stay the time till we have bade Good night
Thou hast both Wind and Tide with thee ; Thy way
As soone dispatcht is by the Night, as Day.
Let us not then so rudely henceforth goe
Till we have wept, kist, sigh't, shook hands, or so.

---

[1] = spice burned at the pyre.   [2] = offer ?
[3] See Memorial-Introduction.

There's paine in parting ; and a kind of hell,
When once true-lovers take their last Fare-well.
What ? shall we two our endlesse leaves take here
Without a sad looke, or a solemne teare ?
He knowes not Love, that hath not this truth proved,
Love is most loth to leave the thing beloved.
Pay we our Vowes, and goe ; yet when we part,
Then, even then, I will bequeath my heart
Into thy loving hands : For Ile keep none
To warme my Breast, when thou my Pulse art gone.
No, here Ile last, and walk (a harmlesse shade)
About this Urne, wherein thy Dust is laid,
To guard it so, as nothing here shall be
Heavy, to hurt those sacred seeds of thee.

The Olive Branch.

SADLY I walk't within the field,
    To see what comfort it wo'd yeeld :
And as I went my private way,
An Olive-branch before me lay :
And seeing it, I made a stay.
And took it up, and view'd it ; then
Kissing the *Omen,* said Amen :
Be, be it so, and let this be
A Divination unto me :

That in short time my woes shall cease ;
And Love shall crown my End with Peace.

Upon Much-more.[4] *Epig.*

M *UCH-MORE*, provides, and hoords up like an
    Ant ;
Yet *Much-more* still complains he is in want.
Let *Much-more* justly pay his tythes ; then try
How both his Meale and Oile will multiply.

To Cherry-blossomes.

Y E may simper,[5] blush, and smile,
    And perfume the aire a-while :
But (sweet things) ye must be gone ;
Fruit, ye know, is comming on :
Then, Ah ! Then, where is your grace,
When as Cherries come in place ?

How Lillies came white.

W HITE though ye be ; yet, Lillies, know,
    From the first ye were not so :
      But Ile tell ye
      What befell ye ;

[4] Like others in these Epigrams, this was no doubt chosen as
expressive of a greedy miserly fellow. Ben Jonson has similar char-
acter-names in his Epigrams. [5] = look pleasant : deteriorated since.

Cupid and his Mother lay
In a Cloud ; while both did play,
He with his pretty finger prest
The rubie niplet of her breast ;
Out of the which, the creame of light,
    Like to a Dew,
    Fell downe on you,
And made ye white.

To Pansies.

A H, cruell Love ! must I endure
    Thy many scorns, and find no cure ?
Say, are thy medicines made to be
Helps to all others, but to me ?
Ile leave thee, and to *Pansies* come ;[6]
Comforts you'l afford me some :
You can ease my heart, and doe
What Love co'd ne'r be brought unto.

On Gelli-flowers begotten.[7]

W HAT was't that fell but now
    From that warme kisse of ours ?

---

[6] "There is pansies, that's for thoughts," [good thoughts]. Hamlet IV., 5.

[7] = gilli-flowers : the " Posie of Gilloflower " (1580) of Humph. Gifford has immortalized the name.

Look, look, by Love I vow
   They were two *Gelli-flowers*.

Let's kisse, and kisse agen;
   For if so be our closes
Make *Gelli-flowers*, then
   I'm sure they'l fashion *Roses*.

The Lilly in a Christal.[8]

YOU have beheld a smiling *Rose*
   When Virgins hands have drawn
   O'r it a Cobweb-Lawne:
And here, you see, this Lilly shows,
   Tomb'd in a *Christal* stone,
More faire in this transparent case,
   Then when it grew alone;   [*than*
   And had but single grace.

You see how *Creame* but naked is;
   Nor daunces in the eye
   Without a Strawberrie:
Or some fine tincture,[9] like to this,

---

[8] See Memorial-Introduction. This was a favourite of Herrick's own. See Glossarial Index under ' christal.'

[9] =colour, as in heraldic language. See Memorial-Introduction on Herrick's feeling for colour.

Which draws the sight thereto,
More by that wantoning with it;
    Then when the paler hieu   [*than*
    No mixture did admit.

You see how *Amber* through the streams
    More gently stroaks the sight,
    With some conceal'd delight;
Then when he darts his radiant beams
    Into the boundlesse aire:
Where either too much light, his worth
    Doth all at once impaire,
    Or set it little forth.

Put Purple grapes, or Cherries in-
    To Glasse, and they will send
    More beauty to commend
Them, from that cleane and subtile skin,
    Then if they naked stood,   [*than*
And had no other pride at all,
    But their own flesh and blood,
    And tinctures naturall.

Thus Lillie, Rose, Grape, Cherry, Creame,
    And Straw-berry do stir
    More love, when they transfer
A weak, a soft, a broken beame;

Then if they sho'd discover   [*than*
At full their proper excellence ;
    Without some Scean cast over,
To juggle with the sense.

Thus let this *Christal'd Lillie* be
    A Rule, how far to teach,
    Your nakednesse must reach :
And that, no further, then we see
    Those glaring colours laid
By Arts wise hand, but to this end
    They sho'd obey a shade ;
    Lest they too far extend.

So though y'are white as Swan, or Snow,
    And have the power to move
    A world of men to love :
Yet, when your Lawns & Silks shal flow ;
    And that white cloud divide
Into a doubtful Twi-light ; then,
    Then will your hidden Pride
    Raise greater fires in men.

To his Booke.

L IKE to a Bride, come forth, my Booke, at last,
    With all thy richest jewels over-cast :

Say, if there be 'mongst many jems here; one
Deservelesse of the name of *Paragon :*[1]
Blush not at all for that; since we have set
Some *Pearls* on *Queens,* that have been counterfet.

Upon some women.

THOU who wilt not love, doe this;
    Learne of me what Woman is.
Something made of thred and thrumme;[2]
A meere Botch of all and some.[3]
Pieces, patches, ropes of haire;
In-laid Garbage ev'ry where.
Out-side silk, and out-side Lawne;
Sceanes[4] to cheat us neatly drawne.
False in legs, and false in thighes;
False in breast, teeth, haire, and eyes:
False in head, and false enough;
Onely true in shreds and stuffe.

---

[1] Herrick, following the French (see Cotgrave s. v.) uses paragon as = peerless one or pattern. Shakespeare has the verb in the sense of to compare as excellent (Ant. & Cl: i. 5) and also to excel (Othello ii. 1 and cf. Henry VIII., ii. 4). See Glossarial Index s. v.

[2] = ends of weaver's warps or coarse yarn.

[3] = the whole and parts.

[4] Used as = screen. See Glossarial Index s. v.

Supreme fortune falls soonest.

WHILE leanest Beasts in Pastures feed,
_ *The fattest Oxe the first must bleed.*

The Welcome to Sack.[5]

SO soft streams meet, so springs with gladder smiles
Meet after long divorcement by the Iles :
When Love (the child of likenesse) urgeth on
Their Christal natures to an union.
So meet stolne kisses, when the Moonie nights
Call forth fierce Lovers to their wisht Delights :
So *Kings & Queens* meet, when Desire convinces[6]
All thoughts, but such as aime at getting Princes,
As I meet thee.   Soule of my life, and fame !
Eternall Lamp of Love ! whose radiant flame
Out-glares the Heav'ns *Osiris ;*[7] and thy gleams
Out-shine the splendour of his mid-day beams.
Welcome, O welcome my illustrious Spouse ;
Welcome as are the ends unto my Vowes :
I ![8] far more welcome then the happy soile,   [*than*
The Sea-scourg'd Merchant, after all his toile,

---

[5] See Memorial-Introduction, on this.   [6] =conquers.
[7] The Sun. H.   [8] =Ay : see Glossarial Index s. v.

Salutes with tears of joy; when fires betray
The smoakie chimneys of his *Ithaca.*
Where hast thou been so long from my embraces,
Poore pittyed Exile? Tell me, did thy Graces
Flie discontented hence, and for a time
Did rather choose to blesse another clime?
Or went'st thou to this end, the more to move me,
By thy short absence, to desire and love thee?
Why frowns my Sweet? Why won't my Saint confer
Favours on me, her fierce Idolater?
Why are Those Looks, Those Looks the which have been
Time-past so fragrant, sickly now drawn in
Like a dull Twi-light? Tell me; and the fault
Ile expiate with Sulphur, Haire, and Salt :⁹
And with the Christal humour of the spring,
Purge hence the guilt, and kill this quarrelling.
Wo't thou not smile, or tell me what's amisse?
Have I been cold to hug thee, too remisse,
Too temp'rate in embracing? Tell me, ha's desire
To thee-ward dy'd i'th'embers, and no fire
Left in this rak't-up Ash-heap, as a mark
To testifie the glowing of a spark?
Have I divorc't thee onely to combine
In hot Adult'ry with another Wine?

⁹ **Folk-lore.**

True, I confesse I left thee, and appeale
'Twas done by me, more to confirme my zeale,
And double my affection on thee ; as doe those,
Whose love growes more enflam'd, by being Foes.
But to forsake thee ever, co'd there be
A thought of such like possibilitie?
When thou thy selfe dar'st say, thy Iles shall lack
Grapes, before *Herrick* leaves Canarie Sack.
Thou mak'st me ayrie, active to be born,
Like *Iphyclus*,[9] upon the tops of Corn.
Thou mak'st me nimble, as the wingèd howers,
To dance and caper on the heads of flowers,
And ride the Sun-beams.   Can there be a thing
Under the heavenly *Isis*,[1] that can bring
More love unto my life, or can present
My *Genius* with a fuller blandishment?
Illustrious Idoll! co'd th' *Ægyptians* seek
Help from the *Garlick*, *Onyon*, and the *Leek*,
And pay no vowes to thee? who wast their best
God, and far more transcendent then the rest?
Had *Cassius*, that weak Water-drinker,[2] known
Thee in thy Vine, or had but tasted one

---

[9] So Virgil of Camilla.   [1] The Moon.   H.
[2] Cassius Iatrosophista, or Cassius Felix?

K

Small Chalice of thy frantick liquor ; He
As the wise *Cato* had approv'd of thee.
Had not *Joves*[3] son, that brave *Tyrinthian* Swain,
(Invited to the *Thesbian* banquet) ta'ne
Full goblets of thy gen'rous blood ; his spright
Ne'r had kept heat for fifty Maids that night.
Come, come and kisse me ; Love and lust commends
Thee, and thy beauties ; kisse, we will be friends
Too strong for Fate to break us : Look upon
Me, with that full pride of complexion,
As *Queenes*, meet *Queenes;* or come thou unto me,
As *Cleopatra* came to *Anthonie;*
When her high carriage did at once present
To the *Triumvir*, Love and Wonderment.
Swell up my nerves with spirit ; let my blood
Run through my veines, like to a hasty flood.
Fill each part full of fire, active to doe
What thy commanding soule shall put it to.
And till I turne Apostate to thy love,
Which here I vow to serve, doe not remove
Thy Fiers from me ; but Apollo's curse
Blast these-like actions, or a thing that's worse ;

[3] Hercules. H.

When these Circumstants[4] shall but live to see
The time that I prevaricate[5] from thee.
Call me *The sonne of Beere*, and then confine
Me to the Tap, the Tost, the Turfe[6]; Let Wine
Ne'r shine upon me ; May my Numbers all
Run to a sudden Death, and Funerall.
And last, when thee (deare Spouse) I disavow,
Ne'r may Prophetique *Daphne* crown my Brow.

Impossibilities to his friend.

M Y faithful friend, if you can see
     The Fruit to grow up, or the Tree :
If you can see the colour come
Into the blushing Peare, or Plum :
If you can see the water grow
To cakes of Ice, or flakes of Snow :
If you can see, that drop of raine
Lost in the wild sea, once againe :
If you can see, how Dreams do creep
Into the Brain by easie sleep :
Then there is hope that you may see
Her love me once, who now hates me.

---

[4] = surroundings, environings.   [5] = play fast and loose or betray.
[6] = peat-fire ?

Upon Luggs. *Epig.*

L*UGGS* by the Condemnation of the Bench,
　　Was lately whipt for lying with a Wench.
Thus Paines and Pleasures turne by turne succeed :
He smarts at last, who do's not first take heed.

Upon Gubbs. *Epig.*

G*UBBS* calls his children *Kitlings*[7]: and wo'd bound
　　(Some say) for joy, to see those Kitlings drown'd.

To live merrily, and to trust to
Good Verses.

N OW is the time for mirth,
　　Nor cheek, or tongue be dumbe :
For with the flowrie earth,
　　The golden pomp is come.

The golden Pomp is come ;
　　For now each tree do's weare
(Made of her Pap[8] and Gum)
　　Rich beads of *Amber* here.

---

[7] ━kittens.　　　　[8] sap.

Now raignes the *Rose*, and now
　　Th' *Arabian* Dew besmears
My uncontrollèd brow,
　　And my retortèd[9] haires.

Homer, this Health to thee,
　　In Sack of such a kind,
That it wo'd make thee see,
　　Though thou wert ne'r so blind.

Next, *Virgil*, Ile call forth,
　　To pledge this second Health
In Wine, whose each cup's worth
　　An Indian Common-wealth.

A Goblet next Ile drink
　　To *Ovid ;* and suppose,
Made he the pledge, he'd think
　　The world had all *one Nose*.[1]

Then this immensive[2] cup
　　Of *Aromatike* wine,

---

[9] = thrown back.

[1] A play on the Poet's name of 'Naso,' and referring also to that amorous disposition which was supposed to be indicated by a long nose. 　　　　　　　[2] = measureless.

Catullus, I quaffe up
   To that Terce[8] Muse of thine.

Wild I am now with heat;
   O *Bacchus !* coole thy Raies !
Or frantick I shall eate
   Thy *Thyrse*, and bite the *Bayes*.

Round, round, the roof do's run;
   And being ravisht thus,
Come, I will drink a Tun
   To my *Propertius*.

Now, to *Tibullus*, next,
   This flood I drink to thee:
But stay; I see a Text,
   That this presents to me.

Behold, *Tibullus* lies
   Here burnt, whose smal return
Of ashes, scarce suffice
   To fill a little Urne.

Trust to good Verses then;
   They onely will aspire,
When Pyramids, as men,
   Are lost, i'th'funerall fire.

[3] = terse.

And when all Bodies meet
In *Lethe* to be drown'd ;
Then onely Numbers sweet,
 With endless life are crown'd.

Faire dayes : or, *Dawnes deceitfull.*

FAIRE was the Dawne ; and but e'ne now the Skies
 Shew'd like to Creame, enspir'd[4] with Straw-
  berries :
But on a sudden, all was chang'd and gone
That smil'd in that first-sweet complexion.
Then Thunder-claps and Lightning did conspire
To teare the world, or set it all on fire.
What trust to things below, whenas we see,
As Men, the Heavens have their Hypocrisie ?

Lips Tonguelesse.[5]

FOR my part I never care
 For those lips, that tongue-ty'd are :

---

[4] —breathed upon. See Glossarial Index s. v.
[5] This little jeu-d'esprit is possibly grounded on the following lines :
> Si linguam clauso tenes in ore,
> Fructus projicies amoris omnes :
> Verbosâ gaudet Venus loquelâ.
>> Catullus. Carm. 52. N.

Tell-tales I wo'd have them be
Of my Mistresse, and of me.
Let them prattle how that I
Sometimes freeze, and sometimes frie :
Let them tell how she doth move
Fore or backward in her love :
Let them speak by gentle tones,
One and th'others passions :
How we watch, and seldome sleep ;
How by Willowes we doe weep :
How by stealth we meet, and then
Kisse, and sigh, so part agen.
This the lips we will permit
For to tell, not publish it.

To the Fever, not to trouble Julia.

TH'AST dar'd too farre ; but Furie now forbeare
    To give the least disturbance to her haire :
But lesse presume to lay a Plait upon
Her skins most smooth, and cleare expansion.
'Tis like a Lawnie-Firmament as yet
Quite dispossest of either fray, or fret,
Come thou not neere that Filmne so finely spred,
Where no one piece is yet unlevellèd.

This if thou dost, woe to thee Furie, woe,
Ile send such Frost, such Haile, such Sleet, and Snow,
Such fears, quakes, Palsies, and such Heates as shall
Dead thee to th' most, if not destroy thee all.
And thou a thousand thousand times shalt be
More shak't thy selfe, then she is scorch't by thee.

To Violets.

1. WELCOME, Maids of Honour,
    You doe bring
    In the Spring;
And wait upon her.

2. She has Virgins many,
    Fresh and faire;
    Yet you are
More sweet then any.   [*than*

3. Y'are the Maiden Posies,
    And so grac't,
    To be plac't,
'Fore Damask Roses.

4. Yet though thus respected,
    By and by
    Ye doe lie,
Poore Girles, neglected.

Upon Bunce.   *Epig.*

MONY thou ow'st me ; Prethee fix a day
  For payment promis'd, though thou never pay :
Let it be Doomes-day ; nay, take longer scope ;
Pay when th'art honest ; let me have some hope.

To Carnations.   A Song.

1. STAY while ye will, or goe ;
    And leave no scent behind ye :
   Yet trust me, I shall know
    The place, where I may find ye :

2. Within my *Lucia's* cheek,
    (Whose Livery ye weare)
   Play ye at *Hide* or *Seek*,
    I'm sure to find ye there.

To the Virgins, to make much of Time.[6]

1. GATHER ye Rose-buds while ye may,
    Old Time is still a-flying :
   And this same flower that smiles to day,
    To morrow will be dying.

[6] See Memorial-Introduction on this.

2. The glorious Lamp of Heaven, the Sun,
    The higher he's a-getting;
  The sooner will his Race be run,
    And neerer he's to Setting.

3. That Age is best, which is the first,
    When Youth and Blood are warmer;
  But being spent, the worse, and worst
    Times, still succeed the former.

4. Then be not coy, but use your time;
    And while ye may, goe marry :
  For having lost but once your prime,
    You may for ever tarry.

Safety to look to ones selfe.

FOR my neighbour Ile not know,
    Whether high he builds or no :
Onely this Ile look upon,
Firm be my foundation.
Sound, or unsound, let it be;
'Tis the lot ordain'd for me.
He who to the ground do's fall,
Has not whence to sink at all.

To his Friend, on the
untuneable Times.

PLAY I co'd once ; but (gentle friend) you see
   My Harp hung up, here on the Willow tree.
Sing I co'd once ; and bravely too enspire,
(With luscious Numbers) my melodious Lyre.
Draw I co'd once (although not stocks or stones,
Amphion-like) men made of flesh and bones,
Whether I wo'd ; but (ah!) I know not how,
I feele in me, this transmutation now.
Griefe, (my deare friend) has first my Harp unstrung ;
Wither'd my hand, and palsie-struck my tongue.

His Poetrie his Pillar.

1. ONELY a little more
     I have to write,
     Then Ile give o're,
  And bid the world Good-night.

2. 'Tis but a flying minute,
     That I must stay,
     Or linger in it ;
  And then I must away.

3. O time that cut'st down all !
    And scarce leav'st here
    Memoriall
    Of any men that were.

4. How many lye forgot
    In Vaults beneath ?
    And piece-meale rot
    Without a fame in death ?

5. Behold this living stone,
    I reare for me,
    Ne'r to be thrown
    Downe, envious Time by thee.

6. Pillars let some set up,
    (If so they please)
    Here is my hope,
    And my *Pyramides.*[7]

Safety on the Shore.

WHAT though the sea be calme ? Trust to the
        shore :
Ships have been drown'd, where late they danc't
        before.

[7] Note the pronunciation to rhyme with 'please'—pyr-am-i-des.
Like statua, apostata, it had not yet been perfectly Anglicised.

A Pastorall upon the Birth of Prince Charles,
Presented to the King, and Set by
Mr. Nic : Laniere.[8]

The Speakers, Mirtillo, Amintas, *and* Amarillis.

Amin. GOOD day, *Mirtillo.* *Mirt.* And to you
no lesse :
And all faire Signs lead on our Shepardesse.
   Amar. With all white luck to you. *Mirt.* But say,
what news
Stirs in our Sheep-walk ? *Amin.* None, save that my
Ewes,
My Weathers, Lambes, and wanton Kids are well,
Smooth, faire, and fat ; none better I can tell :
Or that this day *Menalchas* keeps a feast
For his Sheep-shearers. *Mir.* True, these are the least.
But, dear *Amintas*, and, sweet *Amarillis*,
Rest but a while here, by this bank of Lillies.

---

[8] This was afterwards Charles II : born 1630 : Nicholas Laniere,
painter, engraver and musician, was born in Italy in 1568. He
came early in life to England. One of his chief compositions was
a Masque performed on the marriage of the Earl of Somerset with
the Countess of Essex. His own portrait, by himself, is in the
Music-School at Oxford. He died in November, 1646. This it will
be seen is another early poem. See Memorial-Introduction.

And lend a gentle eare to one report
The Country has. *Amint.* From whence ? *Amar.*

From whence ? *Mir.* The Court.
Three dayes before the Shutting in of *May*,
(With whitest Wool⁹ be ever crown'd that day!)
To all our joy, a sweet-fac't child was borne,
More tender then the childhood of the Morne. [*than*

Chor. Pan pipe to him, and bleats of lambs and sheep,
Let Lullaby the pretty Prince asleep !

Mirt. And that his birth sho'd be more singular, .
At Noone of Day, was seene a Silver Star,
Bright as the Wise-men's Torch, which guided them
To God's sweet Babe, when borne at *Bethlehem ;*¹
While Golden Angels (some have told to me)
Sung out his Birth with Heav'nly Minstralsie.

Amint. O rare ! But is't a trespasse if we three
Sho'd wend along his Baby-ship to see?

Mir. Not so, not so. *Chor.* But if it chance to prove
At most a fault, 'tis but a fault of love.

Amar. But, deare *Mirtillo*, I have heard it told,
Those learned men brought *Incense*, *Myrrhe*, and *Gold*,
From Countries far, with store of Spices, (sweet)
And laid them downe for Offrings at his feet.²

---

⁹ See Glossarial Index s. v. ¹ See Memorial-Introduction on this.
² St. Matthew, ii. 11.

Mirt. 'Tis true indeed ; and each of us will bring
Unto our smiling, and our blooming King,
A neat, though not so great an Offering.

Amar. A Garland for my Gift shall be
Of flowers, ne'r suckt by th' theeving Bee :
And all most sweet ; yet all lesse sweet then he. [*than*

Amint. And I will beare along with you
Leaves dropping downe the honyed dew,
With oaten pipes, as sweet, as new.

Mirt. And I a Sheep-hook will bestow,
To have his little King-ship know,
As he is Prince, he's Shepherd too.

Chor. Come let's away, and quickly let's be drest,
And quickly give, *The swiftest Grace is best.*
And when before him we have laid our treasures,
We'll blesse the Babe, Then back to Countrie pleasures.

To the Lark.

GOOD speed, for I this day
    Betimes my Mattens[3] say :
    Because I doe
    Begin to wooe :
    Sweet singing Lark,
    Be thou the Clark,

[3] = matins.

And know thy when

To say, *Amen.*

And if I prove

Blest in my love ;

Then thou shalt be

High-Priest to me,

At my returne,

To Incense burne ;

And so to solemnize

Love's, and my Sacrifice.

The Bubble. A Song.

TO my revenge, and to her desp'rate feares,
    Flie, thou made Bubble of my sighs, and tears.
In the wild aire, when thou hast rowl'd about,
And (like a blasting Planet) found her out ;
Stoop, mount, passe by to take her eye, then glare
Like to a dreadfull Comet in the Aire :
Next, when thou dost perceive her fixèd sight,
For thy revenge to be most opposite ;
Then like a Globe, or Ball of Wild-fire, flie,
And break thy self in shivers on her eye.

A Meditation for his Mistresse.

1. YOU are a *Tulip* seen to day,
       But (Dearest) of so short a stay ;
   That where you grew, scarce man can say.

2. You are a lovely *July-flower*,
       Yet one rude wind, or ruffling shower,
   Will force you hence, (and in an houre.)

3. You are a sparkling *Rose* i'th'bud,
       Yet lost, ere that chast flesh and blood
   Can shew where you or grew, or stood.

4. You are a full-spread faire-set Vine,
       And can with Tendrills love intwine,
   Yet dry'd, ere you distill your Wine.

5. You are like Balme inclosèd (well)
       In *Amber*, or some *Chrystall* shell,
   Yet lost ere you transfuse your smell.

6. You are a dainty *Violet*,
       Yet wither'd, ere you can be set
   Within the Virgins Coronet.

7. You are the *Queen* all flowers among,
       But die you must (faire Maid) ere long,
   As He, the maker of this Song.

The bleeding hand : or, *The sprig of Eglantine given to a maid.*

FROM this bleeding hand of mine,
   Take this sprig of *Eglantine.*
Which (though sweet unto your smell)
Yet the fretfull bryar will tell,
He who plucks the sweets shall prove
Many thorns to be in Love.

Lyrick for Legacies.

GOLD I've none, for use or show,
   Neither Silver to bestow
At my death ; but thus much know,
That each Lyrick here shall be
Of my love a Legacie,
Left to all posterity.
Gentle friends, then doe but please,
To accept such coynes as these ;
As my last Remembrances.

A Dirge upon the Death of the Right Valiant Lord, Bernard Stuart.[4]

1. HENCE, hence, profane ; soft silence let us have ;
    While we this *Trentall*[5] sing about thy Grave.
   Had Wolves or Tigers seen but thee,
   They wo'd have shew'd civility ;[6]
   And, in compassion of thy yeeres,
   Washt those thy purple wounds with tears.
   But since th'art slaine ; and in thy fall,
   The drooping Kingdome suffers all.

    Chor. This we will doe ; we'll daily come
    And offer Tears upon thy Tomb :
    And if that they will not suffice,
    Thou shalt have soules for sacrifice.

---

[4] Robert Heath, in his " Clarastella " (1650), has a poem in celebration of this Royalist Worthy (" Elegies " p. 8). This was Bernard
Stuart, fourth son of Esme, 3rd Duke of Lennox. He was com-
mander of the King's troop of guards in the Civil Wars, and was
killed at Rowton Heath, near Chester, in 1645.

[5] Originally the Romish office for the dead, consisting of thirty
masses rehearsed for thirty days after the death of the person. Hence,
a dirge, but here used for a funeral song or lamentation.

[6] =civilization.

Sleepe in thy peace, while we with spice perfume thee,
And *Cedar* [7] wash thee, that no times consume thee.

2. Live, live thou dost, and shalt ; for why ?
   Soules doe not with their bodies die :
   Ignoble off-springs, they may fall
   Into the flames of Funerall :
   Whenas the chosen seed shall spring
   Fresh, and for ever flourishing.

Cho. And times to come shall, weeping, read thy
glory,
Lesse in these Marble stones, then in thy
story. [*than*

To Perenna, *a Mistresse.*

DEARE *Perenna*, prethee come,
   And with *Smallage* [8] dresse my Tomb :
Adde a *Cypresse*-sprig thereto,
With a teare ; and so *Adieu.*

Great boast, small rost.

OF Flanks and Chines of Beefe doth *Gorrell* boast
   He has at home ; but who tasts boil'd or rost ?
Look in his Brine-tub, and you shall find there
Two stiffe-blew-Pigs-feet, and a sow's cleft eare.

---

[7] See Glossarial Index s. v.　　　[8] Herb, as before.

Upon a Bleare-ey'd woman.

WITHER'D with yeeres, and bed-rid *Mumma*
     lyes;
Dry-rosted all, but raw yet in her eyes.

·

The Fairie Temple : or, Oberon's *Chappell.*
Dedicated to Mr. John Merrifield,
Counsellor at Law.[9]

RARE Temples thou hast seen, I know,
     And rich for in and outward show :
Survey this Chappell, built, alone,
Without or Lime, or Wood, or Stone :
Then say, if one th'ast seene more fine
Then this, the Fairies once, now Thine.   [*than*

The Temple.

AWAY enchac't with glasse & beads
     There is, that to the Chappel leads :
Whose structure (for his holy rest)
Is here the *Halcion's*[1] curious nest :
Into the which who looks shall see
His *Temple of Idolatry :*

---

[9] Nothing seems to be now known of Merrifield. It is just possible that—as throughout the poem—the name was an invented one,
' Merry Field.'   [1] Kingfisher.

Where he of *God-heads* has such store,
As *Rome's Pantheon* had not more.
His house of *Rimmon*[2] this he calls,
Girt with small bones, instead of walls.
First, in a *Neech*,[3] more black then jet,   [*than*
His Idol-Cricket there is set :
Then in a Polisht Ovall by
There stands his *Idol-Beetle-flie :*
Next in an Arch, akin to this,
His *Idol-Canker*[4] seated is :
Then in a Round, is plac't by these,
His golden god, *Cantharides.*
So that where ere ye look, ye see,
No *Capitoll*, no *Cornish*[5] free,
Or Freeze, from this fine Fripperie.
Now this the Fairies wo'd have known,
Theirs is a mixt Religion.
And some have heard the Elves it call
Part Pagan, part Papisticall.
If unto me all Tongues were granted,
I co'd not speak the Saints here painted.
Saint *Tit*,[6] Saint *Nit*,[7] Saint *Is*,[8] Saint *Itis*,[9]
Who 'gainst *Mabs-state* plac't here right is.

---

[2] 2 Kings, v. 18.   [3] =niche.   [4] =worm.
[5] =cornice: still pronounced ' cornish ' in Devon.
[6] St. Titus.   [7] St. Neot.   [8] St. Idus.   [9] St. Ida.

Saint *Will o'th Wispe* (of no great bignes)
But *alias* call'd here *Fatuus ignis.*
Saint *Frip,*[1] Saint *Trip,*[2] Saint *Fill,*[3] S. *Fillie,*[4]
Neither those other-Saint-ships will I
Here goe about for to recite
Their number (almost) infinite,
Which one by one here set downe are
In this most curious Calendar.
First, at the entrance of the gate,
A little-Puppet-Priest doth wait,
Who squeaks to all the commers there,
Favour your tongues,[5] *who enter here.*
Pure hands bring hither, without staine.
A second pules, *Hence, hence, profane.*
Hard by, i'th'shell of halfe a nut,
The Holy-water there is put :
A little brush of Squirrils haires,
(Compos'd of odde, not even paires)
Stands in the Platter, or close by,
To purge the Fairie Family.

---

[1] St. Fridian or St. Fridolin. [2] St. Trypho. [3] St. Felan. [4] St. Felix. Whilst I have given these Romish saints' names, I am not sure but Herrick would have laughed loudly at my pains, and told me that he merely gave such names as Fairy saints might have had. Certes St. Will o' th' Wispe looks like this.

[5] = Favete linguis, &c. Horace, Od. iii. 1, 2.

Neere to the Altar stands the Priest,
There off'ring up the Holy-Grist :[6]
Ducking in Mood, and perfect Tense,
With (much-good-do't him) reverence.
The Altar is not here foure-square,
Nor in a forme Triangular ;
Nor made of glasse, or wood, or stone,
But of a little Transverce bone ;
Which boyes, and Bruckel'd [7] children call
(Playing for Points and Pins) Cockall.[8]
Whose Linen-Drapery is a thin
Subtile and ductile Codlin's [9] skin ;
Which o're the board is smoothly spred,
With little Seale-work Damaskèd.
The Fringe that circumbinds [1] it too,
Is Spangle-work of trembling dew,
Which, gently gleaming, makes a show,
Like Frost-work glitt'ring on the Snow.

---

[6] = holy grain. The reference is to the offering of the Host.

[7] = begrimed, wet and dirty. Whence is it derived? Nares s. v. suggests 'breeched'; but it is a very unsavoury etymology, albeit not far out here.

[8] = the huckle or pastern-bone of the sheep, used for a game played from classic times.

[9] = codling : apple so called.   [1] = binds it round.

Upon this fetuous [2] board doth stand
Something for *Shew-bread*, and at hand
(Just in the middle of the Altar)
Upon an end, the *Fairie-Psalter*,
Grac't with the Trout-flies curious wings,
Which serve for watchèd [3] Ribbanings.
Now, we must know, the Elves are led
Right by the Rubrick, which they read.
And if Report of them be true,
They have their Text for what they doe ;
I [4], and their Book of Canons too.
And, as Sir *Thomas Parson* [5] tells,
They have their Book of Articles :
And if that Fairie Knight not lies,
They have their Book of Homilies :
And other Scriptures, that designe
A short, but righteous discipline.
The Bason stands the board upon
To take the Free-Oblation :

[2] =fetise, well-made, or neat, elegant.
[3] =watched, dark blue.   [4] =Ay. So in next page, l. 22.
[5] This might be put as a general name for a clergyman ('parson '),
'Sir' being the olden designation of a priest. But the following
line, " that Fairie knight," looks as if some real person were meant.
Who ?

A little Pin-dust; which they hold
More precious, then we prize our gold :   [*than*
Which charity they give to many
Poore of the Parish, (if there's any).
Upon the ends of these neat Railes
(Hatcht,[6] with the Silver-light of snails,)
The Elves, in formall manner, fix
Two pure, and holy *Candlesticks :*
In either which a small tall bent [7]
Burns for the Altars ornament.
For sanctity, they have, to these,
Their curious *Copes* and *Surplices*
Of cleanest *Cobweb*, hanging by
In their *Religious Vesterie.*[8]
They have their *Ash-pans*, & their *Brooms*
To purge the Chappel and the rooms :
Their many *mumbling Masse-priests* here,
And many a dapper *Chorister.*
There ush'ring *Vergers*, here likewise,
Their *Canons*, and their *Chaunteries :*
Of *Cloyster-Monks* they have enow,
I, and their *Abby-Lubbers* [9] too :

---

[6] ═ engraved : " This sword, silver'd and hatcht " : Chapman
(Bailey s. v.)   [7] ═ blade of coarse grass or rush.
   [8] ═ vestry or church-room.   [9] ═ lazy monks.

And if their Legend doe not lye,
They much affect the *Papacie*:
And since the last is dead, there's hope,
Elve Boniface shall next be Pope.[10]
They have their *Cups* and *Chalices*;
Their *Pardons* and *Indulgences*:
Their *Beads* of Nits,[1] *Bels*, *Books*, & *Wax*
Candles (forsooth) and other knacks:
Their *Holy Oyle*, their *Fasting-Spittle*;
Their *sacred Salt* here, (not a little.)
Dry *chips*, old *shooes*, *rags*, *grease*, & *bones*;
Beside their *Fumigations*,
To drive the Devill from the Cod-piece [2]
Of the Fryar, (of work an odde-piece.)
Many a trifle too, and trinket,
And for what use, scarce man wo'd think it.
Next, then, upon the *Chanters* side
An *Apples-core* is hung up dry'd,
With ratling Kirnils, which is rung
To call to Morn, and Even-Song.

---

[10] Is this a reference to some recent Papal election, of which rumours were circulating?

[1] =nuts in Devonshire, as in the local proverb "So many nits [nuts], so many pits [graves]," which seems to point to the indigestible, and so deathly, nature of nuts taken in over-quantity.

[2] See Glossarial Index s. v.

The Saint, to which the most he prayes
And offers *Incense* Nights and dayes,
The *Lady* of the *Lobster*³ is,
Whose foot-pace he doth stroak and kisse ;
And, humbly, chives⁴ of Saffron brings,
For his most cheerfull offerings.
When, after these, h'as paid his vows,
He lowly to the Altar bows :
And then he dons the Silk-worms shed,⁵
(Like a *Turks Turbant*⁶ on his head),
And reverently departeth thence,
Hid in a cloud of *Frankincense :*
And by the glow-worms light wel guided,
Goes to the Feast that's now provided.

To Mistresse Katherine Bradshaw, *the lovely,
that crowned him with Laurel.*⁷

M Y Muse in Meads has spent her many houres,
Sitting, and sorting severall sorts of flowers,

---

³ Who?

⁴ ⸗chip or shiver, and in a plant is the thread-like style and stigma of the flower. Saffron is that part of the crocus. ⁵ Cocoon.

⁶ Italian and Spanish turbante—linen head-dress wreathed⸗ turban.

⁷ Impossible to identify. The Bradshaws were very numerous at this period. No doubt a Devonshire Beauty.

To make for others garlands : and to set
On many a head here, many a Coronet :
But, amongst All encircled here, not one
Gave her a day of Coronation ;
Till you (sweet Mistresse) came and enterwove
A *Laurel* for her, (ever young as love),
You first of all crown'd her ; she must of due,
Render for that, a crowne of life to you.

The Plaudite, or end of life.[8]

IF after rude and boystrous seas,
    My wearyed Pinnace here finds ease :
If so it be I've gain'd the shore
With safety of a faithful Ore :
If having run my Barque on ground,
Ye see the agèd Vessell crown'd :
What's to be done? but on the Sands
Ye dance, and sing, and now clap hands.
The first Act's doubtfull, (but we say)
It is the last commends the Play.

[8] These lines have an evident reference to the *Phaselus* of Catullus, or fifth Carmen. N. Very slight indeed, if any such reference.

To the most vertuous Mistresse Pot,
who many times entertained him.[9]

WHEN I through all my many Poems look,
   And see your selfe to beautifie my Book;
Me thinks that onely lustre doth appeare
A Light ful-filling all the Region here.
Guild still with flames this Firmament, and be
A Lamp Eternall to my Poetrie.
Which if it now, or shall hereafter shine,
'Twas by your splendour (Lady), not by mine.
The Oile was yours; and that I owe for yet:
He payes the halfe, who do's confesse the Debt.

To Musique, to becalme his Fever.

1. CHARM me asleep, and melt me so
      With thy Delicious Numbers;
   That being ravisht, hence I goe
      Away in easie slumbers.
         Ease my sick head,
         And make my bed,

---

[9] Probably another character-name.

Thou Power that canst sever
From me this ill :
And quickly still :
Though thou not kill
My Fever.

2. Thou sweetly canst convert the same
From a consuming fire,
Into a gentle-licking flame,
And make it thus expire.
Then make me weep
My paines asleep ;
And give me such reposes,
That I, poore I,
May think, thereby,
I live and die
'Mongst Roses.

3. Fall on me like a silent dew,
Or like those Maiden showrs,
Which, by the peepe of day, doe strew
A Baptime [10] o're the flowers.
Melt, melt my paines,
With thy soft straines ;

---

[10] = baptism, as before. See Glossarial Index s. v.

That having ease me given,
 With full delight,
 I leave this light;
 And take my flight
 For Heaven.

Upon a Gentlewoman with a sweet Voice.

SO long you did not sing, or touch your Lute,
 We knew 'twas Flesh and Blood, that there sate
  mute.
But when your Playing, and your Voice came in,
'Twas no more you then, but a *Cherubin*.

Upon Cupid.[1]

AS lately I a Garland bound,
 'Mongst Roses, I there *Cupid* found :
I took him, put him in my cup,
And drunk with Wine, I drank him up.
Hence then it is, that my poore brest
Co'd never since find any rest.

---

[1] Imitation of the Pseudo-Anacreon, No. 59 (5 in Bergk's Lyric Poets.)

M

Upon Julia's *breasts.*

DISPLAY thy breasts, my *Julia*, there let me
   Behold that circummortall [2] purity :
Betweene whose glories, there my lips Ile lay,
Ravisht, in that faire *Via Lactea.*

Best to be merry.

FOOLES are they, who never know
   How the times away doe goe :
But for us, who wisely see
Where the bounds of black Death be :
Let's live merrily, and thus
Gratifie the *Genius.*[3]

The Changes to Corinna.

BE not proud, but now encline
   Your soft eare to Discipline.
You have changes in your life,
Sometimes peace, and sometimes strife :
You have ebbes of face and flowes,
As your health or comes, or goes ;

---

[2] = more than mortal. (See Glossarial Index under circum.)
Perhaps a reference to the "glory" of purity that surrounds (the
head of) saints. See "glories" in l. 3.

[3] Used in the Roman sense for guardian spirit or personal Lar

You have hopes, and doubts, and feares
Numberlesse, as are your haires.
You have Pulses that doe beat
High, and passions lesse of heat.[4]
You are young, but must be old,
And, to these, ye must be told,
Time, ere long, will come and plow
Loathèd Furrowes in your brow :
And the dimnesse of your eye
Will no other thing imply,
But you must die
As well as I.

No Lock against Letcherie.

BARRE close as you can, and bolt fast too your
    doore,
To keep out the Letcher, and keep in the whore :
Yet, quickly you'l see by the turne of a pin,
The Whore to come out, or the Letcher come in.

Neglect.

ART *quickens Nature; Care will make a face:
Neglected beauty perisheth apace.*

---

[4] = passions wanting in heat, i. e., depressing passions.

Upon himselfe.

MOP-EY'D [5] I am, as some have said,
　　Because I've liv'd so long a maid :
But grant that I sho'd wedded be,
Sho'd I a jot the better see?
No, I sho'd think, that Marriage might,
Rather then mend, put out the light.　　　　*[than*

Upon a Physitian.

THOU cam'st to cure me (Doctor) of my cold,
　　And caught'st thy selfe the more by twenty fold:
Prethee goe home ; and for thy credit be
First cur'd thy selfe ; then come and cure me.

Upon Sudds *a Laundresse.*

SUDDS Launders Bands in pisse ; and starches them
　　Both with her Husband's, and her own tough fleame.

To the Rose.　Song.

1. GOE, happy Rose, and enterwove
　　　With other Flowers, bind my Love.
　　　Tell her too, she must not be,
　　　Longer flowing, longer free,
　　　That so oft has fetter'd me.

[5] = short-sighted or dim-sighted.

2. Say (if she's fretfull) I have bands
   Of Pearle, and Gold, to bind her hands :
    Tell her, if she struggle still,
    I have Mirtle rods, (at will)
    For to tame, though not to kill.

3. Take thou my blessing, thus, and goe,
   And tell her this, but doe not so,
    Lest a handsome anger flye,
    Like a Lightning, from her eye,
    And burn thee up, as well as I.

Upon Guesse.   *Epig.*

GUESSE cuts his shooes, and limping, goes about
 To have men think he's troubled with the Gout :
But 'tis no Gout (beleeve it) but hard Beere,
Whose acrimonious humour bites him [t]here.

To his Booke.

THOU art a plant sprung up to wither never,
 ·But like a Laurell, to grow green for ever.

Upon a painted Gentlewoman.

MEN say y'are faire ; and faire ye are, 'tis true ;
 But (Hark !) we praise the Painter now, not you.

Upon a crooked Maid.

CROOKED you are, but that dislikes not me ;
  So you be straight, where Virgins straight sho'd be.

Draw Gloves.[6]

AT Draw-Gloves we'l play,
      And prethee, let's lay
A wager, and let it be this ;
    Who first to the Summe
      Of twenty shall come,
Shall have for his winning a kisse.

To Musick, to becalme a sweet-sick-youth.

CHARMS, that call down the moon from out her sphere,
  On this sick youth work your enchantments here :
Bind up his senses with your numbers, so,
As to entrance his paine, or cure his woe.
Fall gently, gently, and a while him keep
Lost in the civill Wildernesse of sleep :[7]
That done, then let him, dispossest of paine,
Like to a slumbring Bride, awake againe.

---

[6] An old English sport or game.   Cf. Strutt s. v.
[7] Cf. Maud :
      "Hast given false death her hand, and stol'n away
        To dreamful wastes, where footless fancies dwell."

To the High and Noble Prince, GEORGE,
Duke, Marquesse, and Earle.of
Buckingham.[8]

NEVER my Book's perfection did appeare,
  Til I had got the name of VILLARS here.
Now 'tis so full, that when therein I look,
I see a Cloud of Glory fills my Book.
Here stand it stil to dignifie our Muse,
Your sober Hand-maid ; who doth wisely chuse,
Your Name to be a *Laureat-Wreathe* to Hir,
Who doth both love and feare you *Honour'd Sir.*

His Recantation.

LOVE, I recant,
    And pardon crave,
That lately I offended,
      But 'twas,
      Alas,
To make a brave,[9]
But no disdaine intended.

No more Ile vaunt,
For now I see,
Thou onely hast the power,

---

[8] *The* Buckingham of History.   [9] — bravado.

To find,

And bind

A heart that's free,

And slave [1] it in an houre.

The comming of good luck.

SO Good-luck came, and on my roofe did light,

    Like noyse-lesse Snow; or as the dew of night :

Not all at once, but gently, as the trees

Are, by the Sun-beams, tickel'd by degrees.

The Present : or, The Bag of the Bee.

FLY to my Mistresse, pretty pilfring Bee,

    And say, thou bring'st this Hony-bag from me :

When on her lip, thou hast thy sweet dew plac't,

Mark, if her tongue, but slily, steale a taste.

If so, we live; if not, with mournfull humme,

Tole forth my death; next, to my buryall come.

On Love.

LOVE bade me aske a gift,

    And I no more did move,[2]

[1] = put it in bondage—as enslave; and so Shakespeare.

[2] = ask.

But this, that I might shift
Still with my clothes, my Love:
That favour granted was;
Since which, though I love many,
Yet so it comes to passe,
That long I love not any.

The Hock-cart, or *Harvest home:*
To the Right Honourable,
Mildmay, *Earle of*
Westmorland.[3]

COME, Sons of Summer, by whose toile,
We are the Lords of Wine and Oile:
By whose tough labours, and rough hands,
We rip up first, then reap our lands.
Crown'd with the eares of corne, now come,
And, to the Pipe, sing Harvest home.
Come forth, my Lord, and see the Cart
Drest up with all the Country Art.
See, here a *Maukin*,[4] there a sheet,
As spotlesse pure, as it is sweet:

[3] See former note on this poet-noble, and Memorial-Introduction.
[4] = maulkin: cloth usually wetted and attached to a pole to clean out a baker's oven-floor. In Devon, a cloth or clout generally.

The Horses, Mares, and frisking Fillies,
(Clad, all, in Linnen, white as Lillies.)
The Harvest Swaines, and Wenches bound
For joy, to see the *Hock-cart* [5] crown'd.
About the Cart, heare, how the Rout
Of Rurall Younglings raise the shout;
Pressing before, some coming after,
Those with a shout, and these with laughter.
Some blesse the Cart; some kisse the sheaves;
Some prank [6] them up with Oaken leaves:
Some crosse the Fill-horse; [7] some with great
Devotion, stroak the home-borne wheat:
While other Rusticks, lesse attent
To Prayers, then to Merryment,   [*than*
Run after with their breeches rent.
Well, on, brave boyes, to your Lords Hearth,
Glitt'ring with fire; where, for your mirth,
Ye shall see first the large and cheefe
Foundation of your Feast, Fat Beefe:
With Upper Stories, Mutton, Veale
And Bacon, (which makes full the meale)
With sev'rall dishes standing by,
As here a Custard, there a Pie,

---

[5] See Glossarial Index s. v.
[6] =adorn.   [7] =the shaft or fill horse.

And here all-tempting Frumentie.[7]
And for to make the merry cheere,
If smirking [8] Wine be wanting here,
There's that, which drowns all care, stout Beere; *remember only you are hire.*
Which freely drink to your Lords health,
Then to the Plough, (the Common-wealth)
Next to your Flailes, your Fanes,[9] your Fatts;[1]
Then to the Maids with Wheaten-Hats:
To the rough Sickle, and crookt, Sythe,
Drink, frollick, boyes, till all be blythe.
Feed, and grow fat; and as ye eat,
Be mindfull, that the lab'ring Neat[2] *men identified with beasts*
(As you) may have their fill of meat.
And know, besides, ye must revoke
The patient Oxe unto the Yoke,
And all goe back unto the Plough
And Harrow, (though they'r hang'd up now.)
And, you must know, your Lords word's true,
Feed him ye must, whose food fils you.
And that this pleasure is like raine,

---

[7] = hulled wheat boiled in milk and variously seasoned.
[8] We say ' winking ' = sparkling.
[9] = fanners or fans, for winnowing: or perchance 'vanes' to mark the wind = weather-cocks. I add the alternative because it is used provincially in both senses. [1] = vats. [2] = oxen.

Not sent ye for to drowne your paine,
But for to make it spring againe.

The Perfume.

TO-MORROW, *Julia*, I betimes must rise,
    For some small fault, to offer sacrifice :
The Altar's ready ; Fire to consume
The fat ; breathe thou, and there's the rich perfume.

Upon her Voice.

LET but thy voice engender with the string,
    And Angels will be borne, while thou dost sing.

Not to love.

HE that will not love, must be
    My Scholar, and learn this of me :
There be in Love as many feares,
As the Summers Corne has eares :
Sighs, and sobs, and sorrowes more
Then the sand, that makes the shore :   [*than*
Freezing cold, and firie heats,
Fainting swoones, and deadly sweats ;
Now an Ague, then a Fever,
Both tormenting Lovers ever.

Wods't thou know, besides all these,
How hard a woman 'tis to please?
How crosse, how sullen, and how soone
She shifts and changes like the Moone.
How false, how hollow she's in heart;
And how she is her owne least part :[3]
How high she's priz'd, and worth but small;
Little thou'lt love, or not at all.

To Musick. A Song.

MUSICK, thou *Queen of Heaven*, Care-charming spel,
    That strik'st a stilnesse into hell :
Thou that tam'st *Tygers*, and fierce storms (that rise)
    With thy soule-melting Lullabies :
Fall down, down, down, from those thy chiming spheres,
To charme our soules, as thou enchant'st our eares.

To the Western wind.

1. SWEET Western Wind, whose luck it is,
        (Made rivall with the aire)
    To give *Perenna's* lip a kisse,
        And fan her wanton haire.

---

[3] Meaning — very little herself, but chiefly and more usually some-
body or something else : or perhaps more correctly " for every passion something, and for no passion truly anything," as says Rosa-
lind in As You Like It.

2. Bring me but one, Ile promise thee,
   Instead of common showers,
   Thy wings shall be embalm'd by me,
   And all beset with flowers.

Upon the death of his Sparrow.
An Elegie.

WHY doe not all fresh maids appeare
   To work Love's Sampler[4] onely here,
Where spring-time smiles throughout the yeare?
Are not here *Rose-buds, Pinks*, all flowers,
Nature begets by th' Sun and showers,
Met in one Hearce-cloth,[5] to ore-spred
The body of the under-dead?
Phill,[6] the late dead, the late dead Deare,
O! may no eye distill a Teare
For you once lost, who weep not here!

---

[4] See Glossarial Index s. v.   [5] = hearse-cloth (at funerals).

[6] The use of 'Phil' for the 'sparrow' by Sir Philip Sidney, has led to ludicrous misunderstanding of his "Astrophel and Stella." Whence did Phil originate? Probably from their note, which was represented in English by 'phip, phip.' So in Skelton's elegy on Philip Sparrow :

> "And when I sayd Phyp Phip
>   Then he wold leape and skip."

See Lyly's Mother Bumbie.

Had *Lesbia* (too-too-kind) but known
This Sparrow, she had scorn'd her own :
And for this dead which under-lies,
Wept out her heart, as well as eyes.
But endlesse Peace, sit here, and keep
My *Phill*, the time he has to sleep,
And thousand Virgins come and weep,
To make these flowrie Carpets show
Fresh, as their blood ; and ever grow,
Till passengers shall spend their doome,
Not *Virgil's* Gnat had such a Tomb.[7]

To Primroses fill'd with morning dew.

1. WHY doe ye weep, sweet Babes? can Tears
  Speak griefe in you,
  Who were but borne
  Just as the modest Morne
  Teem'd [8] her refreshing dew?
Alas, you have not known that shower,
  That marres a flower ;
  Nor felt th'unkind
  Breath of a blasting wind ;
  Nor are ye worne with yeares ;

---

[7] Spurious : but Spenser translated it.   [8] = poured out.

Or warpt, as we,
Who think it strange to see,
Such pretty flowers, (like to Orphans young,)
To speak by Teares, before ye have a Tongue.

2. Speak, whimp'ring Younglings, and make known
The reason, why
Ye droop, and weep;
Is it for want of sleep?
Or childish Lullabie?
Or that ye have not seen as yet
The *Violet?*
Or brought a kisse
From that Sweet-heart, to this?
No, no, this sorrow shown
By your teares shed,
Wo'd have this Lecture read,
That things of greatest, so of meanest worth,
Conceiv'd with grief are, and with teares brought forth.

END OF VOL. I.

PRINTED BY ROBERT ROBERTS, BOSTON, LINCOLNSHIRE.

www.ingramcontent.com/pod-product-compliance
Lightning Source LLC
Chambersburg PA
CBHW031816270326
41932CB00008B/445